BATMAN UNAUTHORIZED

OTHER TITLES IN THE SMART POP SERIES

BATMAN UNAUTHORIZED

VIGILANTES, JOKERS, AND HEROES IN GOTHAM CITY

Edited by
DENNIS O'NEIL
with LEAH WILSON

BENBELLA

BENBELLA BOOKS, INC.
Dallas, Texas

"Keeping It Real in Gotham" © 2008 by Robert Brian Taylor
"Two of a Kind" © 2008 by Lou Anders
"Frank Miller's New Batman and the Grotesque" © 2008 by Geoff Klock
"Holy Signifier, Batman!" © 2008 by Nick Mamatas
"The Cost of Being Batman" © 2008 by Darren Hudson Hick
"Ra's al Ghul: Father Figure as Terrorist" © 2008 by Michael Marano
"The Dubious Origins of the Batman" © 2008 by Alan J. Porter
"Why Doesn't Bruce Wayne Retire Already?!" © 2008 by Monkeybrain, Inc.
"The Madness of Arkham Asylum" © 2008 by Paul Lytle
"Robin: Innocent Bystander" © 2008 by Jake Black
"Batman in Outer Space" © 2008 by Mike W. Barr
"Gotham's First Family" © 2008 by Mary Borsellino
"What's Wrong with Bruce Wayne?" © 2008 by Robin S. Rosenberg
"The Batman We Deserve" © 2008 by Daniel M. Kimmel
"To the Batpole!" © 2008 by Alex Bledsoe
"Heroes of Darkness and Light" © 2008 by John C. Wright
"Batman in the Real World" © 2008 by Kristine Kathryn Rusch
"Batman, the Failure" © 2008 by David Seidman
Additional Materials © 2008 by Dennis O'Neil

BenBella Books, Inc.
6440 N. Central Expressway, Suite 503
Dallas, TX 75206
www.benbellabooks.com
Send feedback to feedback@benbellabooks.com

Printed in the United States of America
10 9 8 7 6 5 4 3 2 1

Library of Congress Cataloging-in-Publication Data

Batman unauthorized : vigilantes, jokers, and heroes in Gotham City / edited by Dennis O'Neil with Leah Wilson.
    p. cm.
  ISBN 1-933771-30-5
  1. Batman (Fictitious character) 2. Comic books, strips, etc.--United States--History and criticism. I. O'Neil, Dennis, 1939- II. Wilson, Leah.

  PN6728.B363B37 2008
  700'.451--dc22

                    2007046504

Proofreading by Emily Chauvier and Yara Abuata
Cover design by Laura Watkins
Cover illustration by Big Time Attic
Text design and composition by Laura Watkins
Printed by Bang Printing

Distributed by Independent Publishers Group
To order call (800) 888-4741
www.ipgbook.com

For special sales contact Robyn White at robyn@benbellabooks.com

CONTENTS

INTRODUCTION

In the beginning was the meme, and the meme belonged to Jerry Siegel and Joe Shuster. But not for long.

I'll be happy to elucidate.

I'll begin with a bit of history that may already be familiar to you. It concerns a young man who was living in Cleveland in 1934 and loved science fiction. One sleepless night, he had an idea. As he later described it, "All of a sudden it hits me. I conceive of a character like Samson, Hercules, and all the strong men I ever heard of rolled into one—*only more so.*" The next day, he described his brainstorm to an artist friend and together they created a fictional character who became an international icon and, among other accomplishments, created an industry that spawned hundreds—thousands?—of imitations. The youthful brainstormer was writer Jerry Siegel, his artist friend was Joe Shuster, and their creation was Superman, a meme—call it the *costumed superhero meme.*

Meme?

Allow me to offer a definition from no less an authority than the Oxford English Dictionary: "An element of a culture that may be considered to be passed on by non-genetic means, especially imitation." So architecture is a meme. Fashion's a meme. The birthday song is a meme. Anything you pass on by imitation is a meme.

A moment's thought will convince you that costumed superheroes are memes and Jerry Siegel and Joe Shuster created one when they created Superman. Of course, they had no way of knowing that's what they did because Richard Dawkins wouldn't coin the word for another forty-two years or so. Dr. Dawkins, a geneticist, posits that these incorporeal *memes* behave a lot like biological *genes*: that is, they mutate and evolve, and in the process affect the world around them.

To end the Superman creation story quickly (the better to get to the subject of this book): Four frustrating years after Superman's creation, Joe and Jerry finally sold their baby to a new publishing medium, comic books. To call the character's reception a sensation would not, for once, be an exaggeration. Superman's publishers had themselves a smasheroo and pretty soon they began to attempt a duplication of their success.

And at last, panting slightly and just a bit impatient, we come to our real subject, Batman.

It would be nice to say that Bill Finger and Bob Kane, flushed with youthful creative energy, got together and decided to produce a classic hero for this new medium, comic books, and devised a character and an iconography that would endure for generations. Nice, but wrong. Particulars are blurred by time and by the fact that probably these early comics guys weren't thinking about posterity—may not have been aware that they were creating a language, a genre, and a publishing form, so they weren't making notes, even mental notes, and may not have been concerned with much beyond solving the problems in front of them. But we can feel safe in saying that Batman exists because Superman was suc-cessful. Liberal arts majors of my generation, those who have managed to avoid working in the media, may feel that art is pure—"a holy chore," as one writer put it. Holy it may be—the jury's still out—but whatever else it may be, it is also, often, a business. This is not new. Writers, painters, sculptors, actors—anyone whose work does not involve food and shelter—need patrons who can supply them with roofs and dinner, which is why Virgil wrote the *Aeneid*, Shakespeare wrote *The Merry Wives of Windsor*, and Michelangelo painted the big ceiling, to cite just three of many obvious examples.

I didn't know either Bill Finger or Bob Kane well enough to ever engage in soul-baring with them, but I'd bet the mortgage money that one of the reasons they got into comics was as old as rocks: the need to eat. Both were Jewish and career opportunities for Jewish storytellers were limited in the '30s. Radio might have seemed, and maybe was, the domain of theater people and ex-vaudevillians; the pulps offered scant opportunities to Jews; book publishing then and now is generally iffy.

2

There were the movies, for those willing to gamble on a move west, but these were young men for whom a trip to an unknown land—California—might have been daunting.

And suddenly, there were comic books. Maybe really not all that suddenly; comics had been around for a few years, mostly reprints of newspaper material. But this new outfit, National Allied Publications, was buying original stuff: action, adventure, cowboys, airplane pilots, detectives, all staples of the pulps, but now there was another market for this kind of derring-do story. It was a strange market, to be sure; no one knew what the rules were, or if there even were rules, and the money wasn't great. But it *was* money. And these were young guys, in their teens and twenties, some of them still living with their parents. They didn't need much. And besides, if they were anything like the young guys of my comic book generation, they were happy to be getting any reward at all for writing stories and drawing pictures.

So an editor at this Jewish owned and operated publishing house, National Allied Publications, which had no prohibitions against Jews and was seeking the next Superman, asked a cartoonist known as Bob Kane to generate a caped and costumed do-gooder. Bob enlisted the help of his friend, a writer named Bill Finger, and . . . what happened next? Who did exactly what, and when? Accounts vary. But somehow, together, Messrs. Finger and Kane presented the editor with the Bat-Man, who made his debut in *Detective Comics* #27, dated May 1939, and . . . lightning struck twice. Another hit! Another Superman?

Well, no. Oh, there were, and are, similarities: the double identity, the cape and tights, the devotion to crime-fighting. But the meme created by Siegel and Shuster was already mutating. This Bat-Man bore far more resemblance to one of Bill Finger's favorite pulp heroes than to his stablemate, Superman. That hero was the Shadow, an extraordinary man but a man nevertheless. He was born on Earth; he couldn't fly; he was tough as tungsten but not impervious to bullets, explosions, car crashes, or even really enthusiastic clunks on the head. His tools were enormous detective skills, a certain ruthlessness, a cadre of helpers, a disguise, a vast knowledge of his city. Subtract some of the ruthlessness and decrease the size of the cadre and I've just described Batman. I doubt that anyone realized how basically different Batman was from his older brother, the one with the red

3

cape, nor cared. They were making it all up as they went along, inventing a faux mythology and the means to express it by meeting deadlines and getting the job done.

Comics and superheroes were popular during the war years and immediately after, and then, change began in earnest. The characters of Superman and Batman and their home medium, comic books, began an ongoing process of parallel evolution. The medium went from being considered okay entertainment for children, a perception encouraged by the publishers; to, in the witch-hunting '50s, being considered pap for the semi-literate and encouraging antisocial behavior among the young; to being a source of campy humor in the '60s; to, finally, a slow recognition of its identity as a valid narrative venue and—dare we whisper it?—an art form.

At the same time, Superman and Batman (and Wonder Woman and other superdoers) were undergoing their own evolution. Superman's story will have to wait for a collection of essays about him.[1] As for Batman . . . here it is, by decades, quick and dirty: '30s: playboy detective with a double identity. '40s: mostly, an ex officio cop—at times he carried a "platinum police badge." '50s: Gotham's leading citizen whose adventures sometimes involved things like time travel. Call it "science fiction lite." '60s: a comedian in the early part of the decade, because of a popular television show that played him for laughs. In the latter part of the decade and on to the present, a dark, obsessive avenger, a persona that was always implicit in the mythos, but often ignored.

How dark and obsessive? Depends on who's writing, drawing, and editing the stories. This topic is covered by several of our contributors and I suggest that if you have questions about it, they'll likely supply your answers. All I want to add is that without the evolution I doubt that these characters would still be with us. Remember the costumed superhero meme? You can consider each of Batman's iterations a mutation. Some were evolutionary dead ends, like the badge-toter, and some, like the dark avenger, seemed to have great survival potential. Each, I would suggest, was appropriate for its own era, and when that was no longer true, it morphed into the next adaptation. None were permanently lost.

[1] Like *The Man from Krypton* (BenBella Books 2006).

Even the silliest lurks in the mythos, ready to be resurrected if and when a storyteller finds a use for it.

Well into his sixth decade, Batman is, belatedly, respectable, recognized not only as a pop culture icon, but also as a classic character, a good subject for speculation and examination—a good subject, that is, for a book of essays by knowledgeable and thoughtful writers. You're holding that book.

Dennis O'Neil
Nyack, NY
2007

Robert Brian Taylor labels Batman's genre — accurately, I think — "pulp noir." This is a very small club; few characters are members, and there are uncommon problems in taking those characters from the printed page to the big screen, which Mr. Taylor will tell you about. Along the way, he'll speculate on the difficulties of reinventing classic heroes, whether to make them acceptable to contemporary audiences or to export them to different media. It's a thoughtful, interesting look at pop culture and a good introduction to everything that follows it.

KEEPING IT REAL IN GOTHAM

ROBERT BRIAN TAYLOR

I t was early 2005. Christopher Nolan's *Batman Begins* was well into post-production and slated to open that June. Meanwhile, filming on Bryan Singer's *Superman Returns* was underway for a summer 2006 release. And it seemed like every fourth day I would find myself embroiled in a heated debate over which would end up being the better film. Though I had high hopes for both, I figured the safer bet was *Superman Returns*. My argument was a simple one, and went something like this: Both directors were up to the task, and the casts for each movie looked solid on paper. However, Nolan was making one huge mistake choosing Ra's al Ghul—a power-hungry scientist who discovers the secret of immortality—to serve as the film's primary villain. Ra's was an awful choice, not because of the non-comic-reading public's total unfamiliarity with him (though that had to be a concern of the studio's), but rather because no Batman movie featuring a guy who can live forever could be taken all that seriously.[1]

---

[1] Before the geek uprising begins, let's get this out of the way up front: For the sake of

Of all the mega-popular superheroes, it is Batman and his universe that are the most grittily realistic. He is not faster than a speeding bullet. He doesn't swing around Manhattan with the proportional strength of a spider. Batman cannot fly, shoot laser beams from his eyes, or regrow damaged body tissue. He's a guy who puts on a mask, blocks out the pain, and takes to the streets of Gotham City every night to beat evil into a bloody pulp. The world Batman inhabits isn't the same fanciful, brightly colored comic book macrocosm of Superman or Spider-Man, at least it shouldn't be, despite several attempts to turn it into one. I'm looking at you, Adam West and Joel Schumacher. Batman thrives in a pulp-noir universe, where his acts of heroism are more mundane and yet more titillating—the brutal disarming of a knife-wielding thug, with the snap of broken bone, deep in the shadows of some Gotham back alley. The characters who occupy Batman's universe can get hurt, even paralyzed—just ask Barbara Gordon. Sometimes they die.

More often than not, the villains Batman fights, from the street hoodlums up to the major heavies, aren't fantastically gifted, either. The most memorable, the most enduring, of Batman's rogues gallery are the ones who are merely human. They are sociopaths, thieves, and gangsters to be sure, but they're made of the same flesh, blood, and guts as Batman. The Joker. Two-Face. The Penguin. The Riddler. Black Mask. These are men who certainly do great harm . . . but without the help of telekinesis or being able to shapeshift. Sure, reading a comic that has Superman and Darkseid pummeling the crap out of each other can be fun, but it's ultimately two indestructible gods whaling on each other in space. Reading a comic that has Batman matching wits and then punches with the Joker operates on a much smaller scale, but in the end makes for a more intense and dramatic experience.

That's why sticking Ra's al Ghul in a Batman movie seemed like a very bad idea. In the Batman funny books, throwing in a guy who can live

this essay, we'll be labeling Ra's as an immortal. To be nitpicky, he needs his beloved Lazarus Pits to continue his eternal regeneration, and it's been said that the Pits have less and less an effect the more Ra's uses them, mea ning that eventually, someday, far, far into the future, Ra's could finally reach his life's end. But come on—it's been written that Ra's is at least 450 years old in current DC continuity. Plus, one of the guy's nicknames is the Immortal. So he's *virtually* unkillable, which is good enough for me to stick that immortal tag on him.

forever is at least understandable. Batman's comic universe contains hundreds of characters, overflows into the DC Universe at large, and has been in existence for more than sixty years—of course an immortal is eventually going to show up. (This doesn't entirely let Batman comic writers off the hook, but we'll get to that a bit later.) The Batman films, however, are extremely condensed peeks into Batman's world that should be built upon the most basic and powerful of the Dark Knight's major thematic elements. The tone of the comic has wavered over the years—there was a sci-fi infusion in the late '50s, and the campiness of '60s live-action television series carried over into comics for a while as well—but the character has always worked best when writers return him to his pulp roots: Batman's a regular guy with a scarred psyche who uses his skills as a fighter and as a detective to protect the people of Gotham from the same fate that befell his parents—to be murdered by a cold and cowardly thief allowed to run the streets freely because the system doesn't work. The police department is crooked. The judicial system is a mess. In Gotham, Batman is the common man's only hope against the same type of senseless violence that plagues many real-world cities.

Director Tim Burton may have had this in mind when, in 1989, he released his first Batman film—a solid take on the Batman mythos brought down by too much Prince music and a ridiculous final act—but he'd all but forgotten it three years later when *Batman Returns* featured a Catwoman who literally had nine lives. It was the first hint of the supernatural in a big-screen version of the Caped Crusader and the biggest annoyance in a movie that moved Batman from the darkly logical universe that best serves the character to more of a standard comic book world where anything is possible, including Michelle Pfeiffer surviving two falls from Gotham skyscrapers, four gunshot wounds, and a self-inflicted Taser to the mouth. There is also the makeover Tim Burton gave Oswald Cobblepot, a.k.a. the Penguin, to consider. In the original comics Cobblepot was no more than a greedy, power-mad mobster who earned his nickname because of his appearance. He was a short, fat guy with a thing for nice tuxedos. The Penguin in *Batman Returns* has no supernatural powers, but is remade into more of a grotesque, inhuman creature who has more in common with the Lord of the Rings's Gollum than the refined Cobblepot from the comics. Certainly, Gollum and the

Returns version of Cobblepot both have a taste for raw fish heads. *Batman Returns* is an appropriately dark film, but it also remakes Batman's world as more of a fantasy construct—complete with subservient penguins, deadly circus performers, and a touch of the metaphysical. The filmed versions of Catwoman and the Penguin may have served Burton to that end, but they further removed Bruce Wayne from a more tangible reality.

Then Joel Schumacher took over the franchise . . . and things got worse. There's no need to discuss in detail Schumacher's awful remaking of Gotham as a neon-splashed, amusement-park wonderland. That's not the point of this essay. But it is necessary to note here that 1995's *Batman Forever* hinges on a storyline that further drives the series into an illogical fantasy world. In *Forever*, Jim Carrey's Riddler invents a device that literally sucks brainwaves from people's minds, allowing him to exponentially increase his own intelligence. The brain-stealing is represented visually by a greenish beam of neural energy that jumps from the heads of the Riddler's victims to his own—essentially a blast of '50s sci-fi hokum. *Forever* was followed two years later by the much reviled *Batman & Robin*, which introduced to the movies Poison Ivy—the sexy villainess who wields a deadly kiss, super-pheromones, and telekinetic control over plant life. Granted, she exhibits similar superpowers in some of her comic incarnations, but these things tend to come across as ludicrous on the big screen. Heck, even Paul Dini and Bruce Timm knew the Batman universe was better served by scaling back on the fantasy elements whenever possible. Their *Batman: The Animated Series* featured a Poison Ivy whose only superpower was a more plausible immunity to poison. In the cartoon, the poison kiss came courtesy of a synthesized lipstick created from plant toxins. Schumacher, however, had a tendency to focus on the magical claptrap—the more far-fetched, the better—and *Batman & Robin* gave us a Poison Ivy who could sprout killer shrubbery from the ground at will. Yes, they're only comic book movies. But the further the filmmakers drift away from the real world, the less of an impact Batman makes as a character.

That's why it was so disheartening to hear that Ra's al Ghul would serve as Bruce Wayne's main adversary in *Batman Begins*. It was assumed that Nolan's version of the Batman universe would be a return to the more starkly grounded Gotham popularized in comics such as *Batman:*

Year One, Frank Miller's down and dirty prequel. How would Nolan reconcile that levelheaded approach with Ra's al Ghul's more fanciful comic book background, his immortality? Turns out, the solution was easy. In *Begins*, Ra's al Ghul can't actually live forever. His supposed immortality is still integral to the character, but it's cleverly incorporated into the film as a bit of sleight of hand—the real and very mortal Ra's moves about in shadow while a series of disposable decoys front Ra's's army of assassins. It's brilliant how these lines of dialogue from the film, spoken as Liam Neeson's Henri Ducard reveals himself to be the authentic Ra's al Ghul, maintain Ra's's key character trait while still preserving the realism Nolan does indeed strive for in his film:

> BRUCE WAYNE: (to a Ra's imposter) You're not Ra's al Ghul.
> I watched him die.
> DUCARD: (entering from behind Wayne) But is Ra's al Ghul
> immortal? Are his methods supernatural?
> WAYNE: (turning, realizing the solution to the Ra's riddle) Or
> cheap parlor tricks to conceal your identity, Ra's?

And with that Nolan seamlessly integrates Ra's al Ghul into his no-supernatural-crap version of the Batman universe that is far superior to Burton's and Schumacher's takes on the character. (Not only that, *Begins* ended up being a supremely better movie than Singer's plodding *Superman Returns*—boy, did I back the wrong horse there.) And it's not just Ra's that Nolan gets right. From the Batmobile—extrapolated from real-world tank design—to the other villains in the film—brutish mobster Carmine Falcone and sociopathic psychologist Jonathan Crane, a.k.a. the Scarecrow—Nolan properly reins in the outlandish elements to a point where Batman's universe is only one or two steps removed from our own. There are no supermen from other planets who can save our world here, only a human being with enough determination and loose screws to roam the city dressed like a bat for our protection. Boy, it makes for great drama when things are that simple.

It's a lesson that all caretakers of the Batman mythos would do well to follow, not just those tasked with bringing the character to movie screens. Frank Miller knows this. In an interview conducted by Kim

Thompson and published in *The Comics Journal Library, Volume Two: Frank Miller*, Miller talks about how, in his celebrated Dark Knight series, he strived to restore the human context in the Batman mythos and present the American city in more realistic terms. Miller goes on to say: "As dramatic as it was when Superman teamed up with Batman, or Spider-Man met the Fantastic Four, these were steps taken toward ruining the superhero. Now, modern superhero comics have reached the point where there are so many damn superheroes and so damn much superpower flying around that there's no room left for anything human."

It's too bad the folks at DC don't always listen to Frank. In the last few years, the people in charge of the Batman comics have made a couple of truly boneheaded decisions that further remove the humanity from the Dark Knight's universe. Sometimes it's a little thing—a minor reworking of a character that may look cool on the page but is enough to drive a serious-minded Batman enthusiast crazy. Consider, for example, the 2004 transformation of the Scarecrow into some hideous monstrosity called "the Scarebeast." Jonathan Crane has always been one of the more low-key members of Batman's rogues gallery. He's a meek-looking, spectacled professor who preys on the fear of innocents using a harmful combination of drugs and psychological tactics. He's a very cool, very nasty, very *human* character. Cillian Murphy played him brilliantly in *Batman Begins*—coldly calculating but totally insane. Yet in the 2004 story arc *As the Crow Flies*, beginning with *Batman* #627, the Penguin succeeded in mutating Crane, turning him into the Scarebeast—a creature that is ten feet tall, possesses super-strength and -agility, has claws instead of fingers, and can release a hallucinogenic gas biologically. He's essentially one of J. R. R. Tolkien's Ents crossbred with a werewolf. The transformation was incredibly dopey and turned the Scarecrow into a superhuman, larger-than-life menace that, quite frankly, Batman already has too many of in the comics. Look no further than Clayface and Man-Bat . . . and hope you never see any of them in a Batman film. To defeat the beast, Batman donned a thickly armored Batsuit that would make Tony Stark proud and proceeded to punch the mutated Crane senseless. Though Alfred did pitch in at the end with a well-timed tranquilizer shot. But these punches lacked the thrill of Batman's more visceral rounds of fisticuffs. When you have a gigantic screeching monster on one side of a fight and a man wearing a seemingly indestructible suit of techno-armor on the other, it's all too easy to remember that you're just reading a silly comic book where nothing much matters besides the *Bang! Pow! Zap!* of it all. Writers blessed with the opportunity to pen a Batman title should aspire to more.

The Scarebeast eventually turned back into skinny little Jonathan Crane, though the beast within has occasionally emerged to do more damage, adding a Jekyll-and-Hyde dimension to the Scarecrow that the character certainly didn't need. And Crane isn't the only Batman villain who has undergone this kind of misguided reinvention. Killer Croc was originally Waylon Jones, a man afflicted by a rare medical condition that gave him reptilian-like skin and made him an outcast of society. People shunned him because of his strange appearance, which in turn drove him to a life of crime. It isn't exactly Shakespeare, but it's a compelling enough backstory. These days, however, Croc is usually written as 95 percent dinosaur—a lizard-headed abomination with more teeth than soul. And when fighting these exaggerated villains, Batman often abandons the skills that make him an intriguing hero: his wit, his gift for strategy, his resourcefulness. Those things tend to get tossed in favor of a clunky metal Batsuit. (And riddle me this: If Batman can take down a rampaging Scarebeast with a simple costume change, why is the Joker always so much of a problem?) Still, the transfigured Scarecrow and amped-up Killer Croc are minor in the grand scheme of things and easily retconned down the line. What about intrusions of the fantastical that aren't easily erased? Ones that permanently alter the fabric of Batman's universe for the worse? DC has erred here recently as well—and in a big way.

The 1988 death of Robin #2, Jason Todd, was originally the result of a cheap gimmick. DC Comics set up a toll-free number where Batman fans could call and vote on whether Jason should live or die in the *A Death in the Family* story arc (which ran from *Batman* #426–429). Death won, and Jason was viciously murdered by the Joker. Then something interesting happened. Over the years, Jason's death grew in meaning as it weighed heavily on Bruce Wayne's mind. Remember, Bruce takes to the streets at night as Batman to prevent the tragedy of his parents' murders from happening to others. So what does it say that he couldn't save his own protégé? What is the purpose of Batman if he can't even protect the ones he loves? The effects of Jason's loss have been effectively explored by many writers in the years since his death, always symbolized by Jason's Robin costume hanging solemnly behind glass in the Batcave. Bruce remains haunted by Jason's death, and it informs many of his decisions later on (for example, his reluctance to take on Robin #3, Tim Drake). What started as a publicity stunt ended up adding yet another human dimension to Batman as a character. That is, until DC went and ruined it all by bringing Jason Todd back to life in a blaze of retconning and mind-blowingly ridiculous fantasy/sci-fi drivel (culminating in Judd Winick's *Under the Hood* story arc, *Batman* #635–641).

Rather than attempt to personally explain how Jason Todd came back to life some fifteen-plus real-world years after his death, let us instead turn to Wikipedia for the full story. And I quote:

> . . . Jason indeed had died at the hands of the Joker, but when Superboy-Prime alters reality from the paradise dimension in which he is trapped (six months after his death), Jason is restored to life and breaks out of his coffin, but collapses thereafter and is hospitalized. After spending a year in a coma and subsequently as an amnesiac vagrant, he is recognized by Talia al Ghul, who restores his health and memory by immersing him in a Lazarus Pit in which her father Ra's al Ghul is also bathing. ("Jason Todd")

Superboy-Prime? Paradise dimension? Lazarus Pit? God, I hate this stuff. But looking past all the supernatural bullshit, the biggest crime committed here is that bringing Jason Todd back to life snuffs out one of the harshest, most brutally real chapters of Bruce Wayne's life—makes it as if it never happened. One of the inspired things about Jason's death was that it was (seemingly) permanent, unlike most other comic book demises, where you roll your eyes and say sarcastically, "Yeah, right. That'll last." Heck, DC used to print a quote on the back of the *A Death in the Family* trade paperback from former *Batman* writer Denny O'Neil that said, "It would be a really sleazy stunt to bring him back."

Sleazy? Sure. Also monumentally stupid, especially when you're liberally using alternate dimensions and characters from other timelines just to dramatically legitimize the fact that Jason is breathing again. (Note to DC: It didn't work.) The resurrection of Jason Todd is the strongest example of what happens when you mix Batman's universe with too much fantasy hogwash—the whole endeavor becomes laughable. And that's the one thing you never want with Batman's world, a place where the all-too-real screams from Arkham Asylum pierce the air, where criminals use knives and guns instead of superpowers to threaten innocents. But if the Joker can't really kill anyone without them being magically reborn, what's the point of Bruce Wayne putting on the Batsuit in the first place? Even worse, what's the point of us caring?

This is the third of ROBERT BRIAN TAYLOR's Smart Pop essays, as he has previously written about the kickass women of Joss Whedon's *Firefly* and how Brian Michael Bendis spins better Spider-Man tales than Sam Raimi. He writes a weekly TV column for *The Herald*, the daily newspaper of Rock Hill, South Carolina, although he currently lives in the Pittsburgh area with his wife, April, and daughter, Zoe. You can find him online at www.robertbriantaylor.com.

REFERENCES

"Jason Todd." Wikipedia. 20 Aug. 2007.
   <http://en.wikipedia.org/w/index.php?title=Jason_Todd&oldid=142411709>
Miller, Frank. Interview by Kim Thompson. In *The Comics Journal Library: Frank Miller*, edited by Milo George. Fantagraphics Books: Seattle, 2003.

Anyone who wants to write heroic fiction would do well to pay as much attention to his villains as his heroes. It's a lesson I learned pretty late: your good guy is only as good as the bad guy who gives him his opportunity to shine. In the following piece, Lou Anders speculates on how well the Batman's greatest foe — and, I would argue, the greatest evildoer in pop culture — will fare in his next screen incarnation. Along the way, Mr. Anders gives us a glimpse of the many faces of the Batman and offers an opinion as to which one is the truest.

TWO OF A KIND

Can the Team Behind *Batman Begins* Capture the Essence of the Joker?

LOU ANDERS

Once upon a time, when the mention of the Caped Crusader would invoke singing of the Batman Theme from the campy Adam West TV show or recollections of the Hanna-Barbera *Super Friends* series, I would protest that, no, these cartoon and live-action media representations of the Dark Knight Detective weren't the *real* Batman. They were silly Hollywood corruptions and not what I meant when I told you I was a fan. There was a serious story here, waiting to be told.

And with the debut of *Batman Begins*, it was. For the first time in the life of the character's then sixty-six-year history, the real Caped Crusader came to the big screen. The film was a critical as well as commercial success, winning both comic book fan and widespread mainstream approval and grossing $205 million domestically and $372 million worldwide. The general consensus was that the "definitive" version of the character had finally been done. Now, the team of director Christopher Nolan and screenwriter David S. Goyer are set to do it again. Joined this time by screenwriter Jonathan Nolan (*The Prestige*, *Memento*), they will return to Gotham City in 2008 with *The Dark Knight*, a film that will tackle the Batman's archnemesis and perhaps the most famous supervillain in seven decades of comic books, the Joker. Having given us the definitive interpretation of the Batman, will they be able to capture the Clown Prince of Crime as well? To answer the question, one must first look at who the Batman is, and how they were able to sift through almost a century of material to arrive at the core of the crimefighter.

Of course, there isn't really such a thing as a "real" Batman. Leaving aside the obvious contention that he doesn't exist, we must further concede that there has been a multitude of variations and interpretations since his inception. Like many characters who have achieved immortality through their popularity, James Bond and Sherlock Holmes among them, tales of his exploits range far beyond the decades of his conception. The Batman who fought Nazis in World War II and mobsters in the '40s and '50s is not the same Batman who fought terrorists in the '70s or Al-Qaeda in 2007.[1] The Batman of *The Dark Knight Returns* is not the same as the Super-Batman of Planet X (also known as planet Zur-En-Arrh, as recounted in *Batman* #113). Director Tim Burton's Batman is not Joel Schumacher's Batman is not Christopher Nolan's Batman. Batman is a myth, a symbol, a legend like King Arthur or Robin Hood. There are as different iterations as there are writers who have crafted his adventures, his exact nature depending on who is doing the writing and the time in which each tale is set. Batman creator Bob Kane—who was much more of an artist than he was a writer—deserves the most credit, not for his words, but for crafting an enduring iconography—the cowl, the cape, the cave, the car, the butler, the signal, the rogues gallery—that lasts and lends itself to a multitude of interpretations across the decades and now across the centuries. And the version of Batman that delighted small children in the adventures of the *Super Friends* back in 1973 is no less valid than the grittiest noir retellings of the character appearing from Frank Miller in 1986 or Grant Morrison today.

My own introduction to the character came through the Adam West series of 1966–1968, and from a largely forgotten animated series called *The New Adventures of Batman* (1977), which featured Adam West and Burt Ward as the voices of the Dynamic Duo, along with Lou Scheimer as Bat-Mite—a character I loved then as much as I loathed it later. But

---

[1] Frank Miller's *Holy Terror, Batman!*, which might not appear on time as scheduled.

even as a small child, I was aware of the evolution of the Batman character. My parents had given me a nice hardcover volume called *Batman: From the '30s to the '70s* (Crown Publishers, 1971). It reprinted choice selections from the Dark Knight Detective's career, from his very first appearance (*Detective Comics* #27, "The Case of Bat-Man & the Chemical Syndicate"), to the first appearances of the Joker and Robin, and continuing through important moments such as Dick Grayson's departure for Hudson University and beyond. Poring through this volume, my childhood self was exposed to the entire progression of the superhero genre in microcosm. I was able to track as both art and story grew in depth and sophistication, and though I lacked the vocabulary to describe it, I could sense how Bob Kane's genius lay in creating a character who was so visually memorable that he could be pulled back and forth like taffy and still survive. And I began to get a sense, even then, that within this history there was a serious depiction of the character at odds with some of its more lamentable renditions. What's more, the character had actually begun life on a serious footing, only to slide into parody before a return.

Introduced in 1939, "the Batman" began life as a noir vigilante, very much in the vein of the earlier pulp hero, the Shadow. In fact, he executed criminals without compunction with twin-six guns in a manner that would have made Lamont Cranston proud. But within a year, the Boy Wonder was introduced, World War II was looming large in the American consciousness, and dark-toned stories fell out of favor in lieu of more lighthearted fair. Batman and Robin soon revealed they had a code against killing, the guns were gone (in part to play down the inevitable Shadow comparisons), and their mythos rewritten such that the Batman had never killed.

Truth be told, through much of the '40s and '50s, Batman's comic book exploits were pretty much inline in tone and temperament with those of his camp '60s television show counterpart. To this day, you'll never find a better Penguin than Burgess Meredith or a more accurate rendition of the Riddler than that offered by Frank Gorshin. (Oddly, the only major Bat-villain to be absent from the television show was Two-Face, perhaps because his scarred countenance was too horrific. However, of all the stories from that era, it's interesting to note that the

Two-Face encounters are the least camp, the most poignant—drenched as they were in the character's guilt and steadfast refusal to believe in the possibility of redemption. As such, they hold up the best in light of today's more sophisticated readers' standards.) Still, the Batman TV series and the era that spawned it are generally regarded as the low point in the character's history.

However, it was as the camp television show was in its final days that a writer named Denny O'Neil (born the same month and year as the Batman himself, May 1939) took over the reigns of the comic book and changed everything. Partnering with the soon-to-be-legendary artist Neal Adams, who brought a hitherto unseen level of realism to the depiction of superheroes, O'Neil revamped the Batman legend, either reinventing the character or returning it to its 1939 roots, depending on your perspective. Robin (who was previously presumed to be thirteen) was swiftly aged and sent off to college. Gone mostly were the costumed villains, replaced by international terrorists, corrupt politicians, and mafia bosses. O'Neil's Batman was a Darknight Detective—emphasis on "detective"—more akin to Sherlock Holmes than a superhero, who employed his wits and credible criminology methods in the apprehension of evildoers. Rolling with the times, Bruce Wayne moved out of Wayne Manor into a penthouse apartment atop the Wayne Foundation in the heart of Gotham, and the Batmobile itself was often depicted as little more than an unmarked dark blue sports car, not dissimilar to a Corvette of the era. Occasionally it would have the suggestion of the Batman's cowl in the lines of its hood, but gone were the fins, bubble domes, rocket engines, and Bat-insignias of previous models. The mysterious Ra's al Ghul was introduced at this time as well, his daughter and Batman-love interest Talia and his Himalayan headquarters both directly inspired by the James Bond film *On Her Majesty's Secret Service*. O'Neil also worked in Batman-inspiration the Shadow, first in *Batman* #253 in a storyline called "Who Knows What Evil—?" and again in "The Night of the Shadow," appearing in *Batman* #259, which explained that Batman abstained from guns because of a phobia resulting from a childhood encounter with the Shadow. (Since the Shadow was only temporarily licensed to DC, the brilliant *Batman: The Animated Series* later replaced Wayne's childhood inspiration with a similar character called the Grey

Ghost, voiced, appropriately enough, by Adam West. Ah, the tangled webs. . . .) Suffice to say, the O'Neil and Adams era established the Batman (not Batman, but "the Batman" as he was originally called) as a serious comic book icon, and their tales remained for many years the quintessential depiction of the character.

But a three-decades long backstory weighs heavy, and in the wake of O'Neil's departure from DC Comics, the costumed villains, one by one, came marching back in. The late '70s and early '80s were a schizophrenic time for the character, with writers and fans maintaining the "seriousness" of Batman while parading out an assortment of costumed crazies, with everything from dueling versions of the Mad Hatter to the Calendar Man making an appearance. Slowly, the legend of the Batman began to ebb, if not back toward camp, toward a muddle from which little work of lasting significance emerged. (An exception to this is a brief but significant run in *Detective Comics* by Steve Englehart and Marshall Rogers, *Detective Comics* #471–476, August 1977 to March–April 1978, which revived the 1939 villain Professor Hugo Strange and duplicated the Joker's original killing spree from his first appearance. More on this later.) This is not to say no good work was crafted in this period, but everything that came before was about to be overshadowed by a landmark event in comic book history.

Everything changed when Frank Miller's *The Dark Knight Returns* burst on the scene in 1986. In this tale of an aging Bruce Wayne emerging from retirement for one last showdown against crime and corruption, Miller chose to play up the "dark" in *Dark Knight*. His Batman was obsessed, seething with a barely contained rage that forced out any chance at companionship or peace and overwhelmed Wayne. To recount *The Dark Knight Returns*'s influence on and importance in the entire comics industry would take another essay entirely. The prestige format was created for its release, and it almost single-handedly launched the "graphic novel" format as well — to say nothing of the emphasis it caused to be placed on adult storytelling, nor the respect for comic books it engendered in the mainstream. But suffice it to say that *The Dark Knight Returns*, along with Miller's later *Batman: Year One*, soon became the definitive rendition of the character, and while it has become somewhat diluted by recent poor efforts on Miller's part — his woefully inferior *The*

21

Dark Knight Strikes Again reads more like a parody of Frank Miller than Miller himself—still, the 1986 work has characterized the view of Batman that is now entering its third decade of dominance.

It was the initial success of *The Dark Knight Returns* that prompted Warner Bros. to put forth a darker, "serious" cinematic version of the character—it's been rumored a comedy starring Bill Murray had previously been in development—that resulted in the 1989 Tim Burton film, *Batman*. Praised at the time for being the most serious depiction the Batman had yet received in film or television, and impressive in its striking visual surrealism, it nonetheless wasn't right in the eyes of many fans, eschewing reality for Dali-esque surrealism and prompting Frank Miller himself to say that there were many versions of the Batman character, and obviously he and Tim Burton were depicting different ones. Nonetheless, the film made the character hotter than ever, and the success of the Burton film prompted Warner Bros. to launch a new cartoon franchise, conceived in more sophistication than any previous animated version. *Batman: The Animated Series* (later *The Adventures of Batman and Robin*, 1992–1995) drew its inspiration not from cinema but from comic books. The brainchild of producers Paul Dini and Bruce Timm, this series accomplished the daunting task of synthesizing six decades of comic material into a coherent narrative. For many, it became the new definitive.

Meanwhile, the live-action cinema franchise quickly degenerated. Michael Keaton, who portrayed the character in *Batman* and *Batman Returns*, turned down a then-unheard-of thirty-five million dollars to reprise his role in *Batman Forever*, dissatisfied that the script was lighter in tone than the previous two films. Under the helming of director Joel Schumacher, the franchise that Tim Burton launched ended in the almost universally loathed *Batman & Robin* in 1997. Resembling little more than a decadent, incoherent, and overblown version of the camp '60s television series, the film was so indisputably bad that even star George Clooney opinioned, "I think we might have killed the franchise" (Daniel).

And for a while all was quiet. Once again "Batman" was no longer cool, a dirty word, a silly franchise as ill-regarded as the Adam West series had been decades earlier. And any chance of seeing the "real"

Batman on the big screen seemed hopelessly remote. But, again, what is the "real" Batman? "Right" is and will always be subjective, and I wouldn't begrudge the children of yesterday one iota of their enjoyment when Batman and his super friends save the day. But I contend that we can speak in terms of levels of sophistication of various Batman interpretations, as well as pinpoint key works as having had the most profound and lasting influences on the canon, as determined by writers and fans over years. And by acknowledging that the canon of any long-running franchise is a dialogue between fans and creators, and assembling those stories that have had the most significant lasting impact, we can arrive at something like a Batman "ideal," even while acknowledging the impossibility of such a goal.

To date, the "great works of the Batman canon" would certainly include O'Neil and Adams' original run, the aforementioned Englehart & Rogers collaboration, Frank Miller's *The Dark Knight Returns* and *Year One*, Alan Moore's *The Killing Joke*, *Batman: The Animated Series* and related animated movies and spin-offs (*Mask of the Phantasm, Batman Beyond, Justice League,* etc. . . .), and Jeff Loeb and Tim Sale's *The Long Halloween* and *Dark Victory*. These works have informed and fed into each other, such that bits of *Year One* were transcribed directly into *Mask of the Phantasm*, themes from *The Killing Joke* found their way into *Batman Beyond: Return of the Joker*, characters from *The Animated Series* worked their way into official DC comics continuity, etc. Therefore, with allowances to the character's variegated history, and apologies to Adam West, a "definitive depiction" of the Dark Knight might look something like this.

First and foremost, an accurate rendition of the Batman must acknowledge the extreme force of will of the character. Michael Keaton's Batman was a frustrated and confused little guy who suited up in stiff armor and used an arsenal of impossible gadgets to vent his frustration, then came home and had trouble sleeping. He was dark all right, but his anger was unfocused, his motivation unclear, his methods unrefined. The Batman of the comics, as he is portrayed today, is a "normal" human being who can enter a room full of super-powered beings and command their attention and send a chill down every spine there—despite having no powers of his own—by his mere presence and force of personality.

This is a man who believes, as he said in *The Dark Knight Returns*, that "the world only makes sense when you force it to" (192), and has the will to carry out that objective. An accurate presentation, therefore, has to understand this sense of will, and presence, and discipline, and tightly restrained force.

Secondly, it's important to understand that the Batman has something to prove. Legendary artist Dick Giordano once said of Batman, "The Batman does what he does for himself, for his needs. That society gains from his actions is incidental, an added value . . . but not the primary reason for his activities" ("Graphic Novel Reviews"). Consider: Young Bruce Wayne was the prince of Gotham City, a billionaire's son living a life only the top 1 percent of the world could enjoy. Then, in an instant, his happiness and security were yanked away from him. That realization, the realization of the inevitability of death as the great equalizer—that no matter who you are, you can step outside and be hit by a bus, be struck by lightning, choke on an olive pit, be shot by a petty thief, and it can all end—struck the young Wayne at an age way earlier than most of us ever encounter it. (I still remember being seventeen and seeing how close I could drive my car to a retaining wall on a curving mountain road. And the exact moment, a year later, when I realized the foolishness of that action, when I suddenly understood with stunning certainty that I was not immortal.) This knowledge—and accompanying fear—of death at such an impressionable age terrified him. Too much, too soon, and he was over the edge. Like Captain Ahab, who lost his leg (and more if you read between the lines) to the White Whale, Wayne set out to prove to the universe that death could not catch him unawares again. He chose as his territory Gotham City, and as his target the criminal underworld (as Ahab chose the whale), but his real target (and intended audience) was the cosmos itself. In a Batman story from the early '70s, a trained martial artist studied Batman in combat and then attempted to take him down. Later, looking out the window of Commissioner Gordon's office, Batman mused that somewhere out there, some other punk was readying himself to take his shot. Gordon asked if that made him depressed, and Batman responded that, no, he could hardly wait. In "Ghost of the Killer Skies" (*Detective Comics* #404), he even challenged a cornered opponent to a duel in the air in biplanes, a rather pointless bit of theatrics when a simple punch would have sufficed, until

24

we remember his motivation—proving to himself and the universe that no matter what form death takes, it will find him ready. This theme played out in full in Frank Miller's *The Dark Knight Returns*, in which every possible death was evaluated by the Batman until he settled on one grand enough to lay his spirit to rest—that of beating the Man of Steel, here very deliberately a stand-in for God, in a fistfight. Throughout the graphic novel, Superman was built up in divine terms, the President of the United States even saying in a televised address, "We have God on our side . . . or the next best thing" (119). When Batman beat Superman senseless, he declared, "In all the years to come . . . in your most private moments . . . I want you to remember . . . my hand . . . at your throat. . . . I want . . . you to remember . . . the one man who beat you . . ." (195). And with that, he "died" with a heart-stopping concoction of his own making. When he was later revived, it was only Bruce Wayne who emerged, by and finally himself, at long last free of the spirit of the "burnt remains of a crimefighter whose time has passed" (199).[2]

Thirdly, essential to the Batman character is a refusal to kill and an aversion to guns in particular. Not to pick on him excessively, but in the second Burton film, *Batman Returns*, Michael Keaton's Batman sits inside the protection of his armored Batmobile and burns alive an unprotected man with a flame from his rocket engine, after the other ineffectually menaced him by breathing fire in a cheap circus stunt. This dick-wagging scene, which drew a chuckle from the audience I saw it with, not only flew in the face of seventy years of continuity, but was the most cowardly act the Batman has ever been seen to enact on film. In contrast, the Batman of Frank Miller's *The Dark Knight Returns* shut off his weaponry and emerged from his Batmobile to take on a younger, stronger, seemingly superior foe bare-handed because "I honestly don't know if I could beat him" (77) (see the second point above). The Batman absolutely cannot kill, even in self-defense. In fact, especially

---

[2] Miller undermined this himself twelve years later when DC Comics paid him to write the three-issue sequel, *The Dark Night Strikes Again*. Controversial, and largely considered an inferior repudiation of the original, I don't think much of it myself. The kindest thing that can be said of it is that it may be a deliberate satire of the past decade of grim and gritty adult works that Miller himself helped to set in motion. Editor's Note: See Geoff Klock's essay following this one for another interpretation.

25

not in self-defense. Since he is acting out of selfish motivation, as Giordano notes above, and placing himself into situations in which he must prove his superiority over death on a nightly basis, he would be a monster if he condoned killing in self-defense. His entire perception of his own sanity, therefore, and his ability to circumnavigate Gotham's laws in favor of a higher, personal justice, rests on his interpretation of this razor-thin line.

Finally, any accurate depiction of the Batman must include the understanding that, unlike the vast majority of costumed crime fighters, Batman's secret identity is not his core persona. Bruce Wayne, the millionaire playboy, is the disguise, whereas "the Batman" is his true nature. In Grant Morrison's *Arkham Asylum*, when asked by a henchman if they can unmask the captive Batman to see his true face, the Joker snapped, "That is his true face." In an episode of the animated spin-off series *Batman Beyond*, when a criminal named Shriek used a chip implanted in his skull to try to drive the elder Bruce Wayne insane by making him hear voices in his head, Batman confessed that he maintained his grip thusly: "the voices kept calling me Bruce. In my mind, that's not the name I call myself" ("Shriek," 1-6). Wayne is a prop, a place for Batman to hide during the day. Unlike other heroes, who fear exposure of their private lives, if Bruce Wayne were ever revealed to be the Batman, Wayne would merely disappear, and six months later another alter-ego would emerge to serve a similar function, but the Batman would continue unaffected. Inconvenienced, sure, but unchanged.

Certainly, expecting Hollywood to get all the subtle nuances of the above is a tall order, so it's little short of a miracle that they found a team who did. Director Christopher Nolan and screenwriter David S. Goyer took as their inspiration the aforementioned seminal works, relying heavily on Denny O'Neil's original stories of Ra's al Ghul, Frank Miller's *Batman: Year One*, a 1989 comic book story called "The Man Who Falls," which was itself a retelling/compilation of several classic stories (originally published in the *Secret Origins* trade paperback collection), and Loeb and Sale's *The Long Halloween* and *Dark Victory*. Star Christian Bale even kept copies of the latter works on set with him for reference when he needed help maintaining his focus on the character. Drawing from these seminal works, all of which were already feeding off of and into each other, they produced *Batman Begins*. And as to our criteria for a "definitive" Batman?

They nail the force of will of the character when Henri Ducard says to Bruce Wayne, "Your training is nothing. The will to act is everything." If this sounds a bit like Friedrich Nietzsche's concept of the Will to Power, that's probably the intent, as witness Ducard's words about the strong and the weak. As to the juggle between personal vendetta and the ancillary benefit to society, see the film's ongoing dialogue with Alfred Pennyworth. As to the Bruce Wayne persona, Rachel Dawes has it right when she says the face the criminals see is the real one. And as for his code against killing, the entire film is an exploration of how close to that line Bruce Wayne will go without crossing over ("I won't kill you. But I don't have to save you either"). And the success of the film—which had the daunting task of relaunching a dead and lampooned franchise and did so triumphantly—was testament to the validity of this interpretation of the character. Simply put, by crafting what is the most faithful-to-the-comics adaptation of Batman to date on film, Nolan and Goyer created in *Batman Begins* what has emerged as the new definitive rendition of the Batman, as well as raised the bar for comic book adaptations henceforth.

Now, this Dynamic Duo, together with Nolan's brother and screenwriting partner Jonathan, are setting up to do it again with *The Dark Knight*, a film that will see them return to Gotham City to tackle the Batman's archnemesis, the most famous supervillain of them all, the Joker. So, who is this Joker and where did he come from?

The Harlequin of Hate, as he is sometimes called, was first introduced in "Batman vs. the Joker" in *Batman* #1, spring 1940. In his first appearance, he was a deadly serious murderer, who announced his intended victims' fates and dared the police to stop him. He was ghastly, ghostly, nothing to laugh about. In fact, he racked up quite a body count in his first twelve appearances, killing almost thirty people before being sent to the electric chair. But the Joker developed a knack for cheating seeming-deaths, and this was far from the end for the character, despite being originally conceived as a one-off. However, the editors of *Batman* began to fear that leaving a murderer on the loose undermined the Detective's image, and so instituted a policy of only letting one-shot villains kill. For this and other reasons, the Joker was softened, dwindling into a clown-ish buffoon more interested in pranks than killing sprees. In fact, he wasn't even officially crazy. There was actually a comic in which the resolution involved Batman and Robin temporarily convincing the Joker that he was going mad. "The Crazy Crime Clown" (*Batman* #74) saw the Joker placed in a padded cell, but ended with Bruce Wayne musing, "I see where the Joker's recovered from the confusing night we gave him! They're transferring him to the state prison!" To which Dick Grayson replied, "Yes—he finally had to tell the authorities where Derek's money was hidden, in order to prove that he himself was sane!" To prove he was *sane*? Are you sure?

The character then disappeared almost entirely for much of the '60s, and it wasn't until the aforementioned Denny O'Neil and Neal Adams run, in a now-famous story in 1973 entitled "The Joker's Five Way Revenge" (*Batman* #251), that he was returned to the level of a serious and murderous threat. It was in this issue that his lack of sanity was established. When he was incarcerated, we learn that it was not in Gotham Penitentiary as previous tales had it, but in a place called Arkham Asylum for the Criminally Insane. (The name is a nod to the horror fiction of H. P. Lovecraft, Arkham being the fictional Massachusetts city that features heavily in his horror writings about the Cthulhu mythos.)

This notion that the Ace of Knaves is "criminally insane" was given more depth in the Steve Englehart and Marshall Rogers run in a 1978 story entitled "The Laughing Fish" (*Detective Comics* #475), which combined a deliberate reworking of the Joker's original 1940's appearance with a severely demented personality. To date, this issue remains one of the best portrayals of the character's madness. Superman writer Kurt Busiek, in an article in *Wizard* magazine, remembers, "Hands down, the best Joker bit ever, to my mind, is when he tries to copyright fish. . . . It's such a demented thing to do, but he pursues it so intently, so matter-of-factly—pausing only to wonder if it might not work because people might stop eating fish, but reasoning that vegetarians won't go for it—that it really makes him feel like a madman, rather than like a criminal with daffy overtones" (quoted in "Joker [comics]").

From that point forward, the Joker was always depicted as being, if you will pardon the pun, batshit crazy. But it was Alan Moore's landmark graphic novel *The Killing Joke* that truly established the definitive version of the character, retelling his origin story while allowing for differences in continuity. As the character himself said of his history, "Sometimes I remember it one way, sometimes another . . . if I'm going to have a past, I prefer it to be multiple choice!" Despite some confusion as to his former life, the idea that the Joker suffered a personal tragedy beyond just his physical scarring and equal to Bruce Wayne's own loss was introduced as explanation for the character's madness. As recounted here, that tragedy was the death of his wife and unborn child. In this story, the Joker shot Barbara Gordon in the stomach, paralyzing her for life, then kidnapped and brutalized her father Commissioner James Gordon, forcing him to look at photographs of his naked and traumatized daughter in an effort to drive him insane, an attempt to prove that anyone can have "one bad day" and become as the Joker is now. This unprecedented graphic violence escalated post-*Killing Joke*, with the Joker going on to murder Jason Todd, the second Robin, as well as Commissioner Gordon's second wife, Sarah Essen. By 2007, the Joker was indisputably one of the most dangerous and insane villains in DC's entire universe. This is in evidence in the 1995 three-issue *Underworld Unleashed*, in which Flash-nemesis the Trickster said, "When supervillains want to scare each other, they tell Joker stories."

So in the same way that we have crafted a definitive Batman, can we come up with a set of guidelines for what a definitive portrayal of the Ace of Knaves should look like?

To begin with the obvious: the Joker is dangerously insane. Far from being Cesar Romero in greasepaint and armed with a joy buzzer, this is Charles Manson meets Hannibal Lector. A modern portrayal of the Joker needs to understand this and show us someone truly terrifying, worthy of the villain said to have killed more than 2,000 people, including, as recounted in a 1996 issue of *Hitman*, an entire kindergarten class. In short, he needs to be truly frightening.

Secondly, and this is minor but please indulge me, the Joker's face is *not* fixed in a grin. True, the character was modeled on Conrad Veidt from the 1928 silent film, *The Man Who Laughs*, based on the novel by Victor Hugo, about a boy whose face is mutilated into a permanent smile. Bob Kane and Bill Finger took inspiration for the Joker's look from this character, but nowhere was it on record that his face was fixed. This misassumption found its way into the 1989 film, in which the Joker's face is frozen from a gunshot wound, but had stayed out of the comics until just this year, when Grant Morrison introduced the heresy in *Batman* #663. Hopefully, Nolan and Goyer will know better and won't saddle Heath Ledger with any cumbersome and unnecessary prosthetics.[3]

But most important is that the Joker is the one person who truly understands the complex nature of the Batman's code against killing. In fact, he is the single character in the Batman mythos who understands this as well as Batman himself, who grasps how tight a line it is that the hero walks and who knowingly pours as much pressure on this line as he can in a calculated effort to force Batman to cross over.

In Frank Miller's *The Dark Knight Returns*, the Batman says, "I'll count the dead, one by one. I'll add them to the list, Joker. The list of all the people I've murdered—by letting you live . . ." (117). For his part, while poisoning a troop of boy scouts, the Joker says, "They could put me in a helicopter and fly me up in the air and line the bodies head to toe on the ground in delightful geometric patterns like an endless June Taylor dancers routine—and it would never be enough. No, I don't keep count. But *you* do. And I love you for it" (140). His "affection" for the Batman, whom he calls "darling" more than once, comes precisely from knowing how much the mayhem he causes wounds the other man. He knows exactly what he is doing, tormenting the Batman with his crimes, deliberately attempting to force Batman to take a life preemptively. Finally, in the end, when the Batman broke his neck but failed to do so with enough pressure to kill him, he chided, "I'm really . . . very disappointed with you, my sweet . . . the moment was . . . perfect . . . and you . . . didn't have the nerve. . . . Paralysis . . . really . . . they'll kill you for this . . . and they'll never know . . . that you didn't have the nerve . . ." (150–151). And the Batman lamented, "voices calling me a killer . . . I wish I were" (150). The Joker finished himself off, and as the Batman hobbled away, the clown's corpse seemed to mock him for his lack of nerve.

---

[3] After I wrote this, an early publicity shot of Heath Ledger released to the Internet indicates that their Joker will have a scarred mouth and may *not* have white skin. As much as this upsets the canon-keeper in me, the intent of the filmmakers seems to be in presenting the Joker as anything but comical, recasting him as a seriously disturbed psychopath familiar to viewers of films like the Saw films. I applaud this intent.

But why this game? Why does the Joker so desperately want to die at Batman's hands? For that we have to turn to Alan Moore's *The Killing Joke*. When explaining his rationale for brutalizing Barbara Gordon and then forcing her father to witness the footage, the Joker said, "You see, it doesn't matter if you catch me and send me back to the asylum . . . Gordon's been driven *mad*. I've proved my point. I've demonstrated there's no difference between me and everyone else! All it takes is one bad day to reduce the sanest man alive to lunacy. That's how far the world is from where I am. Just one bad day."

Most of us don't hinge our entire sense of sanity on one single facet of character. We don't anchor our identity on a single razor's edge. But the Batman does. Taking the methods of a criminal—breaking and entering, assault, vigilantism, etc.—into his hands, the line he has drawn is his only self-justification, his only proof that the darkness has not completely swallowed him. But if the Joker can get the Batman to bend, just once, he can prove that anyone, even a person of towering force of will, will snap if subjected to enough pressure—i.e., the Joker himself is blameless for his crimes, as he was just someone who snapped after a sufficient amount of tragedy. In *The Further Adventures of the Joker*, in a story by Mark L. Van Name and Jack McDevitt called "Happy Birthday," the Joker tries to demonstrate this once again. He calls in favors and threats all over town, pouring criminals onto the street, subjecting Gotham to a week of utter chaos. This takes a predictable toll on the Caped Crusader. Then, at the culmination, he disguises himself as a cop and dresses a kidnapped cop up as the Joker. Accompanying Batman on a raid, he asks the Dark Knight if he shouldn't just do the world a favor and pull the trigger, and for a moment, the Batman considers. Then Batman sees through the game. But at the story's conclusion, the Joker remarks, "So I won that one. And sometimes at night, when the moon is high, and I know he's out there, I feel a little better. The distance between us isn't as great as it used to be" (290).

This is spelled out again in "The Clown at Midnight" (*Batman* #663): "You can't kill me without becoming like me. I can't kill you without losing the only human being who can keep up with me. Isn't it ironic?!" Later in the issue, he mused, "I could never kill you. Where would the act be without my straight man?"

31

Grant Morrison's *Arkham Asylum* is, even in Morrison's admission, not a great portrayal of Batman, but it does get one thing right about the Joker. At the graphic novel's resolution, the Batman agrees with the Joker and acknowledges the necessity of his own insanity. The result? The Joker is satisfied. Having finally gotten the admission he's *always* wanted, he shuts everything down, surrenders, and walks Batman out of Arkham with an arm around his shoulder, promising him, "Enjoy yourself out there. In the Asylum. Just don't forget—if it gets too tough . . . there's always a place for you here."

Just like Batman, the Joker has something to prove. Their motivations are locked like opposite poles of a magnet. That Batman draws such a clear line in the sand is irresistible to a psyche desperate to see only shades of grey. He's willing to murder the entire world if that is what it takes to make the Dark Knight relinquish his last, tenuous, and tiny finger-hold on sanity. His own salvation rests on proving his point. If Nolan, Nolan, and Goyer understand even half of this, we'll be alright. Given their track record, I suspect we will be, and the most famous supervillain in the history of comics will finally be given his full cinematic due. After all, when you have this level of material to draw upon, anything less would be crazy.

A Hugo and World Fantasy Award nominee, LOU ANDERS is the editorial director of Prometheus Books's science fiction imprint Pyr (www.pyrsf.com), as well as the anthologies *Outside the Box* (Wildside Press 2001), *Live Without a Net* (Roc 2003), *Projections: Science Fiction in Literature & Film* (MonkeyBrain December 2004), *FutureShocks* (Roc January 2006), and *Fast Forward 1* (Pyr February 2007). He is the author of *The Making of Star Trek: First Contact* (Titan Books 1996), and has published more than 500 articles in such magazines as *The Believer*, *Publishers Weekly*, *Dreamwatch*, *Star Trek Monthly*, *Star Wars Monthly*, *Babylon 5 Magazine*, *Sci-Fi Universe*, *Doctor Who Magazine*, and *Manga Max*. His articles and stories have been translated into Danish, Greek, German, Italian, and French. Visit him online at www.louanders.com.

REFERENCES

Bridwell, E. Nelson. *Batman: From the '30s to the '70s.* New York: Crown Publishers, 1971.
Daniel, Mac. "Behind the Masks." *Boston Globe.* 22 Aug. 2007. <http://www.boston.com/ae/movies/articles/2005/06/12/behind_the_masks>
"Graphic Novel Reviews." *Cats Illustrated.* 22 Aug. 2007. <http://cats.english-mist.com/reviews_graphic.html>
"Joker (comics)." Wikipedia. 22 Aug. 2007. <http://en.wikipedia.org/wiki/Joker_comics>
Van Name, Mark L., and Jack McDevitt. "Happy Birthday." In *The Further Adventures of the Joker*, edited by Martin H. Greenberg. New York: Bantam, 1990.

One of the things a critic can do is let us see familiar material from a fresh perspective. That's what Geoff Klock does in the following essay. He argues that some of Frank Miller's later stories, which some readers thought were mistakes, if not frauds, were in fact the fruits of a "subversive genius." After reading Dr. Klock's essay, you may want to revisit the works he writes about, and see it and some of Mr. Miller's other Batman efforts in a new way.

FRANK MILLER'S NEW BATMAN AND THE GROTESQUE

GEOFF KLOCK

A long with Alan Moore, Frank Miller is the most important comic book creator in the last quarter century. In 1986, he wrote and drew *Batman: The Dark Knight Returns*, which revolutionized the comic book industry—it created a radical and definitive version of Batman for the new adult demographic and proved once and for all that superhero comic books, though originally created for children, could tell stories rich and complex enough to rival any novel. Frank Miller followed his success soon after with *Batman: Year One*, illustrated by Dave Mazzucchelli—a book that was similarly mature, and tightly plotted and drawn. These works created a new canonical center for Batman, around which Batman history organized itself. Pre-Miller or post-Miller, every story for the character before and after lived in the shadow of Miller's bat.

Nearly twenty years later, Miller returned to writing Batman stories and chose to write sequels to his earlier projects: *Batman: The Dark Knight Returns* was followed by *The Dark Knight Strikes Again* (2002), like its predecessor written and drawn by Miller. *Batman: Year One* was followed by *All Star Batman and Robin the Boy Wonder* (2006), like its predecessor illustrated by another artist, here Jim Lee. Neither of Miller's '80s Batman projects

35

cried out for a sequel, however—*Dark Knight Returns* imagined what a "last" Batman story would look like, and *Year One*, a retelling and expansion of Batman's origin story, ended with an allusion to the first appearance of Batman's major nemesis, the Joker, a story already told many times.

Both of Miller's new millennium Batman projects were attacked by huge numbers of fans as insane, absurd, as trampling the memories of Miller's original works, not to mention Bob Kane's original character. Many fans went so far as to suggest Miller was writing intentionally horrible comics to intentionally screw with fans and laugh at DC Comics for paying him money. The objections are for the most part very simple. The artwork in *DKSA* is grotesque and bizarre—characters are weirdly out of proportion and colored with big, clunky 1980s computer pixels. In *All Star*, the story itself has glaring pacing problems and errors that are hard to ignore. Batman, for example, kidnapped the boy who would be Robin and more than three issues passed before they got from the circus to the Batcave; because of publishing delays, this covered a real-life time period of more than eleven months. To emphasize the absurdity of this, Miller had Robin appear as a missing kid on the back of a milk carton in a different city before the car ride was over. To make matters worse, interviews suggest Miller made these "mistakes" intentionally (Newsarama).

My claim here is simple: Frank Miller's new Batman projects have a subversive genius that conservative fans have missed. Frank Miller is so much of an iconoclast that he breaks not only the stories done by all previous writers of Batman—as he did in the 1980s with his first Batman projects—but his own earlier Batman work as well, by pushing it into the grotesque.

BATMAN: THE DARK KNIGHT RETURNS AND BATMAN: YEAR ONE[1]

Bob Kane invented Batman in 1939. Subsequent writers of Batman either repeated stories in whatever vein they had inherited or updated Batman

---

[1] I have written extensively about *Dark Knight Returns* and *Year One* in my book *How to Read Superhero Comics and Why* (Continuum 2002). This section is largely a summary of what I wrote there, in order to set up how Miller breaks from *Dark Knight Returns* and *Year One* in his new works.

by changing him to fit the time—for example, by introducing Robin and moving the tone of the book out of horror-tinged detective stories and into something much lighter and more kid-friendly. By 1986, however, Batman had almost fifty years of continuity behind him. Miller's innovation is to avoid simply "telling another Batman story"—he looks back at Batman's history and creates something that investigates, analyzes, synthesizes, and criticizes the history of his main character.

Miller is traditional in setting his comic book in the present day, in the mid 1980s, a fact he emphasizes by creating a city that is very much New York (complete with Coney Island) and a country headed by Ronald Reagan (rather than a nameless "Mr. President"). But his innovation is in calling *DKR* a "last" Batman story, in which his main character has aged into his late sixties. His Batman really *has* been fighting crime for almost fifty years, rather than mysteriously not aging through two world wars and Vietnam.

In 1954, Fredric Wertham wrote a book called *Seduction of the Innocent*, in which he argued that comics were ruining the minds of their readers. His main aim was horror comics, and he successfully abolished them for many decades, but in passing he also argued that the Batman and Robin relationship was clearly homoerotic—the older man keeps the younger man in his mansion, Robin's outfit leaves his genital region clearly on display, and so on (Wertham 191). Batman comics at the time ran from this claim—introducing Batwoman[2] to give Batman an adult female love interest—and later simply ignored it as absurd. Miller opens this issue up again by giving his Batman a new Robin, a girl. Batman spoke of her lost innocence, and at one point she straddled his crotch to keep from falling to her death. Miller casts her as a girl to say yes, this kind of relationship is possible, but to argue that there is no reason we should be concerned with it—nothing happens between them when homosexuality is taken off the table. Rather than reject sexuality—and the homosexuality that caught Wertham's eye—he displaces it from the Batman-Robin relationship to the Batman-Joker relationship, playing their fight as a sexually charged battle: the Joker called Batman "dar-

[2] A character who has ironically returned recently as a homosexual herself in the pages of DC's weekly comic book 52.

ling," and their fight culminated in the tunnel of love (141).

Batman has worn many outfits, including one with a yellow bat-shield that has raised eyebrows among fans—why would an outfit designed to blend in with shadows have such a bright target on the chest? Miller answers the question—when his Batman got shot in the chest the blast revealed metal plating: he narrated, "Why do you think I wear a target on my chest—can't armor my head" (51). Miller's Batman does not throw a batarang to knock the weapons out of the hands of criminals—Miller changes the weapon, making it a series of bat-shaped throwing stars that Batman throws into the arms of his opponents, causing them to drop their weapons in pain. Instead of a stylish but impractical Batmobile, Miller's Batman drives a kind of tank. Miller is actively revising Batman's history, reworking it into a new whole.

Finally, Miller fully accepts the political ramifications of the genre's core principle of vigilante justice—superheroes wear masks and are not hampered by legal red tape, such as probable cause, but Miller is the first to amp this up so we can see it for what it is. Miller's Batman is an unapologetic fascist: in the process of an interrogation, he threatened a man he had already left in a neck brace and crutches and mocked him when he claimed, "I got rights" (45). Though characters in the narrative object to Batman's fascism, Miller places the final word with Commissioner Gordon; Gordon compared Batman to Roosevelt, who, he noted, was suspected of knowing Pearl Harbor was going to be attacked and letting it happen anyway, to galvanize America to win World War II. Gordon said Batman and Roosevelt were beyond the judgment of mere citizens. We must accept Miller's Batman as he is, or reject him as he is—knowing that if we reject him, we reject the whole genre. Batman's final opponent in *Dark Knight Returns* is Superman, who has totally sold out and is now just a tool for Reagan-era politics. Miller demands we side with his Batman.

These carefully thought-out revisions of Batman's history created a new whole that is imaginatively persuasive, leaving the reader with the feeling that, yes, this must be what Batman is really like, that all the stories up until now have been merely kids' versions of the real thing.

Paradoxically, however, Miller's second Batman project, *Batman: Year One*, subtly subverts his first—it is an equally definitive and imaginatively persuasive vision of Batman, but its continuity cannot be reconciled with *Dark Knight Returns*. Miller is looking at an inconsistent history of Batman (who never ages and whose stories take place across fifty years), and so he writes an inconsistent history for his own Batman: his Batman is sixty years old in 1980s New York in *Dark Knight Returns* and twenty-five years old in 1980s New York in *Year One*. In a small way, Miller's *Year One* breaks the flawless and definitive portrayal he created in *Dark Knight Returns*; if fans had caught on to this move, Miller's later work, in which he totally breaks the Batman he created in these 1980s works, would have been seen for what it is—the inevitable next step.[3]

SPAWN/BATMAN

In 1994, Miller wrote what is called a "crossover story" in which Batman meets a character owned by another comic book company, Spawn. Todd McFarlane, the character's creator, drew the book. *Spawn/Batman* seems like a minor throwaway story, but by realizing that there are two squarely defined Miller Batman periods, we can locate how Miller's 1994 *Spawn/Batman* crossover fits into his artistic development. It is the transition between the '80s Batman and the present one, falling at almost the exact midpoint between the two periods; *Spawn/Batman* was written eight years after *Dark Knight Returns* and eight years before *Dark Knight Strikes Again*. Todd McFarlane, whose masculine figures all appear to be jacked up on super-steroids, helps Miller to outdo his hyper-masculine, tough-guy Batman. The Batman of Miller's *All Star* book is years away in time, but very close in spirit. McFarlane is famous for drawing grotesque out-of-proportion bodies—his art style is all about hyperbole, which was the effect Miller was after and would explode in his next two Batman projects. McFarlane's cartoon looniness heads straight into *The Dark Knight Strikes Again*. On the inside cover of *Spawn/Batman* is a disclaimer forgotten (or never noticed) by most readers: "Spawn vs. Batman is a companion piece to DC Comics' *The Dark Knight Returns*. It does not represent current DC continuity." This is not a throwaway project but an intimate part of the Batman canon Miller is building.

---

[3] For a more extensive reading of *Dark Knight Returns* and *Year One* see my *How to Read Superhero Comics and Why*, 25–52.

Spawn/Batman is dedicated to Jack Kirby who died the year it came out; the back inside cover features a photograph of Kirby. Once again Miller was looking to comic book history to justify his changes, which are not arbitrary as fans have objected. Jack Kirby was one of the founding fathers of comic books, the major figure of the Silver Age of comic books in the 1960s—in which he revolutionized comics with the creation of the X-Men and the Fantastic Four. Kirby brought two things to comic books: he coupled his prodigious imagination with realism and angst (his characters, like the Thing, were the first superheroes to wonder if their powers were a blessing or a curse), and he introduced a dynamic art style that included huge blocky hands with square fingers reaching right out to the reader in absurd but fun poses. The ghost of Jack Kirby hovers over Miller's whole later Batman work, because Kirby's emotional realism leads to Miller's political realism,[4] and it is Kirby's out-of-proportion bodies that are the origin of Miller's Batman and Lex Luthor—both of whom have giant Kirby hands in *Dark Knight Strikes Again*. Miller is looking for a new, aggressive direction to take his artwork, and so he looked toward Kirby while playing with one of Kirby's then high-profile artistic inheritors, Todd McFarlane.

THE DARK KNIGHT STRIKES AGAIN

Ironically, *Dark Knight Returns* was responsible for a host of "serious" imitators who took from the book only violence and "adult" themes, resulting in a lot of pretentious nonsense, comics whose main characters were grim figures in trench coats in the rain reciting monologues to themselves and quoting Nietzsche. *Dark Knight Strikes Again* returned to correct this trend by using the same character to strike a note of absurd exuberance. Miller's *Dark Knight Returns* certainly has elements of parodic art—Miller's Batman is unrealistically huge, and at one point he is displayed holding a dead General wrapped in an American flag—but the overall tone is serious, if operatic. *Dark Knight Strikes Again* dangerously veers between, and combines, the sublime and the ridiculous. The art is garish and intentionally loose and sloppy, but also communicates a lot

---

[4]We may identify this as faux-realism in both cases, but the gesture toward realism is the same.

of energy, enthusiasm, and fun, which should be at the core of the super-hero genre. The coloring is insane, often falling outside the lines in huge swathes of large, pixilated blocks, but it is also audacious and fantastic. It is designed to appear to us, now, the way big four-color comics of the 1930s must have looked like to kids then—garish and fun. A handful of details serve as examples.

I argued that Miller looked critically at the history of Batman's outfits, revising that yellow bat-shield. In *Dark Knight Strikes Again*, it is the Joker whose outfits resonate with comic book history. Every time Miller's Joker appears, he wears a different outfit, or an outfit constructed from a combination of several different outfits. All his outfits are references to other characters: Mr. Mxyzptlk's yellow outfit and purple derby hat, Cosmic Boy's pink outfit and white fins, even boots worn by Spider-Man, a character from another company. Miller here is breaking with his earlier investigation and synthesis of Batman's history—here he takes the history of the whole genre, but instead of synthesizing, he just dumps them on the page as chaotic visual detail, a parody of his earlier revisionary aim.

Superman and Wonder Woman have sex in the air over seven pages and then fall to earth together, smashing into the ocean and knocking over an aircraft carrier in the process. Miller is a big fan of pulp novels, and though the scope of the pulps is very different, he uses their overwrought sensibility: where a pulp novelist would have written "and the aircraft carrier was knocked over, the planes falling into the ocean like toys," Miller draws them like little toy planes with barely any detail—they are just plane-shaped gray things with little cockpit windows. The image is childish because it is the visual equivalent of a cheesy (but lovable) metaphor. Similarly, Lex Luthor is a monster, and so Miller draws him as a hulking ape, with huge square hands as big as his torso. He doesn't go for "cool" dark shadows (as McFarlane on *Spawn* would) because he doesn't want us to be in awe of Luthor—he wants us to hate him as a fun but not over-serious monster, which is also how many fans (picking up on the fascism inherent in Miller's Batman) saw the hero of *Dark Knight Returns*.

In the scene at the end of the first issue, Batman gave Superman a severe beating with a pair of Kryptonite gloves; the issue ended with the words, "Get out of my cave" (76). Batman had been narrating the issue, and we had seen him in silhouette, but for many readers this was the first time they had seen Frank Miller's Batman since 1986. The image is grotesquely simple, like a small sketch blown up too big; the garishly green kryptonite gloves on his hands are absurdly huge, the fingers especially. As Batman beats Superman, the movement of the gloves is captured by large pixilated green swathes of color, a bold choice by Lynn Varley—one of the best colorists in the industry, alongside Laura Martin (née DePuy) and Jamie Grant. Lynn Varley knows what she is doing; this must have been intentional. To drive home the moment even more, this scene at the end of the first issue is a mockery of *Dark Knight Returns*'s famous ending—Batman fought Superman early in *Dark Knight Strikes Again* just as he fought Superman at the end of *Dark Knight Returns*. That first fight, as I argued, represented an important ideological battle—Superman's law and order and *status quo* versus Batman's benevolent fascism and above-the-law higher morality. In *Dark Knight Strikes Again*, this is more like a parody—a sudden, violent beat-down that immediately gets out of the way the rematch fans have been drooling for and leaves ideological nuance behind. Miller draws on his earlier work only to break it—to smash it into fragments. He has come to show us something new and so violently swerves from what we are expecting.

There is an American literary tradition of the grotesque, including William Faulkner and Flannery O'Conner, and we should judge Miller's Batman in this context. As an instance of the grotesque, Miller's work succeeds brilliantly. The word "grotesque" comes from "grotto," a cave, because we imagine that cave dwellers, like Tolkien's Gollum, become deformed and weird; Miller's genius was realizing that Batman, who spends the better part of his time in the Batcave, was ripe for this kind of grotesque treatment. Miller created an aggressive, garish, and bizarre comic book because comic book fans are addicted to the *status quo*—he wanted to break from the past to get a fresh start. The final words of the book are Miller's Batman saying that his blown-up cave was not history—it was just a souvenir. "I was sentimental," he says, "back when I was old" (*DKS* #3). Miller's Batman is grotesque in order that he may dismiss his history as souvenirs and find the will to continue; his renewed youth is the effect of Miller giving him a fresh start. *Dark Knight Strikes Again* looks weird and wild, stylish and unique, and these are good things. Batman must be invented again and again, and we should applaud bravery in this arena—and condemn unimaginative stuff like *Batman Begins*. Miller does not compromise, as that movie did, to please the die-hard fans.

ALL STAR BATMAN AND ROBIN THE BOY WONDER

All Star Batman and Robin the Boy Wonder is a hard book to love. Like most fans, I hated the first three issues, but stuck with it out of faith that Miller should be trusted on all things Batman. With the fourth issue, I was rewarded with the realization as to how this book fits into his development. The key to appreciating *All Star Batman*, written by Frank Miller but drawn by Jim Lee, is to connect the STORY of *All Star* with the ART of *Dark Knight Strikes Again*. The plotting and details of *All Star Batman* are grossly out of proportion, like Lex Luthor's gigantic hands. And that's really wild, and a really good thing.

The first issue includes five full pages—nearly 25 percent of the comic—in which Vicki Vale dances around in bra and panties. It is the storytelling equivalent of drawing a woman with huge out-of-proportion breasts (a drawing style that reached its peak in the '90s with artists such as Jim Lee himself): the time devoted to her is as out of proportion as Miller's women usually appear visually.

Exacerbated by the slow publishing of *All Star Batman*, Robin rode in the car with Batman for eleven months of real-world time. We shouldn't just consider it a publishing issue: even monthly, four issues is a long time to keep your two title characters in a car. Miller intended this. Drawing attention to the gap, Batman is shown as having grown stubble between issues one and two, though surely very little time has passed. *That's how much of a man he is.* Miller jacks up his already famously hyper-masculine characters, and the result is hilarious and fun.

The proportions of issue three are similar to the Vicki Vale pages from the first issue: the first fifteen pages are dedicated to a new character, Black Canary, an aside that violently interrupts the Batman-meets-Robin story with fish-net stockings and nonsense; the book ends with two pages about Superman; in between, we get a full-page shot of the Batmobile, a full-page shot of Batman and Robin in the Batmobile, and a two-page splash image of the Batmobile underwater. (The advanced technology of the Batmobile is also intentionally out of whack for a book that is supposed to be a sequel to *Year One*, which starred a very low-tech Batman just starting out.) Those three images, which have minimal dialogue, hardly advance the story at all even though they are the only images that star the title characters. It is even more audacious to do this only three issues in.

The hilarious greatness of all this hit me when I saw, in the fourth issue, the six-page gatefold glamour shot of the Batcave, followed by one more single-page glamour shot of the same thing. In a twenty-two-page comic book, these pages—two images of the same thing—take up near-ly *a third of the book*. Even the title, eight words long, is, like Lex Luthor's hands, completely out of proportion. It's hilarious. Everything is wrong here, but Miller insists this is the same Batman he has been writing all along: in the cave, robots are making the robot T-Rex that Batman will use to attack Superman in *Dark Knight Strikes Again*.

The writing is not just repetitive, it's absurdly repetitive. To quote from the first issue (copying the book's repetitions rather than repeating myself), Robin says, "They're always there for me. They always catch me. Mom and dad. They always catch me. They're always there for me. They're always there for me" (2). The identical sound of "They're" and "there" makes it much worse; this is intentional. In the next scene, Vicki Vale says, "I'm hav-ing a date with Bruce Wayne. I'm having a date with Bruce Wayne. I'm hav-ing a date with Bruce Wayne. I'm having a date with Bruce Wayne. How cool is that? I'm having a date with Bruce Wayne. How cool is that?" (6-8). Cut back to Robin: "They're always there for me. They always catch me" (9). Cut to Vale: "I'm having a date with Bruce Wayne. Hot damn" (12). Miller wrote those words on paper before they were put into word balloons in the comic books. Try typing them out in Word, as I just did. No one can write like that and intend it to be taken seriously. Miller knows what he is doing, which should not surprise anyone who has read *Dark Knight Returns*. His writing is absurd in *All Star Batman* for the same reason the art is absurd in *Dark Knight Strikes Again*—because it breaks from the past and gives him imaginative breathing space to do what he wants.

Complaining about the weird proportions of, say, issue three, or the dialogue, is like complaining about the weird proportions of the eyes of anime characters, or how ugly *Rugrats* looks. Miller is developing a new kind of story here, one to match the grotesque proportions so many superhero characters are drawn with, one to match his own visual weirdness in *Dark Knight Strikes Again*.

BATMAN VS. AL-QAEDA

Batman has been done to death, even by Miller himself. So this is the next step: absurdity and the grotesque. Great superhero creators reinvent the genre. Frank Miller has reinvented the genre TWICE. He is an iconoclast—a word that means breaker of images. Frank Miller's 1980s Batman work smashed the received image of Batman and created the definitive version from the remaining shards of the *status quo*. His work with the character in the new millennium responded to the fact that his 1980s Batman work had created a new *status quo*—every Batman writer after Miller either repeated him or tried desperately to get away from him. Miller is such an iconoclast that he breaks his own Batman, because it is the fresh act of catastrophe-creation, rather than the finished project, that is the important thing. Miller's mode in *Dark Knight Strikes Again* and *All Star Batman and Robin the Boy Wonder* is the grotesque because the grotesque is absurdly aggressive and bold: Batman is figuratively and literally twisted, warped, smashed, and shattered. Miller breaks the inertia of the *status quo* with a shockingly insane portrayal of Batman. After perfection, the only place to go is ruination—glorious and exuberant ruination.

Frank Miller's next Batman project is a straight-to-graphic-novel he has written and drawn called *Batman vs. Al-Qaeda*. "It is, not to put too fine a point on it, a piece of propaganda," says Miller, as quoted by the BBC, "a reminder to people who seem to have forgotten who we're up against" (BBC News). Fans have claimed that Miller has lost his mind—he has certainly revealed that his overblown politics in *Dark Knight Returns* were not a parody, but his belief that heroic fascism is the answer to our current political problems. Whether you agree with his politics or not, you have to admit that Miller is as audacious as he ever was. With a title like *Batman vs. Al-Qaeda*, it is hard to know what the book will look like, but it seems that once again Frank Miller is out to break Batman—and demonstrate that Batman is beyond breaking.

GEOFF KLOCK (D.Phil., Oxford University) is the author of *How to Read Superhero Comics and Why* (Continuum 2002) and *Imaginary Biographies: Misreading the Lives of the Poets* (Continuum 2007). The first applies Harold Bloom's poetics of influence to comic books; the second argues that the bizarre portrayal of historical writers in nineteenth- and twentieth-century poetry constitutes a genre (and will be followed by a companion book on film). For BenBella, he has written on *Veronica Mars*, *Firefly*, and *House*. His blog—*Remarkable: Short Appreciations of Poetry, Comics, Film, Television and Music*—can be found at geoffklock.blogspot.com. He lives in New York City, where he is a freelance academic.

REFERENCES

BBC News. "Comic Book Hero Takes on al-Qaeda." 15 Feb. 2007. <http://news.bbc.co.uk/2/hi/entertainment/4717696.stm>

Klock, Geoff. *How to Read Superhero Comics and Why*. New York: Continuum, 2002.

Miller, Frank, Klaus Janson, and Lynn Varley. *Batman: The Dark Knight Returns*.

National Comics Publications (DC Comics): March 1986.

Miller, Frank, Jim Lee, Scott Williams, and Alex Sinclair. *All Star Batman and Robin the Boy Wonder*. National Comics Publications (DC Comics): September 2005–present.

Miller, Frank, Dave Mazzucchelli, Richmond Lewis, and Todd Klein. *Batman: Year One*. National Comics Publications (DC Comics): 1987.

Miller, Frank and Todd McFarlane. *Spawn/Batman*. Image Comics: 1994.

Miller, Frank and Lynn Varley. *The Dark Knight Strikes Again*. National Comics Publications (DC Comics): 2002.

Newsarama. "Jim Lee Talks Worldstrom/All Star Batman: Part 2." 30 Apr. 2007. <http://forum.newsarama.com/showthread.php?t=90535>

Wertham, Fredric. *Seduction of the Innocent*. New York: Reinhart and Company, 1954.

Okay, exactly what do we mean by "Batman"? Do the word, and the images and marketing detritus attached to it, actually stand for something? And if so, what? These questions apply not only to Batman but also to any character who has been incarnated in sundry media for decades. Nick Mamatas explores them in the thoughtful essay below, and has a surprising answer or two.

HOLY SIGNIFIER, BATMAN!

NICK MAMATAS

Batman, as one of the most iconic and enduring of comic book heroes, is ultimately nothing more than a bundle of images that have proven themselves to be far more valuable and compelling than any storyline, movie, or book of essays on the character. Batman is a Pez dispenser; he is a bat-shaped belt buckle. Batman is not a hard-ass vigilante, nor is he a duly deputized crime fighter; he is a stamped silhouette on a box of cereal.

And that is why I am here today with a proposition: of all the decades of Batman stories in a huge variety of media, there is only one that will forever be tied to the character. I am speaking, of course, of the live-action TV show, which aired twice weekly on ABC from January 12, 1966, to March 14, 1968. The show, featuring Adam West as Batman, was explicitly campy and humorous, with a sensibility in design, plotting, and cinematography that was pure Pop art. William Dozier, the producer of the TV show, actually detested comics and felt that the show would only work as Pop art. And he was right. Batman only works as Pop art. Because Batman is nothing but a logo, and because we are all soaking in logos and commercial messages and not-quite-real (or too-real-to-be-real) realities, the campy TV Batman of the 1960s is the most compelling version of the Caped Crusader of them all.

The Dozier-produced *Batman* is the ultimate in branding. It's Pop art for the boob tube. Susan Sontag noted in "The Aesthetics of Silence" that Pop is a form of art where authorial perspective essentially disappears. The author hasn't created anything; rather the author is simply collecting the pop cultural elements we're all already soaking in, and (re)presenting them as art. Getting some experience out of Andy Warhol's Brillo boxes depends on one having seen Brillo boxes lined up on supermarket shelves. Trademarks get their power in the same way—the consumer's participation in the culture of consumption is what makes a trademark valuable. We are responsible for giving the trademark meaning. Hello Kitty is worth billions because we look at Hello Kitty and say "Yay! Cute!" and Batman has value because we look at Batman and say "Tough" or "Cool" or "Funny" or "Hero" or "Bad-ass."

Roy Litchenstein in 1963 explained that Pop art is:

> . . . the use of commercial subject matter in painting, I suppose. . . . Everybody has called Pop art "American Painting," but it's actually industrial painting. America was hit by industrialism and capitalism harder and sooner. . . . Europe will be the same way, soon, so it won't be American, it will be universal. (Swenson 42)

Batman was Pop art in reverse; instead of fine art being made out of the brands and images of industrial capitalism (like Warhol's Brillo boxes), it was the height of industrial capitalism—a TV show—made out of fine art. When *Batman* was all the rage in '66, it was said, repeatedly, that "For kids, it's real. For adults, it's camp." Lynn Spigel and Henry Jenkins, in a cultural study of Batman, noted that at the time the show aired:

> *Batman* precipitated a questioning of critical hierarchies because it self-consciously placed itself within the Pop art scene. While shows like *Bewitched, Mr. Ed,* and *My Favorite Martian* stretched the limits of TV's realist aesthetic, *Batman*

laughed in the face of realism, making it difficult for critics to dismiss the program as one more example of TV's puerile content. *Batman* presented these critics with the particularly chilling possibility that this childish text was really the ultimate in art circle chic. (Jenkins and Spigel 123)

Childish text as art circle chic. . . . Batman is the sort of thing we used to call a "floating signifier" back in my grad school days. In semiotics, the study of signs, anything that stands for something else is referred to as a sign. Signs themselves are made up of two parts: a signifier (like the outline of a bat on a yellow oval) and a signified (Batman, yay!). The word "open" can signify that a burger joint is open for business, or that you should open an orange juice container on one side but not on the other. Batman, unlike the word "open," is a "floating signifier" because Batman doesn't mean any one thing or even a limited set of things—it means nothing, but instead holds open a space for that which cannot be defined. So Batman can be both a kiddie TV show and worthy of kudos from the art set; he can be a vicious vigilante and also a goofy cartoon character; he can sell us sugary cereal while being portrayed with the physique of a champion bodybuilder.

Batman is so good at being all these things because *he* isn't really anything more than that logo.

Given the noir Batman popularized by Frank Miller, Tim Burton, and Christopher Nolan, though, we have a problem, at least when you buy a birthday cake with a Batman logo on it from the supermarket. Batman, as the logo is presented on birthday cakes and boys' underwear and cereal boxes, has nothing to do with the dark vision of urban crime and vigilante justice that Batman, the character, has supposedly always represented. Would we put Pacino's Scarface on a birthday cake? Do kids run around their backyards pretending to be the characters from *Double Indemnity*?

The problem really came to me a couple of years ago, after I went to the theater to watch *Batman Begins*. *Batman Begins* is nearly crypto-fascist: in it young Bruce Wayne's parents are killed by a gunman despite the family's bleeding heart philanthropy and love for Gotham City, and Wayne travels the world, looking for . . . something, when he is found by a group of ninjas who train him to fight crime. He goes back to Gotham to reclaim his birthright and his multi-billion dollar corporation, and outfits himself as the protector of the city. As a member of the wealthy elite and a superior physical specimen with unlimited technological resources, he can take on corrupt mob bosses, and the police, but eventually must fight his old ninja mentor Ra's al Ghul. Al Ghul wants to speed up the decadence and decay of Gotham City, destroying it, in the same way his ninja clan had previously wiped out Rome. (*Batman Begins* is not very historically accurate, by the way.) But *Batman Begins's* *übermensch* Batman can save the city and then remake it in his own image, as the representative of the melding of state and capital. Happy birthday, Timmy!

While some fans claim that the Miller Batman is a "return" to the original spirit of the character, in fact, the whole noir pose is what they call in the comic business a "retcon." Retcon is short for retroactive continuity and involves changing the narrative past of a character to match the needs of the corporation's plans for the property. For example, in the 1989 film *Batman*, we're told Batman "created" the Joker when he sends thug Jack Napier, the same criminal that killed Bruce Wayne's parents, into a vat of chemicals. In the comics, the Joker and the original mugger were unrelated.

Retconning isn't inherently a bad thing, of course. After all, the character of Robin—the "sensational character find of 1940" according to the cover of *Detective Comics* #38—would be a shriveled old man by now if the property holders had held the characters to their first origins. But the noir retcon—which insists that Batman was always a dark character until the 1960s show—is essentially a form of reactionary revivalism.

In the earliest Batman adventures, the hero was very quickly adopted by the police force and became duly deputized. He gave lectures, generally to Robin, about the nature of the criminal element—generally criminals are lazy and greedy, and occasionally just nuts. The great distinction between Batman and the villains he faced was that Batman financed himself through legal wealth and had the authority of the police to violate all sorts of police procedure to protect the wealthy of Gotham City and not infrequently the wealth of Wayne Enterprises or the Wayne Foundation itself. But in *Batman: Year One*—which was supposed to have been not just a re-imagining of Batman, but an attempt to "reclaim" what was originally inherent in the character—there was nothing worth defending. The enemy was Gotham itself, and how the city generated crime at every level of society, from the poor slum areas to the heights of society. And Batman too was a criminal, ultimately fighting federal troops years later in *The Dark Knight Returns*.

This retcon of Batman's entire history to create a "dark knight" figure ends up being self-undermining. In 2005's *All Star Batman and Robin*—a reference to the juvenile Batman; the cover of the first issue also attempts to capture the spirit of the comics of the 1940s and 1950s—Frank Miller scrapped *Batman: Year One's* character origins as well, resetting them via a retroactive continuity. The introduction of Robin was portrayed as a kidnapping, and Batman and Superman met because the superior detective deduced Superman's identity and blackmailed him.

Miller tried to drown out the camp by amping up the volume. When Robin was hungry, Batman told him he could only eat whatever bats or rats he could catch in the Batcave. When the butler, Alfred, served Robin a cheeseburger, Batman flew into a rage and manhandled Alfred. But the Pop aspects of Batman cannot be drowned out, no matter how much black ink is spilled by Miller to depict these bombastic scenes. Batman is nothing in particular and thus nothing at all, and one cannot build something out of nothing. Pop is winking, knowing, and a celebration of the image. We are surrounded by images (bombarded by them, really); we spend much of our time in virtual environments, and spend much of our lives pursuing media-sanctioned fantasies. The Batman of *Year One* and after is as much a four-color fantasy as the *Batman* TV series—most of us, thankfully, do not live in crime-ridden urban blights, and even those blights that do exist in the U.S. are not nearly so violent as noir Gotham. It is simply a less successful one as it doesn't embrace Batman's true essence as just another bundle of corporate-owned images and sounds. In the same way that satire cannot destroy its target because the mere existence of satire affirms the importance of the target, Miller cannot help but acknowledge Batman's Pop art incarnation: in February 2006, Frank Miller announced another Batman project, in which Batman would track down Al-Qaeda and Osama bin Laden. The proposed name of the graphic novel, *Holy Terror, Batman!*, is itself a Pop art wink at Robin's fill-in-the-blank catch phrase.

The famed jazzy theme song from the 1966 TV show is still a perennial, just as the unique Batwipe—in which the scene was spun optically and the Batman logo zoomed in and out quickly—is still seen on other TV shows and even referenced in comics. Today, Adam West lends his voice talents to the primetime animated series *Family Guy*, in which he plays "Mayor West," the mayor of Quahog, Rhode Island. The cartoon image is a stylized version of West, and the character has referred to his past as a crime fighter and his experience with supervillains. And he's performing this Batmanesque element for an audience that may never have actually seen the '60s show, which hasn't been on the air in syndication since the early 1990s, and is not available on home video. But the young audience for *Family Guy* still gets it, because West's voice is part of our common environment. Michael Keaton's nearly asthmatic declaration "I'm Batman!" isn't. Nor are any of the images from *Year One*, or Christian Bale's attempt to smolder sexily under a rubber cowl. We ultimately cannot relate to that Batman; we can, however relate to the Batman of camp and Pop.

The endless recitations and re-imaginings of Batman in the comics themselves (which are again just a loss leader for the logo—the comics must stay in print, no matter how small the profits, or DC loses their rights to license the character) always must tangle with the Pop art Batman as well. Recently, in *Planetary/Batman* by Warren Ellis, the characters in the group Planetary, who do not normally exist in the same narrative universe of any version of Batman, were shown interacting with the Miller Batmans of *Year One* and *The Dark Knight Returns*—they were very similar except the latter, older Batman had more thought bubbles as he narrated his own actions, Frank Miller–style—and, of course, Pop art Batman.

You can't sell soap with crime, but you can sell soap with crime mixed in with wacky hijinks, crazy colors, and guest cameos by Don Ho. Pop art Batman can embrace the noir. Many of the episodes of *Batman*, especially those of the first season of the show, were actually fairly suspenseful, and there was a glance at the darkness, with a few minor characters being killed. The show's Pop art qualities took on a role similar to that of Hitchcock's often humorous trailers for his dark suspense films, or his cameos in the films themselves—they served to relieve tension through nervous laughter, and to explore the connection between suspense and comic timing. In the season one episodes "The Penguin Goes Straight" and "Not Yet, He Ain't," viewers see such nods toward noir such as extended takes—there was a sixty-nine-second shot with Batman, Robin, and Penguin in close up, negotiating the idea that Penguin had become a hero, and a thirty-five-second traveling camera shot that started with Commissioner Gordon and Chief O'Hara and ended with Batman and Robin stuck in the death trap of the week.

The noir Batman, Miller's Batman, cannot, however, embrace Pop art—at least not without undermining its own sense of seriousness, purpose, and claims of "adult content." But more importantly, it cannot by itself sell cereal or beach towels or even, ultimately, the yellow and black logo itself—which many versions of the noir Batman do not even use. The Pop art conception of Batman, on the other hand, can—it is the perfect vehicle for the nothingness that is Batman, the floating signifier designed to make its owners richer than Bruce Wayne.

NICK MAMATAS is the author of the Lovecraftian Beat road novel *Move Under Ground*, which was nominated for both the Bram Stoker and International Horror Guild awards, and which was released free to the Internet via Creative Commons in 2007. His most recent novel, *Under My Roof*, is a book for teens about building one's own nuclear device and declaring independence from the United States. In 2008, his short fiction will be collected by Prime Books under the title *You May Sleep. . . .* Nick lives near, but not in, Boston, Massachusetts.

REFERENCES

Jenkins, Henry, and Lynn Spigel. "Same Bat Channel, Different Bat Times: Mass Culture and Popular Memory." In *The Many Lives of the Batman: Critical Approaches to a Superhero and His Media*, edited by Roberta E. Pearson and William Uricchio. New York: Routledge, 1991.
Swenson, Gene R., ed., "What Is Pop Art?" *Artnews*, Nov. 1963, 42.
Sontag, Susan. "The Aesthetics of Silence." In *Styles of Radical Will*. New York: Picador, 2002.

Admit it: there's a musty, cobwebby part of our souls wherein lives the wish that superheroes were real. In an essay that's both amusing and informative, Darren Hudson Hick honors that wish by showing how it might come true, if only we had really, really serious financial resources.

THE COST OF BEING BATMAN

DARREN HUDSON HICK

When I was a kid, I had every intention of growing up to be a superhero. This wasn't an idle wish; this was *The Plan*. Now, I had long since given up any illusions that I was a foundling, rescued by my parents from a crash-landed space capsule. And my home chemistry kit had yet to provide me with any Flash-like super-speed. So, while I could still hope that a dying alien would bequeath me a magic ring, if I wanted to carry through with *The Plan*, I had to move in a different direction. No problem. I could be Batman.

That was what was so great about Batman. You didn't need to be born on a distant planet and you didn't need a magic ring. All you needed was determination and a massive cave under your house, and you too could be a superhero. What I didn't factor into *The Plan*, however, was the cost. After all, Bruce Wayne was a millionaire, and I had a two-dollar weekly allowance.[1]

Eventually, having discovered girls, I shelved *The Plan*. But decades have passed and I've earned myself a meager income, so perhaps it's time

---

[1] Although writers tend to be very vague about Bruce Wayne's fortune, he has through the decades been upgraded from millionaire, to multi-millionaire, to billionaire.

to dust off the calculator and revisit *The Plan*. The question is, what sort of bread would you need to spend to become the Caped Crusader? Could you transform yourself into the Dark Knight? Could you become Batman? Well, that depends on what you're willing to spend.[2]

THE COSTUME

The first step to becoming Batman is obviously the costume, for what better way to strike fear into the hearts of criminals than by dressing up like a giant bat? Assuming your spandex-sewing skills are sub-par, however, you'll need to hire a professional, and who better than Corey Sosner of the New Jersey–based Action-Actors Costume & Character Design?[3] Sosner can sell you a nice, spandex, underwear-on-top-of-your-leggings outfit, with cape and cowl, for a mere $150, and if you want to slap a trademarked logo on the chest, that's nobody's business but yours and the courts'. (Logo designers, incidentally, are a dime a dozen, and the field is very competitive. A prospective superhero could reasonably get an attractive logo designed for his chest for $100.)

The problem with spandex, of course, is that nobody can help but look goofy in it. There's a reason you don't see a lot of spandex in the live-action Batman films. If you want to look like you stepped out of a Batman movie, you'll want to go with a molded foam "muscle" suit, which Sosner can custom design to your body for about $5,000. Unfortunately, while it might make you *look* buff, molded foam offers about enough protection to ward off a Wiffleball bat. So, unless you're planning on sparring exclusively with such dastardly villains as the Wiffler and Dr. Feather-Duster, you'll want an upgrade.

To really protect yourself, you're going to have to consider a variety of

---

[2] As a caveat, I should mention right off the bat that I'm looking to calculate the cost of being Batman, not the cost of being Bruce Wayne. We can quibble over identity conditions, but being Bruce Wayne carries substantial costs over and above those of being Batman. In 2005, *Forbes* put together their own calculation of what it would cost to be Batman, but included in this study the cost of being a swingin' playboy (about $1.1 million, though what *Forbes* included in this calculation seems more than a little arbitrary) and the cost of an experienced butler like Alfred ($200,000 annually). To find the *Forbes* study, go to www.forbes.com and run a search for "Batman."

[3] Among other things, Sosner was hired to design and fabricate the costumes for the second season of *Who Wants to Be a Superhero?*

threats. You'll want your costume to be fireproof, bulletproof, and knife-proof, and yet still allow for reasonable mobility. And that's going to cost you. First, you'll need to build your suit in multiple layers. The outermost layer would most likely be a spandex suit sprayed with a flame-retardant material such as Flamex, produced by National Fireproofing, Inc., and surprisingly cheap at about $35 per gallon. Next, we'd need to worry about bullets and edged weapons. Using a blend of ballistic-resistant materials, the bodysuit would consist of twenty-five to thirty layers of Nomex or Kevlar,[4] Spectra,[5] and Dyneema,[6] each layer adding increased protection against the baddies' bullets. As a rough guide, standard Kevlar tends to run about $18 per linear yard, and a bodysuit consists of about twenty to thirty yards of material per layer. Your final layer of protection would consist of molded ceramic plates like those used in ballistic industries and military-grade bulletproof vests. And, as with the muscle suits, Sosner can custom-mold your crime-fighting costume to your body, so there's no need to worry about looking clunky. Finally, we'll need to include your cape, cowl, gloves, and boots, all made from the same materials. Add in Sosner's estimate of a month's labor at $500 per hour, and you're looking at a total cost of between $45,000 and $50,000.[7]

TRAINING AND EDUCATION

So, you've got protection and you look cool. It's a good start, but if you want to trade fisticuffs with the local hooligans, you're going to need some training. In the Batman mythos, our hero spends ten years abroad, turning

---

[4] Nomex and Kevlar are brand-names for Aramid heat- and impact-resistant fibers used in bulletproofing body armor.
[5] Spectra, produced by Honeywell, is spun from a gel of ultra-high molecular weight polyethylene plastic, and is, pound-for-pound, ten times stronger than steel.
[6] Produced by DSM, Dyneema is the highest-grade (SK76) continuous filament yarn available, designed to quickly absorb energy and dissipate shock waves.
[7] I owe great thanks to Corey Sosner, who put an enormous amount of work into researching what would be required for such a high-end costume. To find out more about Sosner and his amazing work, visit www.action-actors.com. Incidentally, the aforementioned *Forbes* article on becoming Batman suggests a ProMAX OTV bulletproof jacket (to protect your torso and arms) and a Kevlar helmet, for a total cost of $1,585, which is all well and good if you want to look like a football-playing vigilante and don't mind getting your kneecaps shot off.

himself into the greatest hand-to-hand combatant alive. Unfortunately, determining the cost of a decade of traveling and training with Shaolin monks and ninjas is a bit difficult. So let's assume you're going to do this domestically. Fortunately, if you want to learn to kick ass and protect your own, there are plenty of opportunities to be had. As a sample, let's consider a few of the techniques you'll need to master.

In the early twentieth century, Hélio Gracie invented what has become known as Brazilian or Gracie jiu-jitsu, based on traditional Japanese jiu-jitsu taught to his family. Decades later, Hélio's eldest son, Rorion, a 9th-degree black belt, opened the Gracie Jiu-Jitsu Academy in Torrance, California, and would later become integral to the foundation of the Ultimate Fighting Championship. The Gracie Academy trains countless military and police officers, and they can train you, too. As an adult, you'll want to start with your blue belt qualification, based on the thirty-four most important techniques of Gracie jiu-jitsu. The thirty-four techniques are taught in the school's "Gracie Combatives" course, composed of twenty-two classes, each of which must be completed twice before the student can move on to the next level. The course lasts twelve months, at $165 per month, for a total of $1,980. Beyond that, students can progress to the Advanced Gracie Jiu-Jitsu program, from blue, to purple, to brown, to black belt status. The course costs $185 per month. Over nine years, that amounts to $19,980, or $21,960 total.

Next, you might consider judo, and what better place to start training than with Professor Willy Cahill. Holding 7th dan Judo status, and 10th dan status in traditional Japanese jiu-jitsu, Cahill has trained nearly 1,000 national and international judo medal award winners. A student typically takes about four years to reach the 1st dan black belt in judo, with daily training and classes three to four times per week. At Cahill's Judo Academy, adult classes cost $75 per month for four weekly classes, plus a $10-per-visit mat fee. Black belts owe dues of $45 per month, and students will have to purchase a gi (the traditional training uniform), with the average gi running about $80. Additionally, you may owe a further $50 annual fee to the United States Judo Association. Assuming you can reach black belt status in four years, ten years of study will cost you $65,780.

Last, but certainly not least, you'll want to learn the "sweet science" of pugilism—boxing. And if you want to learn to box, you can't do much better than "Smokin' Joe" Frazier's Gym in north Philadelphia, the City of Brotherly Gloves, owned and operated by the former world heavyweight champion. Boxers are trained by Frazier's son, Marvis, himself a heavyweight boxer, and a small staff of floor trainers. Initial membership costs include $150 for the first month and $75 per month thereafter. Of course, you will also need to purchase the requisite gloves ($30), shoes ($49), and hand wraps ($5), with good equipment expected to last through years of punishment. At the bottom line, ten years of boxing at Frazier's Gym will run you a mere $8,859.

In all, ten years of concurrent study in these three arts will top out at $96,599. Of course, Batman isn't merely a premier fighter, but also the World's Greatest Detective, and that requires training, too. Specifically, you'll want an education in forensic science.

To begin, you'll want to start with an undergraduate education in chemistry, biology, or biochemistry. The average tuition at a four-year public college or university is $5,836 (or an average of $12,796 including room and board).[8] Tuition multiplied by four years is $23,344. Next, you'll want to move on to graduate school to top off your training, and for forensics, there's probably no better choice than the Forensic Science Masters program at Michigan State University, comprising thirty-eight credits and ordinarily taking about two years to complete. Courses cost $222.50 per credit for Michigan residents and $450 per credit for non-residents, plus $288 in fees per semester. Assuming for the sake of argument that you're not a Michigan state resident, your total grad school bill will be $18,252. Added on to your undergraduate bill, that's $41,596.

THE BATCAVE

The next major element in the Batman mythos is his home base, his secret hideout, his Batcave. Now, if you're lucky, there's an enormous cavern hiding right under your very own home. If you're not so lucky, you may need to build one.

Building caves is big business in some parts of the country. In particular, Californians have started a rage in "wine caves," custom-tunneled enclosures suitable for storing wine and hosting dinner parties. But you've got

---

[8] According to CNN (http://money.cnn.com/2006/10/24/pf/college/college_costs/index.htm).

other plans. Assuming stable rock conditions, a basic wine cave will cost upwards of $150 per square foot—quite reasonable considering the price of housing in California. Being Batman though, you're thinking big. After all, you're going to need at least 2,500 square feet simply to accommodate the Batcomputer (more on this below). At $150 per square foot, that will run you $375,000. Of course, that doesn't leave you much in the way of room for moving around or parking the Batmobile, so you'll certainly want a larger space. Doubling the size means doubling the price, to $750,000. Not cheap, but not bad for your very own Batcave.

However, rather than large, open caverns, wine caves tend to consist of crisscrossing thirteen-foot-wide tunnels. Good for confusing trespassers; bad for that batty ambiance. After all, you don't want the Bat*tunnel*; you want the Bat*cave*. Construction of large underground caverns, however, is the domain of rock engineering, and tends to push construction costs into the millions, if not billions, of dollars, depending on size, use, and ground conditions. Today, the construction of large underground caverns is primarily for purposes of energy storage, with the specific needs of such a construct built into the cost. Not so long ago, however, large underground spaces were being built primarily for the purposes of human occupation. In particular, the British built several large, underground air-raid shelters during World War II to temporarily house endangered citizens, a fine model for a suitable man-made Batcave.

In 1943, Portsmouth City commissioned the design, engineering, and construction of an underground facility comprising two main shelters connected by a tunnel, for the housing of some 5,100 people. Overall, the facility measured 1.8 miles in length, certainly enough room for you and some toys. With construction costs of £73,298, and allowing for 1943 exchange rate and inflation (according to the Consumer Price Index), your ready-made air-raid-shelter-*cum*-Batcave would cost about $3.5 million. Again, not bad when you consider the price of traditional housing and downright cheap when compared with the price tag on the Batcomputer.[9]

---

[9] *Forbes* recommends steering away from a cave and renting a warehouse instead, at the meager cost of $24,000 per year (Manhattan prices). But seriously—the "Batwarehouse"?

THE EQUIPMENT

Having built your Batcave, you now have somewhere to put your gadgets. But *which* gadgets? Certainly, the heart of the Batcave, and Batman's primary gadget, is the Batcomputer (granted, nobody has called it the Batcomputer in decades, but we all know what we're talking about). And unless you're willing to settle for the Batlaptop, you're going to want the best on the market, which means you're not going shopping at Best Buy for Batman's computer needs.

If you want the top-of-the-line, absolute best, absolute fastest computer on the planet, you want IBM's Blue Gene/L. Let's talk processing speed. In terms of crunching out scientific calculation, computer performance is measured in FLOPS (FLoating point Operations Per Second). The central processing unit of your home computer probably tops out at about ten gigaFLOPS, while your Playstation 3 has a theoretical peak performance of 2.18 teraFLOPS (though it's only running one program at any given time). Comparatively, the Blue Gene/L has a theoretical peak performance of about 360 teraFLOPS (165 times the speed of your Playstation; 18,000 times the speed of your home computer). No waiting around for this one to download movies. However, the world's fastest supercomputer is not without its drawbacks. First, it occupies 2,500 square feet of floor space (the size of a nice, three-bedroom home—good enough reason to get a Batcave). Second, it consumes 1.5 megawatts of power, the output of a wind turbine, and would cost about $30 to $90 per hour to run (depending on your power source). You won't be too worried about the operating cost, though, when you consider the U.S. government paid $290 million for this monster. Ouch.

Of course, the Batcomputer isn't going to do all the work for you; you're going to need some other helpful gadgets to fill out the Batcave. In particular, you're going to need some forensics equipment. The two primary tools for this job are a blood-analysis system and a DNA analyzer, not unlike what you'd see on CSI. The Picolo xpress from Abaxis is a portable chemistry system about the size of a shoebox that provides detailed on-site blood testing. Used by hospitals, the military, and government agencies across the U.S. and around the world, a single unit has a list price of $24,000. Even more fun for do-it-yourself biochemistry is a top-of-the-line

DNA analyzer, like Applied Biosystems's 96-capillary 3730x/DNA Analyzer. What better way to find out who the Joker really is? The price? $365,000.

Out in the field, things are much cheaper. A complete Crime Scene Kit for evidence collection and documentation runs $340, available from Evident Crime Scene Products in Union Hall, VA. A Blood Splatter Kit runs $190, and the high-end Master Forensic Entomology Kit (including maggot motels—fun!) from Evident runs $325.

THE TOYS

That's fine for the big-ticket gadgets, but where would Batman be without his belt of wonderful toys? It seems he has everything he needs whenever he needs it. Heck, in the 1966 Batman movie, our hero wards off a shark with a handy can of Bat-shark-repellent. Perhaps that's best put aside for the moment. Instead, let's consider some of the Bat-toy staples you'll want to have at hand.

The 1989 Batman movie introduced the handheld grappling gun, a priceless gadget. Literally priceless, because no such thing exists. Portable grappling guns *have* been developed by Smith and Jewell in the U.K. (the AL-54 air launcher) and by Battelle in Columbus, Ohio (the Tactical Air Initiated Launch System, or TAIL), the latter specifically for use by the U.S. Navy and Special Operations. At $15,000, the TAIL System's not cheap, but it's not ridiculously expensive, either. However, each is about the size of a high-powered rifle, and so not the sort of thing one straps to one's belt. As easily portable grappling guns really are the stuff of fiction, you may need to rely on more conventional means of swinging from rooftops. As such, the ideal choice would be the Capcwell Retractable Grappling Hook, designed for military applications by the Army Natick Soldier Center, and available for $189.95. Three hundred feet of nylon rope capable of holding 550 lbs. will add a mere $15 to the bill.

Next is the batarang. When the batarang first appeared in the comics, it was a black boomerang with scalloped edges, but as time has passed, batarangs have become more like shuriken, bladed projectiles hurled at an opponent. Depending on quality and size, shuriken can be found for anywhere from $2 to $14 apiece. If you're looking to maintain the bat-motif, however, manufacturer AK/MC sells bat-shaped throwing blades, likely infringing on copyright, but available in sets of three for $13.95.[10] Mind you, if you're looking to fight crime, you'll need more than three. We'll put you down for about 1,000 to start ($4,650).

Of course, as a cowled vigilante of the night, you'll be riding the thin line between law enforcement and outlaw, and there are tools available to help you with both sides of that line. Lock-pick tools are surprisingly easy to obtain, with a standard set available for less than $25, and a set of automotive lock-pick tools for about $35. Of course, lock-pick tools require a lot of practice. So while you're getting the hang of them, you can pick up an electric lock-pick gun with rechargeable battery for $129.95.[11]

That's it for the staples. For your miscellany, you might consider adding smoke bombs (available in 12-packs for $96), tasers (about $400–$500), tire spikes (five for $19.95; how does 1,000 sound?), and, heck, why not a can of bear repellent ($35.95)?[12] As for Bat-shark-repellent, it's not yet available, but Eric Stroud, CEO of Oak Ridge Shark Lab in Oak Ridge, New Jersey, is working on just such a product, so keep an eye out.

THE BATMOBILE

With the right costume, training, and equipment, you're ready to take on the baddies. But unless you want to take a cab to the scene of the crime, you're going to need transportation. Specifically, you're going to need a Batmobile.

Since the Batmobile was first introduced in 1941, the Caped Crusader has driven (and in several cases, demolished) a fleet of vehicles bearing that moniker.[13] From non-descript sedans to tricked-out, military-grade tanks and monster trucks, the Batmobile is akin to Air Force One: it's whatever Batman's driving at the time. Of course, unless you're planning on buying off the lot, you're going to need to spend some dough.

Certainly the most recognizable Batmobile is the version driven in the 1960s live-action television show. Originally a Ford concept car, the classic Batmobile started life as the sole 1955 Lincoln Futura. Handbuilt in Italy

---

[10] Available from the Academy of Karate's Martial Arts Supplies at martialartssupermarket.com.
[11] For all your lock-pick needs, visit www.lockpicktools.com.
[12] All available from www.defensedevices.com.
[13] I recommend visiting www.batmobilehistory.com for an exhaustive history of Batman's choices in transportation.

by Ghia, among the most renowned car-design firms in the world, the bubble-domed Futura cost the princely sum of $250,000 ($1.8 million today). Under the supervision of George Barris, the "King of Kustomizers," the retired Futura was transformed into the 5,000-pound land-yacht that would set the bar for every future car hoping to be called the Batmobile. Unfortunately, after modification, the car was held together by Bondo putty and Hollywood magic, and couldn't take much punishment. In other words, not the sort of car one really wants for high-speed chases.[14]

That said, if you want a unique-looking car, a custom concept car is probably the way to go. Unfortunately, most concept cars never get built, at least not as fully functioning prototypes, making pricing such an endeavor difficult. However, at least one recent concept car that did make it to the prototype stage, and just screams "Batmobile," is the 2003 Cadillac Sixteen. Combining elements of modern design and classic 1930s style, the shark-like Sixteen houses a 32-valve V-16 concept engine, capable of 1,000 horsepower. Now, nobody *needs* a car with this kind of power. But if you're Batman, you *want* one, and there won't be anything else like it on the road. The price tag for development, however, is $2 million. So if you want something with the look, feel, and power of the Cadillac Sixteen, you'd better get out your checkbook.[15]

Of course, looking good and going fast are nice, but if the baddies are shooting at you, they aren't enough; you're going to need some protection. And if you want to bulletproof a car, there's no better choice than Custom Armored Vehicles. In ninety days, CAV can turn your sleek sedan into a sleek tank. Capable of repelling shots from AK-47s, M-16s, and 12-gauge shotguns, a full bulletproofing job will run you about $75,000. And if you *really* want to trick out your Batmobile, you can add a smoke-screen system, electric-shocking door handles, ram bumpers, flashing front strobe lights, and a host of other goodies, with the full package totaling about $90,000.[16]

---

[14] Although in less-than-perfect condition, what many think of as *the* Batmobile sold in a 2007 London auction for $233,000 after a fierce bidding war.

[15] Other concept contenders for the Batmobile moniker might include the 2005 Maybach Exelero ($2 million), the 2006 Bugatti Veyron 16.4 ($10 million), and the 2007 GM Efijy ($1.5 million).

[16] For more details, visit www.customarmoring.com.

THE BAT-SIGNAL

You've got the costume, the training, the hideout, and the cool car. You're all set to fight crime. The only problem now is how to find it. Sure, you can skulk on rooftops waiting to swoop down on muggers and jaywalkers, but the seasoned superhero knows the value of good contacts. So you get in with the local fuzz, and let them drop you a line when they need a hand. Yes, you could use a cell phone or a beeper, but where's the drama in that? What you need is a bat-signal!

Portable spotlights aren't too uncommon; you'll find them advertising used car lots, nightclubs, movie premiers, and all other variety of events best advertised by sending a huge beam of light into the sky. The most popular brand of advertising spotlights are SkyTracker units, manufactured by Ballantyne, Inc. Available in single- and multi-beam configurations, and in 2,000- and 4,000-watt outputs, each twenty-four-inch SkyTracker lamp produces a 300-million-candlepower beam, visible for several miles. Unfortunately, even at 300 million candlepower, the beam of light is unlikely to illuminate all but the lowest-hanging clouds.

In the world of spotlights, the bigger, the brighter, the better, and Ballantyne could help you with your upgrade, too. Ballantyne is responsible for the Sky Beam emanating from the top of the Luxor Hotel and Casino in Las Vegas, a 42.3-billion-candlepower column of light purportedly visible ten miles into space. Nice as that would be, your local law enforcement agency would need something the size of a Vegas casino to house and power it.

What seems closest to the bat-signal as depicted in the comics and film, and also the best bet for an actual functioning bat-signal, is the kind of sixty-inch carbon-arc searchlight built by General Electric and Sperry Gyroscope for use in anti-aircraft battles in World War II. Used to illuminate the sky in search of enemy planes, these giants created 800-million-candlepower beams almost six miles long, visible from more than thirty-five miles away—certainly powerful enough to produce a silhouette of a bat on cloud cover that could be seen from the suburbs. With the introduction of radar, however, the searchlights fell out of use, and have not been produced since 1944. At the time, a sixty-inch unit cost $60,000 (more than $670,000 in current dollars). Today, you can search around for a used unit to restore. Depending on condition, you should be able to find one for between $10,000 and $30,000.[17]

TOTAL BILL

Now, we can quibble over exactly what sort of martial arts training you'll need, or over how many batarangs you'll want for your first night of fighting crime, but as a rough tally, this is what you're looking at:

Costume	$50,000
Martial Arts Training	$96,599
Forensic Science Education	$41,596
Batcave	$3,500,000
Batcomputer	$290,000,000
Forensics Equipment	$389,855
Toys	$9,562
Batmobile	$2,090,000
bat-signal	$30,000
	$296,207,612

So, what's the bottom line? *Could* you become Batman? Assuming a certain level of intelligence (not everyone can get a graduate degree in forensic science, after all) and physical conditioning, and assuming you have a spare sixteen years to devote to study, yes, it's possible. Improbable, perhaps, but possible. A price tag of nearly $300 million may sound steep, but a net worth of $300 million won't even put you on the *Forbes* list of the 400 wealthiest Americans (no less than $1 billion will). This, of course, is just as well; with only 400 possible alter-egos, it wouldn't take long for the police or the Riddler to figure out who Batman really is. And, of course, if you opt to downgrade the Batcomputer, you'll save a serious chunk of change, and all but disappear into financial anonymity. So, if you have these meager means and a lot of spare time, yes, you *could* become Batman. As for me, I think I'll

---

[17] As those who restore these classic searchlights tend to do so as a labor of love, getting a price on fixing one up is more than a little difficult. Nevertheless, I'd recommend you pay a little more up front and not have to worry as much about the restoration costs.

reshelve *The Plan* and stick with dressing up in my Batman Underoos (less than $10 on eBay).

DARREN HUDSON HICK is a doctoral candidate in philosophy at the University of Maryland, College Park, and the former managing editor of *The Comics Journal*. He has previously contributed to the Smart Pop anthology, *Webslinger: SF and Comic Writers on Your Friendly Neighborhood Spider-Man*. For more information, visit www.typetoken.com.

For reasons that will be apparent after you've read a few paragraphs of Michael Marano's excellent essay, I found this next piece especially involving. And that leads to another personal note: I often think, these days, that other people know more about the stuff I've worked on than I do. This can be a bit discomfiting, but at the same time, it can also be interesting. At the very least, it's an experience not many people get to have.

RA'S AL GHUL: FATHER FIGURE AS TERRORIST

MICHAEL MARANO

In the 2005 Christopher Nolan movie *Batman Begins*, Ra's al Ghul is first mentioned as a rumor, a whisper . . . a Keyser Söze kind of figure who evolves from phantom to falsehood, from mentor to enemy. That Ra's spoke of himself as a phantom in the guise of his own employee, Henri Ducard, just adds another delicious layer of subterfuge to the guy.

This evolution from rumor to something more tangible and deadly in *Batman Begins* parallels Ra's's evolution in the Batman comics of the 1970s. The first whiff of Ra's al Ghul we got in the Batman mythos was through his daughter, Talia. The lovely Ms. al Ghul made her debut in the May 1971 issue of *Detective Comics* (#411) in a story called "Into the Den of the Death Dealers!" written by Denny O'Neil, who was at the time re-inventing Batman by amputating the overly popish and ridiculous trappings that had smothered the character in the wake of the 1960s ABC TV show in a way that would prove similar to Nolan's reboot of the movie franchise after Joel Schumacher's 1997 horribly be-nippled Batsuit atrocity, *Batman & Robin*.

Talia yanked Batman on a globetrotting adventure, hauling him out of

Gotham, with its gigantically oversized prop advertisements,[1] and into what's described in the comic as an unnamed "tiny Asian nation tucked . . . between two Super-Powers" with gigantically oversized mountain ranges.

Prior to O'Neil's tenure, Batman was more likely to leave the planet than he was to leave Gotham. At times, Batman would leave Earth figuratively, as in 1963's "Robin Dies at Dawn" (in which Batman was the subject of sensory deprivation tests at the local Space Agency). Or he'd leave Earth literally, shifted to other planets by Doctor Light's gadgets or by inter-dimensional tyrant Despero's funky teleporting chessboard in those early issues of *The Justice League of America*.[2]

O'Neil broadened Batman's horizons in the real world, taking him out of the warehouse and factory districts near the Gotham River he used to haunt almost exclusively. One of the landmarks of O'Neil's transformation of Batman is "The Secret of the Waiting Graves" in the January 1970 issue of *Detective Comics* (#395), wherein Batman gets involved in a *Dark Shadows*-like plot in Mexico involving a couple (the not-so-subtly named Muertos) who extend their lives through the alchemical use of a flower with hallucinatory properties, something that catches the attention of Mexican narcotics officers.[3]

Yes, the here and now of the real world in "Waiting Graves" involved a Poe-like plot device and Barnabas Collins–like trappings, but it was the setting of the story that was a breakthrough. Later, when Talia is kidnapped by Dr. Darrk and the shadowy League of Assassins in "Death Dealers!" O'Neil would expand Batman's horizons, and the geographic range of his quest for justice, even further . . . into the realm of the geo-political.[4]

---

[1] Later banned from Gotham's rooftops due to the misadventures of that town's most loveable villain, Humpty Dumpty. See *Arkham Asylum: Living Hell* #3 for Dumpty's full, sad story.

[2] For Despero and his chessboard's debut, see *Justice League of America* #1 (November 1960), "The World of No Return!" by the great Gardner Fox and Mike Sekowsky; Doctor Light and his shifting technology debuted in *JLA* #12 (June 1962) in "The Last Case of the Justice League!" by Fox and Sekowsky. Dig those exclamation points!

[3] In this plot, we can see the seeds of what would come with Ra's: an alchemical means of extending life that brings madness, and a flower with psychotropic properties used as a weapon (like the one Ra's uses against Gotham in *Batman Begins*).

[4] Yes, the Adam West *Batman* movie of 1966 dealt with Joker, Catwoman, Riddler, and Penguin powdering a bunch of dignitaries with a "superhydrator." I'm talking about a geo-political context with a bit more heft, here.

The nameless country to which Talia leads Batman is by its very iconography a quilt of political hotspots. Catwoman, a comparable Batman femme fatale, had never led Batman out of Gotham into, say, the smoldering powder kegs of Suez, Korea, or Kenya, even when she trapped Batman on an unnamed island full of big cats in 1954's "The Jungle Cat-Queen,"[5] in which Batman leaves Gotham through a plot device as void of political overtones as the shifting-to-other-planets moves of Doctor Light and Despero.

There's a gravitas to the setting to which Talia leads him that is new in the Batman mythos. The aforementioned "tiny Asian nation tucked into mountains between two Super-Powers" is a fever-dream comic book collage, evoking images of Bhutan, Nepal, and what was then, in 1971, the region of East Pakistan, which suffered bloody repression by the Pakistani government (called a genocide by some) before declaring itself the independent state of Bangladesh in May of 1971.[6]

"Into the Den of the Death Dealers!" written just a few years after the March 14, 1968, cancellation of the campy Adam West TV show—an era-defining cancellation that coincided with the even more era-defining Tet Offensive[7]—featured Gotham's favorite son getting the shit beaten out of him on flatlands that looked a lot like a rice paddy by assassins

---

[5] *Detective Comics* #211. Dig Catwoman's panther-shaped plane with retractable claws in that issue.

[6] Yeah, the then East Pakistan and current Bangladesh were/is in the lowlands of the region at the mouth of the Ganges, not "tucked into mountains," but I think the proximity of Bhutan and Nepal still might have pushed some buttons, on that count (true, Tibet is also "tucked into mountains," but it's not tiny). Also, I don't know when O'Neil would have written this "May 1971" issue of *Detective Comics*, or when it would have actually been on the newsstands, but the trouble in East Pakistan/Bangladesh that reached its geopolitical climax in May of 1971 had been brewing since 1970. For this essay, I'll be using the cover dates of the comics as lenses through which we can look broadly at the world in which the comics were created. It's worth noting in this context that Christopher Nolan and screenwriter David Goyer chose to set the opening of *Batman Begins* in Bhutan. According to various Wiki articles, the beginning of the movie is set in China, but according to Batman actor Christian Bale (while speaking of his character's development): "And then again the older angry guy in the jail, in Bhutan, and discovering who he is and getting some sense of purpose" (About.com).

[7] To give you an idea of just how dramatically and grimly things were changing during the Tet Offensive, on the very day of *Batman's* cancellation, Viet Cong were sighted for the first time on the Mekong Delta, and the State Department had to warn the South Vietnamese against threatening to invade North Vietnam.

wearing not your standard Ninja gear, but Viet Cong–like pajamas. The NVA stand-ins wielded bo-sticks made from the same kind of bamboo as the punji sticks that mangled so many U.S. troops. Batman had gone from a campy, swingin' '60s icon who danced the Batusi, full of Austin Powers mojo, to a by-proxy frontline soldier in the Vietnam War.

Talia herself was something new, international, and ballsy. She was no Vicki Vale. She was liberated, Baby . . . in a way that put Mary Richards to shame. Talia was a Cosmo girl actualized in a fashion that Lois Lane had yet to be in her fringed-mini-skirt-and-matching-vest, mid-'70s nadir. She wasn't a heroine living in the shadow of a male hero's mythology, the way Batwoman Kathy Kane[8] did with her "utility purse" (by Versace?). Talia was a med student at the University of Cairo. Groovy. In terms of basic narrative function, she was your standard kidnap victim, but she had the Virginia Slims wherewithal to actually pull the goddam trigger of the gun that put the villainous Darrk under the wheels of a train, allowing her to kill a bad guy (horribly) where Batman's code never would have.

Killing Darrk isn't the only line that Talia crossed. In the basement of "the crumbling ruins of a temple" that looked a lot like the Khmer temples of Angkor Wat in Cambodia that had just been hit by artillery fire in February of 1971, she did what would have been unthinkable for any other Batbabe until Catwoman/Selina Kyle became Batman's semi-ally (post-Jeoph Loeb's *The Long Halloween*): Talia crossed the forbidden public/private line and took off the freshly ninja-pounded Batman's mask, something no Gotham doctor or ER tech had ever dared before, even when Batman had to be hospitalized.[9]

---

[8] "Hey, Bruce!"

"Yes, Kathy?"

"As a lark, I'm going to steal the carefully crafted and terrifyingly mythic figure you have created out of yourself through sheer force of will as a means to avenge the brutal murder of your parents that deeply traumatized you as a little boy!"

"That's . . . just . . . great, Kathy. Just . . . swell! Now, please excuse me while I put roses on the grave of my mother, whom I watched bleed to death in a filthy alley after Joe Chill shot her face off. Feel free to appropriate my personal anguish any time!"

(And for the record, I'm cool with Barbara Gordon, as she became Batgirl by accident, . . . while on her way to a costume party.)

[9] In the John Byrne–scripted "Many Deaths of the Batman" in the May 1989 issue of *Batman* (#433), ER techs duked it out when one tried to take the mask off a mortally wounded man they thought was the genuine Batman.

Talia, the daughter of Ra's and the first glimpse of his influence and power, brought Batman into a wider world of turmoil and upheaval while at the same time entering Batman's private world in a way that even dear old Aunt Harriet couldn't.

Batman would meet Ra's himself "a month" later, in the June 1971 issue of *Batman* (#232) in the O'Neil-scripted "Daughter of the Demon." This was yet another kidnap story, and this time it was Dick Grayson/Robin who was kidnapped by unknown assailants in his home (not snatched to provide a false climax by someone like Two-Face and his henchmen after a scuffle at a twin mattress factory on 22 Second Avenue), and was hauled off to the Himalayas (not a hideout in some place like an abandoned Two-Headed Coin factory on the Gotham River).

Ra's continued what Talia had started, taking Batman on another international trek into the political hotbed of India, where, if we continue looking through the cultural lens of May 1971 as the Ground Zero point of Ra's's advent, we see that 160 troops had just been killed on the frontier with Pakistan. In Calcutta, Batman disguised himself as a Muslim holy man, and was accosted by two street toughs in this predominately Hindu city . . . whereupon Batman pounded out of the pair the information he needed in order to track the missing Robin. This may not seem a plot device freighted with political overtones, but consider that in 1969 in Ahmedabad, almost 1,000 Muslims were killed by Hindu fundamentalists, and that in 1970 religiously motivated riots between Hindus and Muslims in Bhiwandi, Jalgaon, and Mahad left scores dead. Suddenly the image of Batman disguised as a helpless Muslim, using himself as bait, gains certain headline-heavy undertone that just doesn't apply, say, to his becoming Matches Malone (the gangster Bruce Wayne/Batman disguised himself as for years when he combed Gotham's underworld for information).[10]

Messing with Batman seemed to be the family pastime for the al Ghuls. Ra's himself crossed a line into Batman's private world that made

---

[10] In the comics, poor Matches was recently bumped off. Batman has taken to using one-armed thug Lefty Knox as his disguise (complete with a mini camera hidden in his prosthetic hook) when prowling the underworld for leads. See the March 2007 issue of *Detective Comics* (#827).

Talia's lifting his mask seem a trifle: in an act of trespass that mirrored the at-home abduction of Robin at the start of that issue, Ra's deduced Wayne was Batman and staked out the Batcave, waiting for Batman to show up. How many villains have tried to break into the Batcave over the years? Yet Ra's just sauntered in and waited, as if he were going to get his teeth cleaned at one of those walk-in places at the mall.

Ra's and Talia not only brought Batman into the wider world, they brought the wider world into the Batman mythology—which, in turn, added a new richness to that mythology. Ra's was himself a new vista beyond the geographic. He was no Gotham native or luggish member of the Gorilla Gang.[11] He was a citizen of the world, and as such, he was a villain formed from the concerns of the time in which he was created, at least as seen through U.S. eyes.

Sure, on one level, Ra's is just a gene-splice of Fu Manchu and the Bond villain Blofeld. In fact, the Batman story arc crafted by O'Neil and Neal Adams for "The Lazarus Pit" and "The Demon Lives Again" borrowed a lot from Fleming's *On Her Majesty's Secret Service*, with Ra's filling in as an ersatz Blofeld complete with an Alpine fortress/retreat reachable only by cable car and a spiffy escape scene on skis.[12] But on another level, the figure of Ra's could be thought of as a bogeyman stitched out of U.S. State Department memos from May and June of 1971, when he and Talia first graced the pages of *Detective Comics* and *Batman*.

Of what kinds of State Department bugaboos are Ra's a collage? There's the aforementioned involvement of Batman, courtesy of the al Ghuls, in a pseudo-Bhutan/East Pakistan/Nepal and India at a time when (all during May and June of 1971) 60,000 refugees a day were pouring from East Pakistan into India (many of whom would die of cholera); India was such a hot-spot on the global stage that according to a poll among non-communist world leaders, India's Prime Minister Indira Gandhi was the most admired person in the world and the U.S. Senate

---

[11] A bunch of bad guys who wisely thought it would be a good idea to dress up as apes to pull capers, as peripheral vision cut off by a rubber monkey mask is a benefit when you're in a pinch, and the ability to really grip things without bulky ape gloves is just a hindrance. Thank God that Ace the Bat-hound was able to end their reign of criminal monkeyshines.

[12] *Batman* #243 and 244, August and September 1972 . . . September 1972, when Black September hit the Munich Olympic Games. Just an FYI.

Foreign Relations Committee voted to end all aid to Pakistan until a relief effort could be mounted for the people in East Pakistan.

Ra's is just a bundle of post-colonial fun. The name "Ra's al Ghul" is Arabic for "the Demon's Head," and he himself is head of a secret international organization at a time when organizations like Black September were first making news. The events of Black September (after which the organization named itself, during which King Hussein of Jordan cracked down on the Palestinian factions that were trying to overthrow him) were fresh on everyone's minds. University of Cairo med student Talia (I'm not sure if the University of Cairo's med school admitted women back then) was studying in Egypt at a time when President Anwar Sadat started the merry month of May 1971 by firing his vice president, just before crushing an attempted coup that nearly destroyed his rule in an act he called a "corrective revolution" on the fifteenth and then jetting down to Saudi Arabia to meet with King Faisal for a week to find ways to strengthen pan-Arab unity against the state of Israel. Ra's is a villain born of an era of international anxiety that would soon allow a guy like Carlos the Jackal to become a freakish kind of celebrity/supervillain-for-real in the press, meshing in popular awareness the real Carlos with the fictional chameleon assassin villain of Fredrick Forsythe's novel *The Day of the Jackal.*

The Buddhist temple in which Talia unmasked Batman was a pretty loaded image as well, evoking a slew of AP newswire implications beyond the aforementioned artillery damage of the temples of Angkor Wat . . . damage from months before the cover date of "Death Dealers!" that the world was only made aware of—you guessed it—in that loaded May of 1971. Because of, or maybe despite, the U.S. war in Southeast Asia, there was a new awareness of Eastern culture in the U.S. May 9, 1971, marked the end of a two-day ceasefire in Vietnam to honor the birthday of the Buddha. Relations with ally Japan were changing, as by the end of that June, the U.S. had pledged to return Okinawa to Japanese control. Let's not forget that in 1970 Fusako Shigenobu had already founded the Japanese Red Army, an organization that in Asia functioned much as Black September did in the Middle East. By the March 1972 issue of *Batman* (#240), "Vengeance for a Dead Man," Ra's was specifically and overtly interested in manipulating U.S. interests in Southeast Asia for the sake of his own agenda.

And what of Ra's's ultimate eco-terrorist agenda, the saving of the planet from human blight? As a guy out to kill billions as part of an extreme environmentalist agenda, he's unique among villains, in that his goal is, ultimately, kinda-sorta noble. As for the means . . . wellllll. Again, let's look at the cultural pressure cooker of May and June of 1971: the FDA warned Americans to not eat swordfish due to mercury contamination; Nixon called for the creation of new and cleaner energy sources for the U.S. (a good idea then, and a really good idea now), and the great conflict over the use of phosphates in laundry detergent was in full swing, with even the Surgeon General getting involved in the debate.

Ra's's agenda was political, in that it dealt with the manipulations of nations and resources. His ultimate goal might be seen as apolitical, or above all politics. Yet it's unquestionable that his tools pushed very specific cultural buttons. Unlike the Joker, who merely had henchmen, Ra's had an international infrastructure for his crimes—an infrastructure that echoed the very real infrastructures used by Black September, the Japanese Red Army (and its affiliated Anti-Imperialist International Brigade), Carlos the Jackal, and later the Baader-Meinhof Gang. It's believable in Mike W. Barr's 1987 graphic novel *The Son of the Demon* to see Ra's with an array of high-tech military hardware at his disposal. But in Jim Starlin's *A Death in the Family* a year later (in *Batman* # 426-429), it was pretty doofy to see the Joker selling missiles to Hezbollah . . . and then see him appointed as an ambassador by the Ayatollah Khomeini. The cultural and political anxieties behind Ra's's villainy were real. The anxieties behind the Joker's were not. That's why the Joker can create mutant fish with his face on them, and still maintain his sense of menace.[13]

Ra's's interactions with Batman reflected, albeit in comic book extremes, real international tensions. And yet, as the villain who has most broadly expanded Batman's horizons to include the international and the political, he's also the villain who has dealt with Batman in the most intimate contexts of all. True, Catwoman Selina Kyle gets pretty darned intimate with Batman and Bruce Wayne once in a while, but Ra's's intimacy with Batman has been a constant. It is uniquely personal in a way that transcends his initial invasion of the Batcave and his daughter's lifting Batman's cowl, and

[13] Steve Engelhart's "The Laughing Fish" and "Sign of the Joker" in *Detective Comics* #475 (Feb. 1978) and #476 (March–April 1978).

defines his function as a character within the Batman mythology. The ultimate goal of other villains is to destroy Batman. Ra's's ultimate goal is to make Batman his son and heir, to have him marry Talia and bring him into his household. He, as the villain who led Batman into the wide world at large, and by implication a little closer into reality,[14] has been the most constant and effective father figure in Bruce Wayne's life. With Ra's al Ghul, the worldly is made dangerous, because through him it is also made so incredibly intimate.

As defined by his and Talia's 1971 debuts, the international becomes the familial with Ra's. These two elements are as inseparable from Ra's as the Joker is from his homicidal gags and the Riddler is from his need to leave obscure clues. Ra's can't function as a villain without this fatherly intimacy in the Batman mythos. Even the grandest plots of this global eco-terrorist are personal, when it comes to Batman.

Let's take a look at some of Ra's's more noteworthy exploits and see how this unique "internationally personal" function of his works.

In the aforementioned *Son of the Demon*, Ra's was faced with a situation that the head of no other terrorist organization, not even Fusako Shigenobu of the Japanese Red Army or Andreas Baader of the Baader-Meinhof Gang, could ever have dreamed of: a conflict between his two surrogate sons. Ra's sought the aid of his chosen successor, Batman, to take on the evil Qayin, whom Ra's raised as his own after his parents were killed and who would later kill Ra's's wife, Talia's mother. Qayin (who styled himself after the biblical Cain), was the malignant counterpart to Batman—having witnessed his parents' death, he vowed not to avenge them, but to bring death to the world. The struggle between him and Batman was a *de facto* struggle between brothers. It was in this story of questionable canonicity that Batman and Talia finally made legit and consummated their marriage begun in the 1978 story "I Now Pronounce You Batman and Wife."[15] Ra's performed the marriage rites in both stories. It was also in this story that Talia gave birth to her and Bruce's son

---

[14] Yes, I recognize the innate absurdity of saying a near-immortal alchemist is of greater reality than, say, a chubby guy with a beaky nose such as Oswald Cobblepot, the Penguin, but I think I've made my point.

[15] *Batman Spectacular*, summer 1978 . . . a story that presages *Batman Begins* in that it features a gas attack by Ra's on Gotham—though *Batman Begins* doesn't feature Talia leading an amphibious assault on Gotham while wearing a bikini.

Ibn al Xu'ffasch (Arabic for "Son of the Bat"), later known as Damian Wayne.

Even when Ra's takes on the whole Justice League, as he did in Mark Waid's *Tower of Babel* story arc,[16] his engagement with Batman has to be *personal*. Integral to Ra's's plot to kill billions was a psychological attack on Batman's familial identity: he dug up the graves of Bruce Wayne's parents and stole the bodies. Not even Blofeld or Irma Bunt would think to mess with Bond's head by pilfering the grave of Tracy Bond, would they? Ra's, the surrogate father, appropriated and by proxy superseded Bruce's birth parents in order to realize his goals. He and Talia also, in the same story arc, destroyed Batman's relationship with his surrogate family, the Justice League, by stealing the files Batman kept on neutralizing each JLA member (should they fall victim to mind control) and implementing the plans therein.

Greg Rucka's 2003 *Death and the Maidens* was a family drama with the scope of a Russian novel. Ra's's long-lost daughter Nyssa sought revenge against her father for leaving her to die in a Word War II concentration camp. She struck out at Ra's, Batman, and Superman to realize her goal of transforming the world emotionally, robbing it of the hope that Superman embodied. Even with the graphic novel's broad geographic and chronological scope, covering hundreds of years and regions as diverse as Russia, Paris, and the Arabian Desert, Batman's involvement was deeply personal: to enlist his aid, Ra's offered Batman a chance to attain a vision of his dead parents. Nyssa's plot was familial and international—an attempt to transform the entire world, beginning with the transformation of a single family member. To attack Ra's, she sought to utterly rewrite the mind of her half-sister Talia, in effect driving her mad and making her emotionally dependant on Nyssa in a way that came across as an amped-up version of Stockholm Syndrome, except here the hostage wasn't dependant on the hostage-taker for her life, but for her repeated resurrection. The resolution of the novel saw Talia, changed by her patricidal half-sister into a much harsher and crueler person, proclaim that she no longer loved Batman, and declare him her bitter enemy. She rejected that which would have made Batman her father's heir and so in effect exiled him from the family . . . even

---

[16] *JLA* 43–46.

after Batman had performed what would ordinarily be a filial duty: cremating Ra's's corpse.

Even with Ra's apparently dead in Devin Grayson's 2005 two-issue *Year One: Batman/Ra's al Ghul* and with the entire balance of life and death on a global scale at stake, Ra's treated Batman as his son, with a deep respect that might just be called "love" if you squint right. A letter from the late Ra's arrived at the Batcave that Ra's had violated the first time he and Batman met. The letter told Batman how to correct the ecological shift incurred by the destruction of Ra's's Lazarus Pits (the alchemical baths that enabled him to live for centuries). Batman was the only person he could entrust with this task, which was the legacy he chose to bestow upon his surrogate son.

It's incomplete to say that Ra's collapses the international with the personal. Even as a father figure, he specifically collapses *terrorism* with the familial, bringing the kinds of conflict fomented by Black September and Baader-Meinhof into the familial conflict of ancient Greek and early modern tragedy. And yet, while terrorism is destructive, fathers are generative forces (consider the original connotation of *genius* in the ancient Roman household: a tutelary, guiding spirit typically passed along paternal lines). It's this *generative* quality of Ra's that has made him integral to not one, not two, but *three* re-generations of the Batman character over the years.

Ra's was integral to the initial salvaging of Batman by Denny O'Neil discussed earlier, which rescued Batman from the dregs of the camp embodied by the ABC TV show of 1966–1968, a cultural legacy that *still* casts a long shadow: witness the Bat-flavored cameos of Adam West on *The Family Guy* and *The Simpsons*. The Bat-Craze and the 1960s camp incarnation of Batman himself had been played out by 1968, made irrelevant by the time of the *Batman* TV show's final broadcast on March 14 of that year. Mid-'60s goofiness didn't fit in a world shifting to the cultural moment of the late '60s. Yeah, we're looking at a difference of only a few years, but think of that moment in these terms: A kid who was a high school freshman in 1965 would see *The Sound of Music*, which featured Julie Andrews dervish-spinning against a bucolic vista, win the Oscar for Best Picture. By the time he was a senior in 1969, getting ready to go to college, or boot camp, he'd see *Midnight Cowboy* win Best Picture . . . which featured Dustin Hoffman dying in a puddle of his own piss.

That last episode of *Batman*, a show that defined much of the TV of that era, aired just a few weeks after another TV-defining moment: the transmission of NBC cameraman Vo Suu's footage of General Nguyen Ngoc Loan—then head of South Vietnam's national police force and future Dale City, Virginia, pizzeria manager—putting a bullet through the brain of Viet Cong prisoner Bay Lop, footage that changed a lot of opinions about the Vietnam War. The exploits of Special Guest Villains in flab-enhancing leotards seem minor when you consider that the week that *Batman* was canceled, news colossi Eric Sevareid, Walter Cronkite, and David Brinkley were all quoted saying that the Vietnam War was as good as lost. When *TV Guide* captioned its listing for the final *Batman* episode (which starred Zsa Zsa Gabor as a villainess), it did so with a kind of specified sign-off that signaled the end of a cultural Bat-era: "Last show of the series, Batfans. Next week, *The Second Hundred Years* takes over this time spot." That's right. *The Second Hundred Years*. ABC saw fit to replace its once mighty and culturally all-pervasive juggernaut with a sitcom starring 1960s stud-muffin Monte Markham as a prospector frozen alive in an Alaskan glacier in the year 1900, only to be thawed out in 1967 to live with his grandson, who's a dead ringer for his long-frozen grandpa. Whackiness and confusion ensue.

O'Neil reanimated Batman from a cultural figure who could be eclipsed by Monte Markham in a dual role by placing that character into a reality colored by the geopolitical and cultural transformations incurred by a post-Tet Offensive world. It was specifically Ra's al Ghul who brought Batman into that transformed world, by bringing that world into Batman's personal life, his domestic reality . . . much in the way that television footage of the Vietnam War was invading and changing domestic realities at the time.

Screenwriter David Goyer and Christopher Nolan resurrected Batman by using Ra's al Ghul just as surely as Ra's himself is resurrected by his Lazarus Pits, collapsing Ra's with another of Bruce Wayne's father figures, Henri Ducard, the French Foreign Legionnaire who taught Wayne the art of man-hunting.[17] True to form in *Batman Begins*, Ra's is an international figure who invades Bruce Wayne's private world, entering his home and burning it down . . . but only after first becoming Bruce's father and mentor, a generative force who guides his growth into becoming the Batman.

---

[17] A character created in the comics by 1989 *Batman* screenwriter Sam Hamm in *Detective Comics* #599 (April 1989).

Ra's again plays on modern anxieties. He's the head of a shadowy international organization hidden in the mountains of central Asia who, at the climax of the film, seeks to overthrow an established social order by driving a multi-passenger transportation device into a skyscraper in the heart of a major American city. Sound familiar?

And in 2006, comic book writer Grant Morrison used the legacy of Ra's for his reboot of Batman, beginning in a story arc entitled "Batman and Son" in *Batman* #656. While Morrison has said that "the idea that superhero comics should reflect the news headlines is not one I tend to subscribe to," he has also said that "Batman will always reflect his times" (Newsarama). Morrison describes "Batman and Son" as "a twisted domestic drama about a playboy confronted with his responsibilities" (Newsarama). The responsibility in question was Damian, Batman's son with Talia. Damian, only eleven years old, but trained from birth by the finest assassins in the world, disrupted and invaded Bruce Wayne's domestic space by injuring the current Robin, Tim Drake, whom Wayne had legally adopted as his son . . . while Talia led a terrorist strike against the British colony of Gibraltar.

As the original confluence of the domestic and the terroristic, Ra's is the keystone of a current trend in the DC comic universe: having traditional villains, who had typically struck at power plants or secret bases, strike at heroes within their home spaces, attacking and overthrowing domestic security. In effect, the "homeland" in "homeland security" is the "home space."[18]

The "Ground Zero" (in more than one sense) of this current trend, of which Ra's is the antecedent, is the JLA story arc *Identity Crisis*, in which Doctor Light—he whose villainy had previously involved goofy dimensional shifting devices—revealed himself to be a villain of a much more base and despicable sort. Striking at the heart of the JLA once entailed menacing Snapper Carr, their jive-talking teenage groupie; in *Identity Crisis*, Doctor Light broke into the "home space" of the JLA headquarters and raped Sue Dibny, the wife of Ralph Dibny, the Elongated Man. The situation escalated and included the murder of Jack Drake, the father of the current Robin, Tim Drake, in his home; this was the event

---

[18] For an interesting collapse of "home space" and "homeland security," check out the Wes Craven movie *Red Eye*, starring cute little Rachel McAdams saving her country and the integrity of her daddy's house from a terrorist played by the Scarecrow himself, Cillian Murphy.

that led to Bruce Wayne legally adopting Tim, creating the household that Talia would disrupt on her way to attack Gibraltar. The planet-shaking crises that the JLA typically faced were now unfolding in the home, with the kind of physical and emotional casualties that their first enemy, Starro,[19] could not inflict. The assault on heroes' home spaces continued in the JLA story arc *Crisis of Conscience*, in which a cabal of villains attacked the JLA by striking at their families, a plot set in motion by Despero, he of the quaint teleporting chessboard of forty years earlier. In the JLA arc *The Tornado's Path*, the android Amazo threatened Red Tornado's wife and daughter in their apartment. In the Justice Society of America story arc *The Next Age*, Vandal Savage recruited neo-Nazis to kill off the bloodlines of various heroes, a plot that included an assault on the family of Commander Steel during that most wholesome and American of functions, a family reunion and picnic. In the Green Arrow arc *Heading Into the Light* (written by Judd Winick), Doctor Light and the evil archer/assassin Merlyn attacked Oliver Queen through his family, going so far as to blow up their house.

How are these assaults terrorist assaults? They reflect a new reality that didn't exist when the JLA first met Doctor Light and Despero. On 9/11, the bastards hit us where we live. The international became by implication domestic, and that new domestic reality has been reflected in the domestic reality of superheroes. According to Brad Melzter, current *JLA* writer and the author of *Identity Crisis*:

> Without question, *Identity Crisis* was a reaction to 9/11. The Norman Rockwell picture of America and firemen and policemen was shattered. And so the popular culture goes too. It was weeks after that I began the series [*Identity Crisis*], determined to remind people of that humanity in heroes. . . . That was always the goal.

Ra's (and by extension Talia) is the source of this trend, as a villain . . . as a surrogate father . . . as a foil who has at least partly redefined the superhero's reality the same way he redefined Batman's reality post-Tet in the comics and

---

[19] An extraterrestrial starfish.

post-9/11 in *Batman Begins*. Why does he function in this way in the Batman mythos? Why is such a familial/antagonistic dynamic impossible, say, between Lex Luthor and Superman?

Because more than any other hero in comics, Batman's quest is personal, to the point that it eclipses all else, and defines who he is as a hero. Batman has no powers, only his personal resolve. Yes, Uncle Ben told Peter about power and responsibility, and yes, Ma and Pa Kent gave Clark All-American Smallville values. But Parker would still be able to climb walls without that guidance from Uncle Ben, and Kal-El would still be a powerful Kryptonian without Ma and Pa Kent's help.

A father and a terrorist/villain—generative and destructive forces, operating in both domestic and international spaces—can subvert the personal resolve of Batman more dangerously than any acid-squirting flower of the Joker's or any trick umbrella of the Penguin's. Ra's strikes at the very core of Batman, just as surely as Kryptonite does the core of Superman.

To strike at the core of one's being is the goal of the terrorist. Ra's has access to that soft target that only a father can attain.

With thanks to Aaron at Comicazi in Boston, for letting me read his copy of "The Secret of the Waiting Graves."

Since 1990, MICHAEL MARANO has been reviewing movies and doing pop culture commentary for the Public Radio Satellite System program *Movie Magazine International*, syndicated in more than 111 markets in the U.S. and Canada. In this capacity, he has seen and ranted on and pontificated about perhaps more than 1,000 genre movies, and is now unfit for most any other form of employment. His articles have appeared in venues like *The Boston Phoenix*, *The Weekly Dig*, *The Independent Weekly*, *Paste Magazine*, and *Science Fiction Universe*. Marano is also a horror writer, with stories in *The Mammoth Book of Best New Horror 11* and *Outsiders: 22 All-New Stories from the Edge*; his first novel, *Dawn Song*, won the Bram Stoker and International Horror Guild Awards. He recently visited the set of the *Batman Begins* sequel

The Dark Knight for the SciFi Channel and saw a lot of cool stuff that he can't talk about. He is a bitter old punk rocker, and can be reached at www.myspace.com/michaelmarano.

REFERENCES

Meltzer, Brad. Personal e-mail dated April 22, 2007.
Morrison, Grant. "Morrison in the Cave: Grant Morrison Talks Batman." Newsarama.
   <http://www.newsarama.com/dcnew/Batman/Morrison/Morrison_Batman.html>
Murray, Rebecca. "Interview with *Batman Begins* Star Christian Bale." About.com.
   <http://movies.about.com/od/batman/a/batmancb060805_2.htm>

In the following essay Alan J. Porter gives some credit where it's due, and in the process rights some historical wrongs. All of that is good. But what I particularly like is his look at a man who has sometimes been demonized. Though he clearly doesn't belong to the man's fan club, Mr. Porter does give us another side of Batman "creator" Bob Kane's story.

THE DUBIOUS ORIGINS
OF THE BATMAN

Who Did What — And Does It Really Matter?

ALAN J. PORTER

I t started with the sound of gunfire echoing across a dark and deserted alleyway. Sudden violence and death. According to some, it happened around the corner from the Monarch Theater as a happy family made their way home after watching Douglas Fairbanks swing across the screen as the inimitable Zorro. Others suggest that it may have been by the opera house, as a concerned father tried to console a young boy disturbed by visions of *Die Fledermaus*.

Perhaps it was a simple mugging gone wrong. Maybe there was a more sinister motive. The gunman could have been a punk named Joe Chill, or a mobster on the rise who went by the name of Jack Napier. To a large extent, the details of what and who are irrelevant, the end was the same. In that dirty place, a place that would, from that point onward be known as Crime Alley, Thomas and Martha Wayne lay dead, the whole grisly deed witnessed by their only son, Bruce Wayne.

The legend says that on that night the boy swore an oath over the dead bodies of his parents—an oath that he would do everything in his power to ensure that no one else would suffer as he did, that no more innocents would die.

On that night, Bruce Wayne set out on the path that would
lead to the creation of the Batman.

The origin story of the Batman is an essential part of his mythos. The
small details may vary with each interpretation, but the underlying
theme of loss and vengeance is as integral to the legend as the cape and
the cowl. From comics to books, radio, television, and the movies,
almost every time[1] the Batman story is told this single event is referenced.

But while Batman's fictional origin story may be well-known, even to
the most casual of fans, what about the origin of the character from a literary perspective—just how did the Batman come about and who were
the men responsible for the creation of one of our greatest cultural
icons?

It's easy to find the answer to the simple question, "Who created
Batman?" It's there on every Batman story, be it in print, TV, or the
movies. Every single one carries the credit—"Batman created by Bob
Kane."

That simple, five-word phrase covers a story full of mystery, betrayal,
opportunism, legal maneuvering, and human misery that would be worthy of investigation by "The World's Greatest Detective" himself.

In fact, it could be said that it was the Batman that created "Bob
Kane."

The story goes that one day young Bob Kane asked his editor, Vince
Sullivan, if "those Siegel and Shuster characters were making good
money with their new Superman strip." Superman had launched just a
few months earlier and had become a massive hit for National
Periodicals—later DC Comics—who, while paying the Man of Steel's
creators reasonable page rates, had bought the rights from Joe Shuster
and Jerry Siegel for a pittance.

National was desperate to find another character who could repeat
Superman's success, so Sullivan asked this opportunistic and inquiring

---

[1] The one notable exception is the classic 1960s TV show starring Adam West. The only
reference to Batman's origin is a passing mention that his parents were "victims of a
crime."

young artist to come up with something over the weekend.

According to Kane's version of events, he came back in the following Monday with the concept for the Batman fully formed and complete with design sketches that resembled the Batman we know today. It was as simple as that.

Over the years, Kane's story about how "he created" Batman grew and each embellishment became more fantastic. At one point, he endorsed a story for a DC fan magazine[2] that showed him having his friend "Larry" dress up in a full Batman costume made by his mother and pose for him while he produced the first Batman model drawings. In later years, he repeatedly told the story of how as a teenager he'd seen a Leonardo da Vinci drawing of a crude flying machine with the inscription "a man shall have no wings other than those of a bat," and it had stuck with him. His 1989 autobiography showed a sketch of the Leonardo machine alongside a sketch of Batman that he had signed and dated "R'bert Kane, '39" as proof of this moment of inspiration. The illustration caption reads, "These drawings were done in 1939, several months before Batman's first published appearance, and were used as a guide when I drew that story" (Kane and Andrae 36). He even produced a lithograph of the piece and signed copies can still be seen for sale at various comics conventions.

For many years, Kane's version of the creation of the Batman was taken at face value by fans and the media; however, those who worked within the early days of the comics industry knew differently. In the 1970s, as the first stirrings of the fan-turned-historian movement started to take shape in the pages of various fanzines and amateur press magazines, and as interviews were conducted and documents studied, it became clear that there were missing names in the true story of the Batman's origin. The one name that was most noticeably absent was that of Bill Finger.

---

[2] *Real Fact Comics* #5, published by DC in 1946. The story is entitled "The True Story of Batman & Robin—How a Big-Time Comic Is Born." It looks as if it were drawn by Win Mortimer, with the text unaccredited and probably done by a staff writer. However, it was narrated in the first person as if Kane were telling the story. Kane would later quote this story as a source in letters to fans.

———

William Finger was showing signs of being a creative and imaginative writer by the time he started at DeWitt Clinton High School a few years ahead of a budding cartoonist named Robert Kahn. It's debatable if the two knew of each other at school, reports vary, but by the time William—now calling himself "Bill"—started working as a shoe salesman, they were firm friends with a shared love of newspaper strips and the pulps.

Young Robert had dreams of becoming a big-time syndicated newspaper cartoonist. While he could think up some basic ideas, his drawing skills were rudimentary at best and more suited to funny animals than illustrative adventure style strips. So he turned to his friend Bill to help flesh out his ideas and write stories for some sample strips to try and break in to the newspaper market. The strips, now signed by "Robert Kane," eventually opened a door for Kane, but not where he expected. Instead of working in the rarified company of newspapers, he found himself involved in the fledgling comic book industry.

Robert Kane was soon landing himself enough assignments to keep himself employed as a jobbing cartoonist, calling on his friend Bill Finger for story assistance when he felt it was needed. Between 1936 and 1938, they produced various stories for a variety of publishers before Robert Kane ended up working for National Periodicals and as they say, the rest is history. But it's history as told by Kane and his growing sense of self-importance.

Even if no one knows exactly what happened, I believe the following scenario—based on various interviews, publications, and my own research—is perhaps as close to the truth as we currently know it.

There is no doubt that Kane was looking to increase his earning potential and probably did ask Sullivan about Siegel and Shuster's pay rate. There also seems to be no doubt that Sullivan asked Kane, and more likely all his artists, to come up with an idea for another hero. Sullivan may have even suggested that Robert think of something using a bat motif. There is no proof that he was given the "weekend" deadline but, given what he turned in, there's no reason to believe that it couldn't have been done quickly over the course of a few days.

Analysis of Kane's work shows a strong propensity to "swipe" poses from newspaper strip artists he admired and aspired to emulate. In particular, Kane borrowed from the work of Alex Raymond's Flash Gordon strip.[3] It's a reasonable assumption that Kane copied a Flash Gordon pose and drew a new costume on to the figure . . . a garishly colored red costume, a domino mask, and fixed, stiff "bat wings" stuck behind the shoulder blades.[4] Sullivan liked the idea but pointed out that Kane needed a story to go along with the concept. Kane turned to his old friend and collaborator, Bill Finger.

When Bill Finger saw Kane's sketch, he felt it looked too much like Superman and suggested a few changes, changes that would be vital in defining the look and impact of the character. According to Finger:

> I got Webster's Dictionary off the shelf and was hoping they had a drawing of a bat, and sure enough it did. I said, "Notice the ears, why don't we duplicate the ears?" I suggested he draw what looked like a cowl. . . . I had suggested he bring the nosepiece down and make him mysterious and not show any eyes at all. . . . I didn't like the wings, so I suggested he make a cape and scallop the edges so it would flow out behind him when he ran and would look like bat wings. He didn't have any gloves on. We gave him gloves because naturally he'd leave fingerprints. (Steranko 44)

Bill wrote that first story, "The Case of the Chemical Syndicate,"[5] and named all the major characters including Bruce Wayne and James

---

[3] The Batman pose in the now iconic image on the cover of Batman's debut, *Detective Comics* #27, is exactly the same as Flash Gordon's in panel five of the January 17, 1937, edition of the Flash Gordon newspaper strip.

[4] Comics art historian Arlen Schumer recreated Kane's original sketch based on analysis of Kane's art style and descriptions given in various interviews by Kane, Finger, and Sullivan. The resulting image was published on the cover of *Alter Ego* magazine, vol. 2 no. 5 (summer 1999).

[5] It has recently come to light that Finger's script for the first Batman story was an adaptation of the Shadow pulp story "Partners of Peril" by Theodore Tinsley published a few years earlier—it seems Bob Kane wasn't the only Batman creator to borrow heavily from his influences.

Gordon. As part of the character development, it was Finger who decided to make Batman a detective—"My idea was to have Batman be a combination of Douglas Fairbanks, Sherlock Holmes, the Shadow, and Doc Savage as well" (Steranko 44).

Robert (now signing himself "Bob Kane") took the completed story back to Sullivan and the strip was scheduled to be published in *Detective Comics* #27.

Finger had transformed Kane's derivative, uninspired design for a "bat-man" into the Batman as we know him. If today's standards had applied during the early days of the comics industry, then Bill Finger would have received a co-creator credit. Co-creator credits weren't unknown at the time, as Superman showed. But that was based on how the strip had been represented to the publishers. The problem was that no one at National knew Bill Finger existed. Sullivan had asked Bob Kane to come up with something and, as far as Sullivan was concerned, Bob Kane had delivered. Bob Kane, and his family, would make sure that it stayed that way.

Unacknowledged, Finger continued to lay the foundations of the Batman mythos. In writing the early Batman stories, he not only named Bruce Wayne and Commissioner Gordon, but Gotham City as well. He went on to create Catwoman, the Penguin, the Riddler, and Two-Face, and co-create Robin. Finger wrote the scripts that introduced many of the staples of the series—the Batcave, the Batmobile, the Batplane, and the bat-signal. It was also Bill Finger who introduced the phrases "Dyanamic Duo" and "Boy Wonder" to the pop culture lexicon.

When the Batman appeared in *Detective Comics* #27, he was an immediate hit with readers. Bob Kane, borrowing a model often used by top newspaper artists, set up his own Batman production shop. He hired his first assistant, Jerry Robinson, as early as the third or fourth Batman issue, and started to step back more into the role of general manager than that of creator or artist.

Robinson and Finger soon became the major creative forces behind the Batman. Robinson describes Finger as "a craftsman whose Batman adventures were carefully plotted, as well as being imbued with humor and sprightly repartee." But according to Robinson and several other Golden Age artists I have spoken to, Finger's greatest strength was the fact that he was a "visual writer—he knew instinctively what the artist could translate into compelling pictures and sequential narrative" ("Siegel, Drake . . .").

Bill Finger was also the first comics writer to provide his artists with visual references and to thoroughly research the science and locations of his stories. He plotted the action so that everything worked in a logical manner. However, Bill Finger wasn't a natural writer. According to Robinson, he had a sense of perfection that impacted his ability to meet deadlines: "Bill really worked on his scripts and it didn't come easily . . . [he'd] sweat out every word" (Robinson).

Eventually other publishers noticed the success of the Batman production team and made offers to both Robinson and Finger. According to Robinson, they approached Bob Kane about receiving more recognition and an increased share of the money. Kane refused, so the duo approached DC about moving on staff. Worried that they would lose the Batman team, DC agreed. Robinson and Finger stopped working for Bob Kane directly, but still continued to work on Batman. And apparently, at no point during these discussions did the shy and insecure Bill Finger represent himself as Batman's co-creator, nor inform DC of his role in defining the character. As far as DC was concerned, he was just Bob Kane's ghostwriter. To fill the gap left by Robinson and Finger, Kane agreed that rather than replace Finger with another writer he would start accepting scripts from DC written by Finger and others; while he continued to populate his studio with an increasing army of artists to produce work credited to "Bob Kane."

While working on staff at DC, Finger went on to co-create[6] the original Green Lantern and boxing superhero Wildcat, but it wasn't long before his inability to meet deadlines became more important than the quality of his scripts. His insecurity grew, which caused further delays, and the comics work started to dry up.

One enduring mystery from this period is how Bob Kane managed to get his name to appear on every Batman story right from the start. In the early days of comics, writers and artists went unacknowledged, unac-

---

[6] The artists who created these characters and for whom Bill Finger wrote the first stories have often referred to him as "co-creator."

credited, and even unrecorded. In fact, even now DC sometimes has problems identifying creators of some early stories when compiling reprint books.

The truth may never be known, as even today, nearly seventy years later, the details of any deal are still hidden away behind legal barriers that no one at DC Comics is in a position to discuss. One possible explanation is that the perpetual byline was an exchange for Kane signing over all ownership rights to the character. What does seem clear is that he (or a family representative) negotiated an unprecedented contract that "Bob Kane" would be the only source of Batman stories for the next twenty years. With an amazing piece of timing, negotiations to renew that contract coincided with the 1960s Batmania craze. Recent research[7] seems to suggest that at this point Bob Kane managed to convince the powers at DC that he had in fact been eighteen and not twenty-two when he signed his first contract, and that if he didn't get the terms he wanted he would sue them for exploiting a minor. It appears that the result of these negotiations was an agreement that Batman stories could now be produced in-house by DC and could carry other creator credits as long as they still used the "Created by Bob Kane" stamp, and as part of the deal, Kane would get a regular monthly royalty plus a slice of the merchandising. With this agreement in place, Kane stepped away from any pretence of creating comics. Whatever the truth, the result was that it made Bob Kane a very rich man.

So where was Bill Finger in 1968? Being fired by the same company that was giving out large checks to his erstwhile partner. After a spell working on TV, including ironically the Batman TV show[8] and movies, Bill returned to writing comics at DC. Not long after his return to the industry, he became upset that when DC started a program of reprinting large numbers of Golden Age stories in the '60s they didn't pay the original creators any reprint fees. As they only reprinted the best stories, a large proportion of the reprints were Bill's. But what got him, and several

[7] Reported in Gerard Jones's *Men of Tomorrow: Geeks, Gangsters, and the Birth of the Comic Book*.

[8] "The Clock King's Crazy Crimes" and "The Clock King Gets Crowned" from *Batman*. Co-written with Charles Sinclair. Finger's name was excluded from the on-screen credits.

other veteran creators, fired was asking about (not demanding, just asking) a health care program.

While Bob Kane was living the life of the "millionaire playboy" he had always dreamed of, his old friend was out of a job, and what little work had been coming his way dried up. By the early '70s, he was back writing for DC on a freelance basis. His failing health was further impacting his ability to deliver scripts on time, and by 1974 his health gave out. He passed away at the age of fifty-nine while working on a script that was already two weeks late. Amazing as it seems from today's perspective, Bill Finger never saw his name appear on a single Batman story[9] during his lifetime.

In 1989, just as the second round of Batmania flowed around the Tim Burton movie, Kane once more renegotiated his deal with DC Comics. He also published a ghostwritten (naturally) autobiography in which—for the first time—Bob Kane made mention of Bill Finger, although it fell far short of what most people in the industry had been hoping for. Kane wrote, "Now that my long-time friend and collaborator is gone, I must admit that Bill never received the fame and recognition he deserved" (Kane and Andrae 44). However, beyond that singe conciliatory sentence, Kane never undertook any actions to redress the situation.

In the 1960s, Kane had relocated to Los Angeles. Banking on his name alone, he created and launched an animated TV series, *Courageous Cat*, that was basically a retread of the Batman concepts first created by Bill Finger. After the failure of the show, Kane moved to producing paintings of clowns (that according to former DC Comics editor Julius Schwartz[10] were also produced by ghost artists) and dating a succession of models and actresses, one of whom he later married. In various published anecdotes of comics fans and creators who encountered him during this period, their estimation of Bob Kane went from "hero to zero" within minutes as Kane's ego took over.

Kane was listed as "creative consultant" on the Batman movies and also "produced" a few Batman lithographs for both *Batman* and *Batman*

---

[9] His name did appear on three Batman stories reprinted in *DC 100 Page Super Spectacular* (DC-20), which was published around the time of his death.

[10] A tale told at a panel at San Diego Comic-Con and recounted in Schwartz's autobiography, *Man of Two Worlds*.

Returns. A planned cameo role for Kane in *Batman* as "Bob the Cartoonist" didn't happen, but his wife, actress Elizabeth Sanders, appeared in *Batman Returns* and the two Joel Schumacher-directed Batman movies as newspaper columnist "Gossip Gerty."

When Bob Kane passed away in 1998, he was universally lauded in the popular press articles and obituaries as the "creator of Batman." Even his grave carries Kane's own peculiar take on events:

> Robert Kane a.k.a. Bob Kane . . . GOD bestowed a dream upon Bob Kane, Blessed with divine inspiration and a rich imagination, Bob created a legacy known as BATMAN. Introduced in a May 1939 comic book, Batman grew from a tiny actor into an American Icon. A "Hand of God" creation, Batman and his world personify the eternal struggle of good versus evil, with GOD's laws prevailing in the end. Bob Kane, Bruce Wayne, Batman—they are one and the same. Bob infused his dual identity character with his own attributes: goodness, kindness, compassion, sensitivity, generosity, intelligence, integrity, courage, purity of spirit, a love of all mankind. Batman is known as the "Dark Knight," but through his deeds he walks in the Light of a Higher Power, as did his creator—Bob Kane! . . .[11]

While Kane went on to earn millions from "his creation," Finger died unknown, unacknowledged, and in near poverty. But he wasn't the only one who lived under Kane's egotistical shadow. Kane was notorious for using "ghost artists" even from the earliest days of the strip. Most of them toiled in anonymity for years. In fact, Kane didn't even acknowledge their existence in his 1989 biography. Over the years, researchers have tried to identify and clarify just who did what during the early days of Batman's existence, hoping that these artists and writers would at last get recognition. Over the years, most—if not all—have been identified and are now acknowledged as contributors when their stories are reprinted.

Even Bill Finger has started to receive increasing credit in print for the

---

[11] Inscription on Bob Kane's grave at Forest Lawn Memorial Park in the Hollywood Hills area of Los Angeles, CA (*The Cemetery Project*).

Batman stories he wrote. In fact, Warner Bros. went as far as to recall the early pressings of the *Batman Begins* special edition DVDs because Finger's writer credit was missing on the reprint of the first Batman story, "The Case of the Chemical Syndicate," included in the set's inserted comics collection. Acknowledgment of Finger's role in Batman actually started as early as 1964 when mention was made by editor Julie Schwartz in the letters column of *Detective Comics #327* that it was Finger "who has written most of the classic Batman adventures of the last two decades." A year later, in *Batman #169*, Finger was mentioned again, this time as the creator of the Riddler. Over the following years, occasional mention of him as Kane's collaborator and even "co-creator" has been made in DC publications in editorials, forewords, and essays — but never on a Batman story, where his only published credit remains simply "writer."

Many of the things that Bill Finger and his contemporaries fought for in the 1960s and that cost him his staff job, such as reprint fees and health plans, are now common practice in the industry. It's also now common practice for all creators to get proper bylines and a stake in the characters they produce. Today, Bill is remembered with the annual Finger Award, awarded since 2005 for lifetime achievement and excellence in Comic Book Writing. Fittingly, among the first two recipients were Arnold Drake and Alvin Schwartz, both friends of Bill's and ghostwriters on the early Batman newspaper strips.

While those of us deeply involved and fascinated by the development of such an iconic character feel that the research to uncover just who did what is important to our understanding of the development of the comic book industry, I have begun to ask myself—at the end of the day, does it really matter?

Will the casual moviegoer sitting down to watch *The Dark Knight* in 2008 care about who did what in 1939?

I doubt it.

The Batman is now far bigger than the industry that gave birth to him. In fact, it could be argued that Batman fans who read comic books are probably in the minority. In the overall picture of his impact on pop culture, who did what in terms of his origin actually carries little meaning.

We must also realize that any change to the accreditation for Batman's origin would have a massive financial impact on DC and Warner Bros. While Bill Finger has no known living descendents, the specter of potential future lawsuits and claims for a slice of the merchandising gold mine that the Batman represents is an ever-present one.

Adding to that consideration, I have also come to realize that, as historians, we may be guilty of presentism, a natural tendency to apply the values and perspectives of today to events that happened in the past.

Writer Elmer Kelton postulates that there are three kinds of truth: fact, folklore, and fiction. The "true" story of Batman's origin encompasses all three.

Fact is truth that can be supported by contemporary documentary evidence. The fact is that the Bat-Man first appeared in *Detective Comics* #27 in 1939 with Bob Kane's signature attached to it.

When we take the gaps in between the facts and speculate on the actions of those involved based on memory, we move into the realm of folklore. Most of what I described in the previous pages is perhaps best treated as comics industry "folklore."

The fiction is Bob Kane's exaggerated and often changing stories of his role, and the roles of others, in the birth and development of the legend of the Batman we know today.

On the basis of this combination of fact, folklore, and fiction, in recent years, comics historians and commentators have come to lionize Bill Finger and demonize Bob Kane. But in doing this are we guilty of generational chauvinism? When judging the actions of people in the past, we should do so within the context of their time and place. We have a natural tendency to apply today's standards to past events, and based on that, every Batman story would carry a "Created by Bill Finger and Bob Kane" credit. But we are talking about events of seventy years ago. Should we be blaming Bob Kane, or his family, for being smarter and more forward-thinking than his contemporaries when it came to sharing in the success of "his" creation?

The argument has been made that "today's sensitivity to credits didn't exist in 1939. If a business model could be said to exist for comic books (at that time) it was newspaper strips: One guy signs it no matter how many draw it. This may have been wrong, but it was not perceived as being wrong" (Evanier and Aragones 91).

As mentioned earlier, the status of "creator" in 1939 was a nebulous one at best, based more on who sold the strip than who actually did the work. Even now there are no standard rules, just an understanding of best practices. At that time there weren't any established practices in the fledgling industry.

Kane's stated ambition was to be a newspaper cartoonist with his own studio; it was the only model he knew, and he took it and applied it to the new world of comic books. If we look at his actions in 1939 from that standpoint, they become not only understandable, but—in many ways—defensible.

But by the time of his contract renewal in the 1960s, the model had changed. By then, the comics industry had accepted practices, and creator credits were becoming commonplace, if not yet universally applied. It could be argued that this was the time to step up and do the morally correct thing and acknowledge the part played by others, and Bill Finger specifically, in building the foundation on which his wealth would be built. Again the opportunity arose in 1989 and was still ignored.

For Bob Kane, the fiction had long ago overtaken the folklore and the fact.

ALAN J. PORTER is a writer on various aspects of popular culture with a few books and a variety of articles published in magazine titles in the U.K., U.S., Canada, Europe, and Australia. He knows way too much about the Batman and is the author of *The Unauthorized Batman Collector's Guide*. He also founded Gotham Gazette—The Batman Magazine on the Web and the long-running *Gotham Weekly News* e-mail newsletter, which were published between 1997 and 2006. He is currently researching a full-length biography of Bob Kane and Bill Finger. Read more online at alanjporter.com.

REFERENCES

Cemetery Project, The. 14 Aug. 2007. <http://www.thecemeteryproject.com>

Evanier, Mark and Sergio Aragones. *Wertham Was Right!: Another Collection of POV Columns.* Raleigh: TwoMorrows, 2003.

Jones, Gerard. *Men of Tomorrow: Geeks, Gangsters, and the Birth of the Comic Book.* New York: Basic Books, 2004.

Kane, Bob and Tom Andrae. *Batman & Me.* Forestville: Eclipse, 1989.

Kelton, Elmer. "Fact, Fiction & Folklore." University of Mary Hardin-Baylor Literary Festival, Wells Science Center, Belton, TX. 8 Jan. 1999.

Robinson, Jerry. Interview by Gary Grouth. *Comics Journal* #271, 15 Oct. 2005.

Schwartz, Julius. *Man of Two Worlds: My Life in Science Fiction and Comics.* New York: HarperCollins, 2000.

"Siegel, Drake to Receive First Bill Finger Award." Comic-Con International. <http://www.comic-con.org/cci/cci_finger_1.shtml>

Steranko, Jim. *The Steranko History of Comics, Volume One.* Reading, PA: Supergraphics, 1970.

What's a comic book editor to do when a hero outlives his origin? When his fictional world no longer reflects the world outside the window? Ignore the problem? Find a way to somehow age the character (and his friends and enemies)? Reinvent the character? These are some of the dilemmas comic book editors deal with that make the job both frustrating and interesting. Chris Roberson discusses these and more.

WHY DOESN'T BRUCE WAYNE RETIRE ALREADY?!

CHRIS ROBERSON

There is a long tradition in heroic fiction of passing the torch, of one generation giving way to the next, and of yesterday's hero acting as mentor and guide to tomorrow's. Zorro did it, as did the Green Hornet, the Question, and many more besides. But while Bruce Wayne has been training sidekicks ever since Dick Grayson was the Sensational Character Find of 1940, he's not shown any indication yet of hanging up his cowl and handing over the keys to the Batmobile.

Isn't it about time that the old guy retired, and let some new blood patrol the crime-infested streets of Gotham? Bruce Timm's *Batman Beyond* series and other alternate continuities offer a tantalizing glimpse into futures in which Wayne has done just this, and suggest a possible solution to the problem.

There have been many examples of heroes handing on the family business over the years, in comics, books, films, and elsewhere. Some characters are even predicated on this kind of heroic succession. The Phantom in the Lee Falk comic strips is one of a long line of Ghosts Who Walk, with father passing down skull-ring to son, down through the centuries. The Black Hood in Gray Morrow's Red Circle comics was Kip Burland, whose ancestors had worn the same hood while fighting oppression down through the generations. The current Iron Fist, Daniel Rand, learns in the pages of *The Immortal Iron Fist* that there have been sixty-six bearers of the iron fist before him. The Phantom, the Black Hood, and Iron Fist are part of generational legacies, having received their heroic identities from predecessors, and it can be assumed that they will one day pass on the mantle to the next generation.

Some characters, while not part of such generational legacies, pass on their mantles when they can no longer carry on using the identity themselves. The Prowler, in Tim Truman's Eclipse Comics series of the same name, is an old man who fought crime in the '30s and '40s under that name, who in the late 1980s finds and trains a young man as his replacement. In Ron Fortier's *Green Hornet* series for Now Comics, newspaperman Britt Reid hands down the green mask and gas-gun to a succession of generations of the Reid clan (all of whom are accompanied by martial artists surnamed Kato, naturally). Even Zorro, in the film *The Mask of Zorro* (1998), having long since retired, finds a young outlaw and outsider to train as his successor. Still other characters pick their successors from their own deathbeds, as when Dan Garrett bequeathed the name of the Blue Beetle to Ted Kord with his dying breath on Pago Island (though Garrett took with him the magic scarab that granted his powers, forcing poor Kord to have to invent technological means to replace them).

Bruce Wayne has been Batman since 1939, nearly seven decades. Isn't it about time he found someone else to fill out the cape and cowl?

So why *doesn't* Bruce Wayne just retire, already?

Well, there are two reasons for it, it would seem. There's a fictional reason in the stories themselves, which explains why the *character* won't retire. And there's a real-world publishing reason that explains why DC Comics isn't in any hurry for Bruce Wayne to board up the Batcave. Ultimately, though, neither of these truly prevents the Dark Knight's retirement.

Let's tackle the "real world" reason first, and see how it complicates the story reasons considerably. The short version is that DC Comics and its parent Time Warner simply have too much invested in the character of Bruce Wayne *as* Batman, and see no good reason to deviate too far from the recognizable form. For millions of TV viewers and moviegoers,

Batman *is* Bruce Wayne, and vice versa. To change that would mean diluting the brand, and running the risk of alienating the audience.

Which isn't to say that DC Comics hasn't played around with heroic succession before. Even with Batman himself, from time to time.

Most often, though, the characters that are replaced with successors are the less successful ones, the ones less well-known by general audiences. A great many potential moviegoers or TV viewers, for example, are probably not aware of the existence of characters like the Flash at all, and if they *are* aware of them, probably aren't too concerned with whether the man behind the mask is Barry Allen or Wally West (or Jay Garrick or Bart Allen, for that matter). So when Oliver Queen dies and his son Connor Hawke replaces him as Green Arrow, it is for DC Comics a much less risky proposition than replacing Batman (that said, it may be telling that Queen is back from the dead and pulling back the old green bowstrings once more). Most people, if told that Sandra Knight had retired and trained Dee Tyler as the new Phantom Lady, would most likely respond, "Phantom *Who?*"

Now, Batman and Superman have both had their respective roles filled by temporary replacements, for brief periods, but it was always clear that they would be taking the role back once they were able. Once Batman's back healed, and Superman came back from the dead (which was, let's face it, inevitable), Azrael and Steel (and the Eradictor and Superboy and the Cyborg, for that matter) would be out of a job. Batman and Superman would no more permanently retire than Thor hand the enchanted Mjolnir over to Beta Ray Bill and never ask for it back, or Captain America hand his shield over to the U.S.Agent and wear the yellow and blue of Nomad for good. And Tony Stark not get the Iron Man armor back from Jim Rhodes? Hardly seems likely. In the DC Universe, as in Marvel's, the marquee names remain the same, while the supporting cast is able to change much more freely.

As a result, former Gotham City police officer Rene Montoya can inherit the mask and fedora of the Question from her late friend Vic Sage, and Jack Knight can take up the cosmic rod of his retired father and patrol the skies over Opal City as Starman (and, of course, he can later hang up his spurs and hand the rod over to Stargirl). Comics, and DC Comics in particular, are full of these sorts of heroic legacies, characters taking up the names and costumes of fallen or retired heroes. In the current continuity, nearly every member of the Justice League of America is at least the second to bear their names, having been preceded by similarly named members of the Justice Society of America, and many of the Leaguers are now actually third generation, in some cases former sidekicks made good. But the notable exceptions are the most recognizable and popular characters on the team: Batman and Superman.

(And Wonder Woman, *arguably*, though there's a bit of confused continuity to do with her mother, who temporarily filled in for her, and then traveled back in time and operated as Wonder Woman in the days of World War II, but those stories might not be in continuity anymore, anyway, in which case. . . . Confused continuity, as I've said, and probably best not discussed.)

Superman is Superman, and it makes sense that he'd stick around. He's from another planet, for one, and who can say what his lifespan might be? And he's invulnerable, for another, so arguably he could be effectively immortal. So certainly there's no room to quibble with Clark Kent continuing to wear the red cape.

But Batman? Bruce Wayne? He's not invulnerable. He's a human being. And we human beings have a tendency to get on in years. We get gray, we get wrinkled, we get *old*.

But Batman can't be old. And if Batman *has* to be Bruce Wayne, then that complicates matters considerably. So while Wonder Woman is immortal, and Superman probably is, too, and all the rest of the superheroes in the DC Comics universe can happily grow older and hand off their heroic identities to their sidekicks or children or random passersby, Bruce Wayne *has* to remain young, and he has to remain Batman.

Which tends to complicate continuity, considerably.

Every decade or two, the DC Universe has to hit a kind of cosmic "reset" button. *Crisis on Infinite Earths. Zero Hour. Infinite Crisis.* Now, all these series are designed to address any number of continuity gaffs, naturally, smoothing out the rough edges and so on. But they all share one key component in common, and that's resetting the calendar and keeping the characters young. Bruce Wayne is never much older than his mid-thirties, if even that, and never ages from there, and the same goes for everyone else. Well, *almost.* . . . See, the sidekicks keep getting older. And the other heroes keep having kids who grow up and become heroes in their own right. And the characters' histories get longer and longer every month.

Case in point: the original Robin, Dick Grayson, the Sensational Character Find of 1940. Now, when Dick was first introduced, he was ten years old. He put on a red, yellow, and green costume and fought crime at Batman's side. Eventually he got a bit older, and no longer the Boy Wonder, he became the *Teen* Wonder. He even cofounded the Teen Titans, and had all sorts of adventures on his own. Finally, he got tired of always being the back half of "Batman and Robin," and created a new identity for himself. He became Nightwing, and a young Jason Todd became the new Robin. Then a few years later Jason Todd died (or *seemed* to; more on this in a moment), and a young Tim Drake became the third Robin. For a short time Tim even stepped down, during which Stephanie Brown became the fourth Robin.

Now, all this time, Dick Grayson kept getting older. Having become Nightwing in his late teens, he's now in his mid- to late-twenties, at least. Jason Todd, who didn't die after all (or *did*, but came back from the dead . . . more complicated continuity) is now grown up enough that *he* took over as Nightwing for a while when Dick Grayson took some time off.

So it's been at *least* a decade and a half since Dick Grayson became Robin in the current continuity, possibly more. Maybe as much as twenty years, based on some stories. And in all that time, how much older has Bruce Wayne grown?

Not a bit. Still the same age.

In the current continuity, Dick Grayson is not much more than ten years younger than Bruce Wayne, as near as can be reckoned. Now, that's *possible*, though it stretches credulity a bit to say that Bruce Wayne was only twenty years old when he first took Robin under his scalloped wing, considering the years of training and travel that he'd done before adopting the mantle of the bat. But what happens in another few years, when Dick Grayson gets older still, and even has kids of his own? How close in age will he and Bruce get, and what will that say about the Batman's early career?

DC Comics quite understandably have a great deal invested in Batman, their most successful character in other media, commercially and critically, and arguably the most recognizable of their trademarks.

103

And they have a vested interest in keeping that character recognizable, and that means keeping Bruce Wayne under the cowl.

But might there not be another solution?

Before looking at alternative approaches, let us first take a quick look at the "in story" reasons why Bruce Wayne doesn't retire. It is really quite simple, and devolves from a flaw in Wayne's character. Intellectually, Wayne knows that he's not going to be around forever, and that his high-risk lifestyle is eventually going to take its toll; on a more emotional level, though, he simply *can't* let the fight go. He is driven to pursue his crusade, to every night put on cape and cowl and patrol the streets of Gotham City, trying to prevent anyone else from falling victim to the same sort of tragedy that took his parents from him. That same drive that has pushed him to succeed in his crusade for so many years, however, threatens to damage the long-term success of that crusade after he himself is gone. If he fails to ensure that Gotham will be protected should he fall in the line of duty, if he refuses to let someone else take over before it's too late, then the city might be left defenseless, without a Batman. Though Bruce Wayne doubtless *knows* that what is best for everyone else is to prepare a successor, he feels compelled to do it all himself.

All of which could be addressed by therapy, of course—provided by a timely intervention by Nightwing, Robin, and other concerned members of the Bat-family. So what's stopping Bruce Wayne from getting older, putting up his feet, and letting someone else answer the bat-signal from now on?

We've had a few tantalizing glimpses of Batman doing just that. Or rather, if not *the* Batman, then other Batmen, at least.

For example, in the pages of *Batman and Captain America* and in the various *Generations* comics series, John Byrne built an elaborate continuity of generational Batmen. The conceit of the various series was that Batman and Superman had both appeared in this alternate universe at the same time their comics were first published in ours, and then continued to age in "real time" over the decades. So Superman first appeared over the skies of Metropolis in 1938, and Batman first patrolled the streets of Gotham City in 1939. A few years on, when Bruce Wayne got a little long in the tooth, Dick Grayson took over as Batman, while Bruce's son became the second Robin. A few years after that, Bruce's son took over as Batman, and so on, and so on. (Byrne cheats the concept a little bit by having Bruce Wayne eventually bathe in the Lazarus Pit of Ra's al Ghul, becoming a literally immortal Batman, but that's another matter entirely.)

In the animated *Batman Beyond* series, alternatively, producer Bruce Timm and company had the aged Bruce Wayne, long retired from his role as the Dark Knight Detective, begin to train young Terry McGinnis as the Batman for a beleaguered future Gotham City. Like Tim Truman's elder Prowler and the retired Zorro of *The Mask of Zorro*, the older Bruce Wayne is a recluse, living alone with his memories, haunted by his past and plagued by the knowledge that, without him, his city stands unprotected. Like the younger Prowler and the new Zorro, Terry McGinnis is a young man who accepts the retired hero's invitation to train him for reasons of his own.

So how *could* DC finally age Bruce Wayne and let another person take on the mantle of Batman, whether Dick Grayson, or Tim Drake, or Terry McGinnis, or Bruce Wayne, Jr., or a hundred other possibilities? And how could they do so without diluting the Batman trademark and rendering the character unrecognizable to the larger audience?

Erik Larsen has suggested a possible solution. In a column for the Web site Comic Book Resources (www.comicbookresources.com), Larsen talked a bit about the passage of time in comics, and the problems therein. In a standard discussion about the appropriate audience for superhero comics, and the practical concerns associating with aging fictional characters in "real time," Larsen made this comment:

> Another thought I had (and I'm sure most of you will pooh-pooh this immediately, but wait until you hear me out first) would be to give every character a definite timeline and have them all be set in certain time periods. Superman really worked best as a character set in the late '30s and early '40s. Spider-Man, the FF, Nick Fury work best in the swingin' '60s and the man called Nova as a product of the '70s. What if the FF was set in the '60s? Why not? Then you wouldn't worry about him aging—it would all fit. And you could have an older Spider-Man encountering Nova in the '70s. A Superman in the '30s works so well. If he's from the '30s, he really is the forerunner of all superheroes whereas now, because of the JSA, he's a relatively recent character. Sure, there would end up being gaffs made, but it might be pretty cool.

This approach approximates the *de facto* solution to continuity and "real time" employed in other media with characters like Sherlock Holmes and Zorro. In the early decades of the twentieth century, when people other than Arthur Conan Doyle turned their hands to tell a Sherlock Holmes story (most notably in the movies), they made Holmes a contemporary character. When Basil Rathbone played the character in *Sherlock Holmes and the Voice of Terror*, Holmes pitted wits against the Nazis! It was only as time went on, and the period of Holmes's origin retreated further into the fog-wrapped past, that creators and pastichers came to realize that the character functioned best (and arguably, only) in Victorian England. Ever since, Holmes and his milieu have been inseparable.

A counter example is James Bond. A product of the Cold War, the more distant the character gets from his origins, the more the strain begins to show. Without an Iron Curtain across which to glare at his implacable Soviet foes, Bond is too often left a hero without a villain (to say nothing of the anachronism of his attitudes toward women which, cheeky and roguish in the '50s and early '60s, come off as just creepy and predatory in more enlightened times).

Novelist Michael Chabon, in his mid-'90s pitch for a Fantastic Four movie, opined that the characters worked best in a '60s milieu (a solution later rediscovered by Brad Bird for *The Incredibles*). Many have pointed out that Batman is a creature of the '40s, and that Superman works best in the '30s, as Larsen suggests (though arguably it is in the more optimistic Eisenhower era that Superman seems best to fit).

Cartoonist Darwyn Cooke understands this. His *New Frontier* comic series gets a lot of mileage out of setting the superheroes of the DC Universe within their historical context (much like John Byrne did in his *Generations*, though to different effect). Kurt Busiek, too, in his *Astro City* series, creates some real narrative frisson by placing certain types of characters against various historical backgrounds (like Larsen, Busiek disagrees with the notion of characters like Superman and Spider-Man aging in real time, though both have created their own superheroic "universes" that progress in real time). Alan Moore, in constructing his America's Best Comics universe, added an additional wrinkle, having characters that, while they don't seem to age at an appreciable rate, still experience the passage of real time, even if their settings don't (Tom Strong's Millennium City is a perpetual post-Art Deco '40s, while in Greyshirt's Indigo City it always seems to be the '50s).

Wouldn't it be possible, then, for DC to have their cake and eat it, too?

Suppose, for a moment, that DC Comics had another of their continuity-restoring crossover series, another *Crisis on Infinite Earths*. But instead of simply resetting the calendar, and ensuring that Bruce Wayne remained an eternal thirty-five, the resulting continuity was just a little bit . . . different.

In this new continuity, as in *Generations* and *New Frontier*, Bruce Wayne first became the Batman in the dark days of 1939. Dick Grayson first tied a yellow cape around his neck in 1940. (Superman, for what it's worth, first flew above Metropolis in 1938 and Wonder Woman first left Paradise Island in 1941.)

DC Comics could continue to tell stories about a virile young Bruce Wayne as Batman, patrolling a Gotham City over which airships patrolled, assisting the police in catching a host of strange villains with his wisecracking sidekick Robin. The only wrinkle would be that these stories would take place in the *past*. (Admittedly, though, the past of a fictional city in a fictional universe, which could share more in common with the Gotham City of Bruce Timm's animated Batman adventures than any real-world city of the 1930s.)

DC could also do stories set in the modern day, of course, but these stories wouldn't be about Bruce Wayne as Batman. These stories would be about a *new* Batman, whoever might be under the cowl. And Bruce Wayne, just as in *Batman Beyond*, could be the elder mentor to the young hero. There might even be stories set in the future, about the Batmen of tomorrow, a whole generational legacy of heroics continuing through the centuries and beyond.

Batmen of yesterday, today, and tomorrow, and all points in between. No longer would readers be presented only with stories of one kind of Batman, fighting crime one kind of way. Innumerable alternatives could coexist in the same timeline, at different points in history. Bruce Wayne as young crimefighter; Bruce Wayne as retired campaigner; Bruce Wayne as mentor and teacher. And just like with Sherlock Holmes, when other media came calling, they could always tell stories of the first and original Batman, the familiar and recognizable Bruce Wayne, simply set in his appropriate historical context.

And all it would require would be for Bruce Wayne to retire already (albeit with a healthy bit of continuity shuffling assistance). Because really, isn't it about time?

CHRIS ROBERSON's novels include *Here, There & Everywhere, The Voyage of Night Shining White, Paragaea: A Planetary Romance, Set the Seas on Fire*, and the forthcoming *End of the Century, Iron Jaw and Hummingbird*, and *The Dragon's Nine Sons*. His short stories have appeared in such magazines as *Asimov's Science Fiction, Postscripts*, and *Subterranean*, and in anthologies such as *Live Without a Net, The Many Faces of Van Helsing, FutureShocks*, and *Forbidden Planets*. Along with his business partner and spouse Allison Baker, he is the publisher of MonkeyBrain Books, an independent publishing house specializing in genre fiction and nonfiction genre studies, and he is the editor of the anthology *Adventure Vol. 1*. He has been a finalist for the World Fantasy Award three times—once each for writing, publishing, and editing—twice a finalist for the John W. Campbell Award for Best New Writer, and twice for the Sidewise Award for Best Alternate History Short Form (winning in 2004 with his story "O One"). Chris and Allison live in Austin, Texas, with their daughter Georgia. Visit him online at www.chrisroberson.net.

REFERENCES

Larsen, Erik. "One Fan's Opinion." *Comic Book Resources*. 14 Aug. 2007. <http://www.comicbookresources.com/columns/index.cgi?column=ofo&article=2257>

Ever since Jack C. Harris gave it a name and therefore an identity in 1974, Arkham Asylum, Gotham's facility for the really, really criminally insane, has been virtually as much a character in the Batman mythos as the Joker, Two-Face, or any of the other colorful felons who inhabit it. In this essay, Paul Lytle does an excellent job both of delineating Arkham's history and explaining just what it has meant to Batman and friends.

THE MADNESS OF ARKHAM ASYLUM

Why Arkham May Be Doing More Harm Than Good

PAUL LYTLE

"You're in the real world now and the lunatics have taken over the asylum. 'April sweet is coming in . . . let the feast of fools begin!'"

—THE JOKER

Elizabeth Arkham Asylum for the Criminally Insane opened in the early 1920s in Gotham City. It often lingers about the fringes of Batman comics, making cameo appearances in certain stories. There have been a few times when it has taken center stage, but most of the time you have to be paying attention to notice.

The end of *Batman Forever* featured the building briefly, but if you missed the signs that appeared for that moment, you probably didn't realize what you were looking at. At the time, I didn't. It was an important setting in the first collection of *The Sandman* comics by Neil Gaiman, but again, the sign only appeared in a couple of frames, and one image didn't even feature the whole name. You were expected to know the rest. Often it is mentioned briefly in a Batman comic, usually with a confused Commissioner Gordon saying, "How did he get out of

Arkham?" or something of that nature. We saw it a great deal more in recent works such as *Batman Begins*, but I doubt that most people, at least those who didn't already know what it was, noticed.

Yet Arkham's subtle influence can be recognized in the very nature of Gotham and its inhabitants. The city's mental health, in a way, rests in Arkham's hands. And when we look at the general mental health of the city, we must recognize that Arkham is not doing its job well. In fact, Arkham Asylum seems to be doing much more harm than good.

This is what I mean: Batman (or one of the other heroes of Gotham) will capture a villain. The villain goes to Arkham (there do not seem to be any prisons in Gotham anymore, since all the villains end up in Arkham). Inside its walls, the villain is treated, but treated in a way that is *harmful* to his mental state rather than *helpful*. Before long, the villain is released or escapes, only now he's more delusional, more deranged, and generally loonier[1] than ever before.

Then Batman captures him again and the cycle repeats.

There can be little doubt that the villains of Gotham are getting a little more, um, cuckoo.[2] As an example, you need only take a look at some early Batman comics. There, you'll find a Joker that is rational, intelligent, and witty (and we will look at those comics a little bit later). Now, he's a wackjob.[3]

The opening scene of the graphic novel *Arkham Asylum: A Serious House on Serious Earth* explained the problem better than anything else we could say about the place. The Joker took over the asylum, and he wouldn't release the hostages unless Batman himself took their place inside. Batman was reluctant. He wasn't afraid of Joker or anyone else held in the asylum, but he *was* afraid.

In a surprisingly candid moment, Batman shared those fears. He said, "I'm afraid that when I walk through those asylum gates. . . . When I

---

[1] You must forgive me if my terms are a little on the technical side. I have struggled with the material to keep it on a layman level, but when dealing with this subject, I am forced to use clinical terms on occasion.

[2] Again, I apologize. I really don't have room to define all these terms in detail, but if it helps, I am going strictly by the definitions found in the fourth edition of the *Diagnostic and Statistical Manual of Mental Disorders*. Your local library should have a copy if you are interested in the concrete diagnoses of the various disorders I will be discussing.

[3] Oh, I give up.

walk into Arkham and the doors close behind me. . . . It'll be just like coming home" (Morrison 10).

I mean, seriously. Batman is scared of the place. Batman. *Batman.* The man faces maniacal killers dressed up as penguins and clowns and jesters, and he doesn't want to go to Arkham, because *that* place is scary.

Does that sound like a place of healing?

Batman knows exactly how unhealthy the place is. When speaking with one of the resident psychiatrists later, he stated it very plainly: "You must admit it's hard to imagine this place being conducive to *anyone's* mental health" (Morrison 26).

So what's going on here? The asylum is supposed to be curing these people, and they are only getting worse. But still, is it fair to blame the asylum? Maybe they're just understaffed and overloaded with nutcases. Maybe they don't have the funds to pay really top-notch doctors. Maybe they're trying their best!

Maybe.

But maybe, just maybe, Arkham Asylum is as bad a problem as any supervillain. The fact that Arkham was named after H. P. Lovecraft's infamous city, which Lovecraft himself described as "witch-cursed [and] legend-haunted" (342), may tell us something about its nature. It is a place of horror, not healing.

Let me give you some examples.

THE INMATES ARE RUNNING THE ASYLUM

The typical scene in a normal therapy session is the therapist in a chair, perhaps with a recorder or a pad and pen. The subject may be sitting as well or perhaps even lying on a couch.

That is what we think of when we think about this sort of therapeutic relationship.

Typically, what we find in Arkham is the subject with a gun, tying up the therapist, perhaps killing him later on.

This is not some sort of strange variation on Death Therapy.[4] No, it just seems that most of the time, the personnel of Arkham actually have

---

[4] You know, from *What About Bob?*

no control over the population. It is, in fact, the inmates who generally run the asylum.

Both of the major Batman mini-series that focus directly on Arkham had the inmates taking over. Grant Morrison and Dave McKean gave us our first hard look at Arkham in *Arkham Asylum: A Serious House on Serious Earth*. In this story, as discussed, the Joker was holding the personnel of the asylum hostage with the other inmates. He threatened to kill everyone if Batman didn't come and join them. Once he arrived, Joker forced the caped crusader into an elaborate game of hide-and-seek.

Batman eventually regained control, but only after delving into his very soul and coming out the other side. He set the inmates free, and Joker and Batman stepped out the door together.

The backward nature of Arkham is evident here, since it is the Joker instead of Batman who did the most good. Joker's game even exorcised some of Batman's demons. In his notes on the script, Morrison says of this ending, "In the reversal reality of the Feast of Fools [which was a kind of Medieval version of April Fool's Day], it's the archvillain who does the most good, while the hero is ineffective and lost until the conclusion" (Morrison 181).

Arkham Asylum: Living Hell is a much lighter look at the institution, but a look that reveals more of the true trouble with the place. Here, too, we have a riot, complicated by the appearance of the undead (no, seriously). Arkham seemed controlled, at this point, by the inmates and demons rather than security. To be fair, the security team (except for one member) were busy panicking that the phone line was dead. Forgetting, of course, that they were carrying cell phones.

In fact, things are so bad in Arkham, even on a daily basis, that Dr. Jeremiah Arkham, the chief of staff in *Living Hell*, became worried when he was *not* wakened in the middle of the night with a problem. "I haven't had a full night's sleep in years," he told us. "But tonight? Nothing. Quiet as the grave. This can't be good" (Slott 74).

THE INMATES ARE RUNNING AWAY FROM THE ASYLUM

No asylum is going to function well without patients. If you want to treat the Joker for all his massive problems and he's not there, you're not going to be able to help him. And so one of the main problems with Arkham is its complete inability to keep the criminals within its walls.

Oh, sure, there are some escapes. But we're talking about someone like the Joker. Someone with an incredible criminal mind. Right?

Sometimes, yes. But then there are other times when the ease with which someone leaves the asylum is astounding.

In *The Sandman*, we found John Dee (a.k.a. Dr. Destiny) in Arkham. His mother had just died and sent him Dream's amulet, which would pretty much give him the power to do whatever he wished. It's pretty complicated, but the point is that he wanted to escape. This shriveled-up, naked (apparently they don't give them clothes in Arkham), little man first knocked out a guard and went wandering through the building. The other guards, by the way, were watching television. And how did he finally escape? Did he tunnel under the building? Did he take a hostage? Did he have a helicopter waiting outside?

No.

He climbed out a window.

Seriously.

Yeah, so this is a problem.

"Well," you may say, "Dee had the amulet. He had all sorts of power."

Perhaps. But as he was leaving, he passed Jonathan Crane (a.k.a. the Scarecrow), who was pulling an April Fool's joke by pretending to be hanged in a straitjacket. He indicated that he had pulled another practical joke in the next room, which was that he had really hanged one of the guards.

The other guards were, remember, watching television.

Crane did not have the power of the amulet, and yet he is perfectly capable of not only wandering about the building without being sent back to his cell, but actually committing murder while doing so. And no one, so far, had noticed.

In *Batman Begins* we have yet another escape, except that this time *everyone* is set free. Okay, maybe there were extenuating circumstances in this case. I mean, a nerve toxin in the water supply had just been activated; that alone would have caused everyone in the city to go mad. But, just for good measure, Ra's al Ghul releases all the inmates as well. It seems like overkill, but he's a supervillain; he does stuff like that. The point is that everyone in the asylum got out thanks to an evil and elaborate plot . . .

. . . an evil and elaborate plot that began *in* Arkham Asylum, as the nerve toxin had been developed in the building's basement.

The Joker's escape from Arkham in *The Dark Knight Returns* is notable simply because it is a variation of the theme. No climbing out the window this time! Instead, a psychologist, anxious to blame Batman for the actions of the villains, took Joker out of the asylum so that he could appear on a late night talk show. From there it was easy—Joker simply killed everyone in the studio.

Our last example comes from *Knightfall*, where the intelligent and powerful villain Bane blew up the building and (you guessed it) released all the inmates. Again.

THE PEOPLE RUNNING THE ASYLUM SHOULD BE INMATES

There are times, however, when the patients are actually in their rooms rather than running around the hallways or the streets. It is in these moments, perhaps, that some psychological progress *might* be made.

That might happen, except that the people running Arkham are very rarely any saner than the people locked within.

Some of the trouble here is small. When Warren White was sent to Arkham after committing stock fraud in *Living Hell* (more on that a little later), one of the security personnel took it upon himself to punish White by putting him in a cell with the serial killer Death Rattle. Death Rattle, by the way, is crazy.

That's bad, but it's not *terrible*. I mean, it could be worse.

To prove it, we must go back to the beginning when Amadeus Arkham founded the asylum in the '20s. While he was building it, his wife and daughter were raped and murdered by "Mad Dog" Hawkins, who was later committed to, yes, Arkham Asylum. Amadeus treated him personally for a while, and then strapped him to a machine to administer electroshock therapy and electrocuted him to death.

It was ruled an accident, but later Amadeus attempted murder again—and this time he was committed to, right again, Arkham Asylum.

That trend has never ceased. Dr. Harleen Quinzel was once a psychiatrist at Arkham—until she fell in love with the Joker. How else to prove that love than by going a little crazy and trying to kill Batman? Quinzel became the supervillain Harley Quinn and has made regular appearances ever since.

Back to Warren White, who was uneasily sharing a cell with Death Rattle. His psychiatrist, Dr. Anne Carver, was very sympathetic and promised to get him out and into a much nicer facility if he could, ahem, cover some expenses. He did . . . and that's when she tried to kill him. You see, Dr. Carver had been dead for a while. She had been secretly replaced by Jane Doe, an inmate and master of disguise (who had been missing for, oh, just about as long as Carver had been dead).

What about *Batman Begins*, where Dr. Jonathan Crane, while running Arkham, is secretly working on a nerve toxin in the basement of the asylum? That toxin is what makes Scarecrow dangerous, for it causes a crippling level of fear to overcome its victim. The scene when Falcone, the local mob leader, is finally caught illustrates the danger best. Falcone and Crane had been working together, and Falcone threatens to talk: "I know about your experiments with the inmates of your nut house."

Crane considers his next words carefully:

> Would you like to see my mask? I use it in my experiments.
> Now, I'm probably not very frightening to a guy like you, but
> these crazies,[5] they can't stand it.

The most important part of the conversation for our purposes is how Crane is doing this sort of thing to *multiple* patients. He is using the asylum to *make* people crazy.

Just before he is gassed, Falcone asks a question that is central to our topic here: "So when did the nut take over the nuthouse?"

And finally, did you wonder who let the Joker out of his cell in *A Serious House on Serious Earth*, allowing him to take everyone hostage in the first place? It was Dr. Cavendish, the administrator at the time. He

---

[5] See! I told you I was using the proper terms.

had read a prophecy written by Amadeus Arkham while he was locked up in his own asylum, a prophecy that warned of a bat. The words drove Cavendish mad, and he decided to set a trap for Batman.

TWO TEST CASES: THE JOKER AND THE SHARK

"Okay, Paul," you may say, "you've made your point. Things in Arkham could be better. But does it really make a difference? Is Gotham so much worse off than if the criminals were simply put in jail?"

I'm glad you asked. If you don't mind, I would like to pull out some examples from the Joker's files (read: comic books) to illustrate the point.

The Joker first appeared in 1940. While the look of the villain was already established very early on, his dialogue and demeanor in these early encounters greatly differ than what we are used to now. He was reasonable and intelligent. When considering the Batman, he said:

> Only one person stands in my way—the Batman! He has outwitted me consistently, thanks to the Bat-Mobile, Batplane, Bat symbol and other revolutionary devices . . . but no more! (anonymous 60)

Not *too* crazy. Let's move forward a few decades, to Joker speaking on a similar topic in 1973:

> I'd always envisioned my winning as a result of cunning at the end of a bitter struggle between the Batman and myself—him using his detective skills and me employing the divine gift men call *madness*! (O'Neil 68)

Joker is now certifiably mad, but it seems almost a rational madness. I mean, yeah, he's a loon, but he *knows* he's a loon, so it isn't that bad.

Compare that to 2003, when the Joker meets Warren White in *Arkham Asylum: Living Hell*. He begins the conversation like any normal homicidal maniac, but finally grins his famous grin and whispers, "Y'know . . . I could use your head as a commode and sell it on eBay"

(Slott 23).

My point is—wackjob.

But this is not really something that has to be pointed out, is it? We've all experienced the Joker recently, and he's been just a little more off than normal. In Jeph Loeb and Jim Lee's *Hush*, Joker deliberately taunted Batman while armed only with a cap gun. The old Joker would never do something like that. Face it: his mental state is deteriorating.

And it's not just the Joker. Consider the case of Warren White, mentioned a couple of times above. The real reason he was placed in Arkham in the first place was that he pled temporary insanity to the stock fraud charges against him. He didn't realize at the time where he would be going.

White was terribly evil and all that, but he wasn't insane. Or at least, he wasn't insane when he entered Arkham. Besides being locked up with Death Rattle and almost being killed by Jane Doe, he had a rough stay in the asylum. Jonathan Crane stabbed him in the hand with a fork. In the ensuing riot, he got smacked around a little bit more. Then he decided to team up with Two-Face for a little protection, but Two-Face would only help him half the time (thus the whole point of Two-Face). And Death Rattle was still trying to kill him. In the next riot, he got beat up by one of the guards. Well, actually it was Jane Doe again, who was determined to steal White's identity. To do that, she had to cut on him a little to make her disguise perfect. She left him in a freezer afterward, where he lost his nose and his hair fell out. He groped around, laughing manically for a while—just for fun, I think. And once he escaped, he had to kill some ghosts (don't ask) and then negotiate with demons.[6]

In the end, White had a new look, a new nickname ("Shark"), and powers granted by the minions of hell.

The bottom line is this: White went inside a criminal, but a sane one—greedy and immoral, but sane. Arkham made him into an insane supervillain. Arkham took a normal, white-collar criminal, and turned him into something more akin to the Riddler or Penguin.

---

[6] There is a great deal more going on in *Living Hell*, but this is White's role in it in a nutshell. Those pesky ghosts and demons would take considerably longer to explain.

THE FEAST OF FOOLS CONTINUES

It is clear that Arkham has left its mark on the city, and not in a good way. Its general incompetence continues to make dangerous villains more dangerous than ever before, only then to put them back on the street long before they should be allowed to leave. The Feast of Fools turned Gotham on its head, where it will probably remain for some time.

If the crime problem in Gotham is ever to be brought under control, the city leaders and justice system are going to have to find something else to do with the criminals once they are caught. Arkham seems incapable of performing its role in the city. It seems clear to me that an alternative method of dealing with criminals needs to be put into place.

Until then, Batman can count the asylum itself as one of his greatest foes.

PAUL LYTLE is an author and musician living on the southwest side of Houston, Texas. He earned a bachelor of arts from Houston Baptist University in English and political science with a specialization in creative writing, and will soon earn a master of liberal arts degree. He is an editor and writer for the Webzine Primum Mobile (www.primum-mobile.net) and is amassing quite a collection of comic books and gently used paperbacks. This is his third contribution to the Smart Pop series, the other two in *The Man from Krypton* and *Webslinger*. He hopes that there will be many more in the future, since they provide a good excuse to head over to the comic book shop ("It's research, honey!"). More of his writings, as well as news and other projects, can be found at www.paullytle.com.

REFERENCES

Anonymous and Jim Mooney. "The Joker Follows Suit!" *Batman* #37 (Oct.–Nov. 1946). Reprinted in *Batman in the Forties*. New York: DC Comics, 2004.

Lovecraft, H. P. "The Thing on the Doorstep." *The Thing on the Doorstep and Other Weird Stories*. New York, Penguin: 2001.

Gaiman, Neil, et al. *Preludes & Nocturnes*. Vol. 1 of *The Sandman*. New York: DC Comics, 1991.

Morrison, Grant, and Dave McKean. *Arkham Asylum: A Serious House on Serious Earth*: 15th Anniversary Edition. New York: DC Comics, 2004.

O'Neil, Denny, and Neal Adams. "The Joker's Five-Way Revenge." *Batman* #251 (Sep. 1973). Reprinted in *Batman: The Greatest Stories Ever Told*. New York: DC Comics, 2005.

Slott, Dan, and Ryan Sook. *Arkham Asylum: Living Hell*. New York: DC Comics, 2004.

Well, okay, just what is a demonic, nocturnal avenger doing with a chirpy kid sidekick who wears primary colors? It's what we can call "the Robin question," and it has seldom been asked, much less answered. Here, Jake Black tells us why Batman may need a Robin more than any of the Robins need a Batman.

ROBIN: INNOCENT BYSTANDER

JAKE BLACK

When young Bruce Wayne watched his parents fall to the ground in the dark alley outside the movie theater where they'd spent a pleasant evening together as a family, the mission that would consume his life began. While it is often said that this mission is one of vengeance, a closer examination of the life and times of Gotham's most prominent playboy and superhero will demonstrate that it is not entirely so. While catching his parents' killer certainly provides a solid motivation for the caped crusader, I have come to determine that his work is driven by something much more altruistic: the protection not of innocents, but rather innocence itself.

The Waynes' deaths marked the end of Bruce's innocence. As he began his quest for vengeance, what he ultimately was avenging was not his parents, but the loss of that innocence. And it is to protect others from losing the innocence he himself lost that he continues to fight.

The key evidence of this quest is found not in his crime-fighting, but in his relationship to the Boys Wonder, the many Robins he has taken under his Batwing as wards and sidekicks over the years. Batman sees in the Robins' innocence his own innocence lost. But the only guidance the

Dark Knight can think to give is to place his young sidekicks on the same path he's trodden. And though Bruce Wayne has in the process tried desperately to protect his loyal wards from suffering the same pain he did, his results have often been, at best, mixed.

DICK GRAYSON

Perhaps the most famous of the Boys Wonder is Dick Grayson. He was, after all, the first. In the 1940s, when comics were experiencing their golden age, youthful sidekicks were common in the so-called funny books. Captain America had Bucky, Flash had Kid Flash, Green Arrow had Speedy, and so on. These sidekicks were created primarily to give readers, mostly young boys, an "in" to the stories. Because the main heroes were adults, the comics were assumed to be inaccessible to children; if kids could see someone their own age having exciting adventures alongside the hero, the stories would prove to be more interesting for them to read. Kids were encouraged to see the sidekick as themselves.

With Robin, it was not only the reader who could relate: Batman, too, identified strongly with Robin. Dick Grayson's parents were circus performers, and like Bruce Wayne's folks, were murdered in front of him. Wayne, reliving his own nightmarish childhood, effectively adopted young Dick as his ward. It wasn't long before Bruce revealed his dual identity to the boy and began training him as Robin.

In the 1995 film *Batman Forever*, this story is told, albeit with an older (college-aged) Dick Grayson. In the film, Dick's experience even more closely resembles Bruce's, as he, too, is seeking vengeance for his parents' murder. But even here—not the most popular or successful version of events—Bruce's response is one of reservation. He seeks to protect Dick from the pain he has lived with for years.

In both comics and film, Bruce Wayne is successful in his mission to ease Dick's pain and protect him from further loss of innocence until he reached adulthood. Dick Grayson always found an element of joy in being a superhero; he possessed a childlike happiness that Bruce did not. And when Dick outgrew the mantle of Robin, he assumed a new identity as Nightwing—a darker persona than Robin's, but one that was still lighter than Batman's.

Grayson's ascent to independence as Nightwing is the crowning achievement of Batman's purest mission: while seeing your child grow up to be a vigilante crime-fighter may not be every parent's dream, in this case it was a tremendous accomplishment. Batman had seen Dick Grayson's Robin as a reflection of himself, and so was able to, in effect, change his own history. Dick didn't become as dark as Bruce had. It was as though Bruce gave Dick the best things about himself, without bequeathing the worst.

JASON TODD

Confident from his success with Dick Grayson, Bruce must have felt confident in his ability to do the same with another victim of lost innocence, Jason Todd, an effectual street urchin he ran into as the boy was stealing wheels off the Batmobile in an alley—the same alley where Thomas and Martha Wayne had been killed.

Seeing Jason in the same alley where his own childhood had ended gave Bruce pause; he projected his own lost innocence onto the boy, seeing Jason as his younger self. He took Jason under his wing as he had Dick Grayson, hoping to grant him, too, the life he'd wished for himself. Only, with Jason, it didn't work as well, and to this day, Jason Todd is Bruce's greatest failure.

Bruce saw himself in both Dick Grayson and Jason Todd, so he acted as if he were in fact dealing with his younger self. This was successful with Dick because Dick's story had closely paralleled Bruce Wayne's; it was easy for Bruce to figure out what his own mistakes had been, and keep Dick from making the same ones. Logically, Bruce assumed the same tactics would work with Jason. But clearly, they did not—Jason ended up dead at the Joker's hands, thanks to his own reckless behavior.

What went wrong? Bruce had repeated the same patterns of training that he had used successfully with Dick, but while Dick was a more innocent version of Bruce's younger self and thus susceptible to the guidance Bruce had to offer, Jason was not. The only thing he had in common with Bruce was that they met in the same alley where Bruce's parents were killed.

123

Jason, as the son of a low-level thug, had grown accustomed to fighting for survival on the streets of Gotham. He had lost his innocence long before Bruce arrived on the scene. There was nothing left for Bruce to protect, a fact to which Bruce chose to remain blind. He'd been able to succeed with Dick because he'd met the boy just as Dick's childhood began to crumble. With Jason, he'd never had a chance, and ultimately only furthered the second Robin's descent into darkness.

Jason was not, however, wholly unaffected by Bruce's attempts. It was Jason's search for his biological mother, a search he would never have embarked upon without Bruce's influence, that ultimately led to his demise. Jason had wondered about his biological mother for years, but after discovering his birth certificate listed a different name for his mother than the one he'd always been told, he set out to find her.

Had Bruce failed to find the spark of youth and optimism in Jason, the second Robin would never have foolhardily gone on the worldwide search for his mother. It never occurred to him that she might have been evil or not wanted to see him. When he finally found her, he discovered that she was involved in criminal activity with the Joker. Jason's mother betrayed her son, allowing the Joker to kill them both.

Bruce had managed to restore some of Jason's lost innocence, but it backfired. Jason was dead *because* Bruce had succeeded—and that meant his mission had failed. Never mind that Dick had grown into as strong a hero and as good a man as Bruce could have hoped. Jason's death repeated Bruce's own loss on that fateful night outside the movie theater, and Bruce would not allow anyone else to suffer death—literal or figurative—in his own image. That is, until a boy named Tim Drake appeared in the Batcave.

TIM DRAKE

He wasn't the likeliest of candidates to fill the role of Robin, but Tim Drake quickly earned the position by impressing Bruce with his keen detective skills: he had pieced together by himself that Bruce Wayne was Batman's alter-ego. While Bruce was hesitant to bring Tim into the fold as Robin after Jason's death, he again must have seen himself in the young man—this time, the boy Bruce had been before his parents' deaths. It helped that Bruce wouldn't be the one responsible for protecting the boy's youthful innocence. Tim had parents who were alive and involved in his life, and who could give him the innocent childhood Bruce had wanted for Dick and Jason.

Bruce saw his talent as a detective in Tim, and so took a different approach with him than he had with the others. Without the need to be the boy's parent, Bruce could take him on as his partner, and focus on helping him hone his skills.

Tragically, Tim's real parents were ultimately murdered, and the innocence Bruce had taken for granted in Tim was ripped away, the same way his own had been. This, however, was in a strange way ultimately a good thing (for Bruce, if not for Tim).

In the haunting scene in Brad Meltzer's *Identity Crisis*, in which Tim found his father murdered, Batman arrived and wrapped Tim in his arms. It was clear that Tim had lost his childhood in that moment, just as Bruce had in Crime Alley. And Bruce, while reliving his darkest moment, was able to be the guardian and guide he had longed for in his own youth. Bruce had become what he set out to be those many years before—a protector of himself. Tim's parents' deaths were the closest parallel to Batman's experience that he'd endured since donning cape and cowl, and with Tim standing as proxy for Bruce, he was able to avenge his own abandonment.

Dick Grayson's origin story may have paralleled Batman's the closest in fact, but it is Tim Drake's experience that is most like Batman's. Tim, who started with the same level of childlike idealism as young Bruce, stood to lose it as dramatically and as tragically as Bruce had. Tim's story is still unfolding; with his recent adoption as Bruce Wayne's son, he could end up as much a success as Dick or come to an end potentially worse than Jason's.

There are few motives more powerful in an individual's life than self-preservation, and that is what Batman's primary mission is, above all: to protect others from losing what he lost the night his parents were killed.

But the boys he takes under his wing and into his household are more than symbols of his mission. With each new sidekick he brings in, he renews that solemn covenant he made long ago in Crime Alley. He needs

125

a Robin. It gives him something tangible to fight for, when his true mission is based in the emotional, the intangible. Without Robin, Batman's quest for justice and protection becomes hollow. It is vengeance for vengeance's sake. But with Robin, he can restore and preserve the parts of him that were destroyed long ago, giving his mission meaning and power in his own life, and in the lives of those he helps. Robin's colorful costume reminds the Dark Knight that all is not as bleak as it may appear. There is still innocence out there, and that is, above all other concerns, worth protecting.

———

JAKE BLACK, a native of Orem, Utah, graduated from Brigham Young University with a degree in history. He has spent the last six years contributing to numerous *Smallville* projects, including short stories, DVD features, Web articles, and comics. He has published licensed work on *Superman Returns*, *WWE*, *Star Trek*, and *Teenage Mutant Ninja Turtles*, and has had essays in several academic publications. He is also a prolific comic book writer, having been published by DC, Marvel, and several independent companies. Visit jakeblack.com for more.

For me, Mike W. Barr's essay is the most valuable one in the book because it fills in some gaps in my own knowledge of the Batman mythos. As Mike writes, the science fiction–themed stories, mostly from the '40s and '50s, are often ignored, a sin of omission I've been guilty of. But they're a part of the character's history, worthy of discussion, and perhaps revisiting.

BATMAN IN OUTER SPACE

(Yes, I Said "Outer Space," Deal With It)

MIKE W. BARR

The fate of the Batman franchise is looking pretty good right now. The series, once claimed to be near cancellation due to low sales, is again one of the jewels in the crown of publisher DC Comics, still riding a wave created in the 1970s by such talent as writers Denny O'Neil and Frank Robbins and such artists as Neal Adams, Irv Novick, and Bob Brown. Modern writers and artists such as Frank Miller have continued this treatment and even enhanced it, influencing such directors as Tim Burton and Christopher Nolan, whose films have drawn even more readers to the comics, and carrying over to the modern version of Batman presented in cartoons.

In analyses of how the creators cited above were able to bring new life to a franchise almost seven decades old, the major emphasis is always given to the mood of the stories. After years of acting as almost a costumed adjunct of the Gotham City Police (in some stories of the '50s and '60s, Batman even carried a badge from the GCPD), it was decided to restore Batman to a dark, moody creature of the night, dashing in and out of shadows, much as was the case in the early days of the character's series, when he took a lot of cues from a preexisting inspiration, the Shadow.

Due to the popularity of this handling of Batman—which obtains to this

127

day—it has become common, among both comics creators and fans, to disparage any version of the character that does not hew to this template, including the then immensely popular 1960s television show.

It is for this reason that many—actually, all—of the science fiction–themed stories of the 1940s and 1950s are roundly disparaged. This subgenre, with its use of rocket ships and pseudoscientific gimmicks, along with fantasy, is often considered anathema to a serious handling of Batman, as such elements are believed to dilute the fundamental nature of the character by placing him in a setting in which he is no longer the dominant visual or dramatic element. No better example of this can be found than a text column appearing in the anniversary issue *Batman* #200 (March 1968). This issue, billed as the "200th Smash Issue" (perhaps unconsciously harking back to the sound effects-laden *Batman* television show) contains a text column, "Dialogue Between Two Batmaniacs Upon Reaching Issue #200," the "Batmaniacs" in question being the writer of that issue, fan-turned-pro Mike Friedrich, and the late Biljo White, B.N.F. (Big Name Fan) and creator of the fanzine *Batmania*. After they discussed several of their favorite stories of the early 1940s, White remarked: "The later '40s and '50s weren't so great—"

"WHAT?!" interrupted Friedrich. "Now there I've *got* to disagree!" Friedrich then named several of his favorite stories from that era, finally bringing White around to his way of thinking.

Friedrich was correct on this point. A great Batman story is determined by far more than a story's setting or mood—it is determined by its plot, its pacing, and several other factors. A great Batman story must first of all showcase the relationship between the Dark Knight and his courageous sidekick, Robin the Boy Wonder. Some action is vital, requiring the heroes to put their long hours of training to use, but the action can never be gratuitous—it must serve the narrative, which must test their wits and their crime-solving abilities, and must feature a threat worthy of them, perpetrated by a worthy antagonist (costumed or otherwise), which culminates in a satisfactory resolution in which justice is served, even if ironically.

Any story without at least a majority of these elements is not really a Batman story but just another superhero story, its resolution hinging not on the training Batman and Robin have put themselves through in the cause of justice, but on a collection of coincidences and luck.

It's likely that White's initial disparagement of the Batman stories of the

1950s had to do with the many science fiction and fantasy stories appearing in that decade. However, stories with fantasy elements were being presented as early as 1941, less than two years into Batman's career, a year in which the grimmer Batfans believe the emphasis of the character to have been on mood and darkness. There's a practical reason behind bringing such subgenres into Batman's stories: with the growing popularity of Batman—and let us not forget, Robin—more and more stories about the character were required by his publisher, National Periodical Publications, Inc. (today known today as DC Comics, after the title in which Batman premiered—*Detective Comics*), and an increasing number of writers were forced to derive inspiration from many different sources to satisfy the gaping maw of the ever-present deadline.

Of course, it must be understood that even the best of these stories cannot be considered "hard" science fiction. In nearly every example, Batman and Robin encounter an alien race that is relatively humanoid, breathes oxygen, and speaks English. The reason for this, as in such science fiction series as *Star Trek*, is to facilitate the action, causing the stories to be classified as "space opera," a subgenre of science fiction characterized by high adventure and intense action.

In *Batman* #5 (spring 1941), one of the issues most highly regarded by Batmaniacs as it contains the classic story "The Case of the Honest Crook!", Batman and Robin didn't go into outer space, but they still went nearly as far as they could from their original environs. In "Book of Enchantment," by Bill Finger, Bob Kane, and Jerry Robinson, Batman and Robin were sent, by means of a pseudoscientific device, into the fantasy world of Fairyland inside a book entitled *Anthology of Fairy Tales*, where they encounter Father Time, a dragon, Humpty Dumpty, a one-eyed giant, a witch, and genuine magic. At this point the strip was less than two years old. (This story, an "actual" fantasy, was preceded by an earlier tale in *Detective Comics* #44 [October 1940], "The Land Beyond the Light!", in which the Dynamic Duo entered the strange world of the fourth dimension, but only in a dream of Robin's.)

Once the chroniclers of "Book of Enchantment"—whose writer and penciler were also the creators of Batman and Robin—took the Dynamic Duo into a world of fairy tales, it was inevitable that it would occur to the publisher to take their heroes into a related genre, though one perhaps as far from the Dynamic Duo's roots as was fantasy.

However, it may have been that even Batman's editorial staff wondered if taking the Dark Knight into space would be accepted by fans. It may be that the first major science fiction-themed story appearing in *Batman*, "The Year 3000!" by Joseph Greene and Dick Sprang (*Batman* #26, December 1944–January 1945), was considered a little chancy. That may be why, just as "The Land Beyond the Light!", as a dream, tested the waters for the reception of "Book of Enchantment," "The Year 3000!" didn't actually involve Batman and Robin save as historical inspirations to a band of rebels who marshaled their courage to drive off a band of invaders from Saturn in the year of the title. (Though World War II is never specifically mentioned in the story, the role that conflict played in inspiring this story must be taken into consideration.) It was not until the story's last panel that we learned that Brane, the organizer of the rebels, was a descendant of Bruce Wayne.

Fifteen issues later, *Batman* #41 (June–July 1947) carried the story "Batman, Interplanetary Policeman!" by Gardner Fox and Jim Mooney. (This story was a return to Batman for Fox; he had been only the second writer to script the feature, having written the Batman stories in *Detective Comics* #29–34. Fox, who would later write dozens of science fiction stories for DC's titles *Strange Adventures* and *Mystery In Space*, as well as co-create DC's classic space hero Adam Strange, was a perfect choice to take the Dynamic Duo into space.) In the story itself, Batman and Robin were brought to the planet Mars to thwart an evil scientist's plan to rule the red planet by controlling the flow of water conducted through the Martian canals. Presumably Batman's earlier forays into science fiction and fantasy caused no precipitous drop in sales; this story was featured on the cover of the magazine, depicting the Dynamic Duo using rocket belts to swoop down on a pair of tentacled aliens with green, scaly skin and pointed ears that were firing ray-guns at them.

Having traveled into space while remaining in their present time, the only remaining boundary was travel in both space and time. Earlier, beginning in *Batman* #42 (August–September 1944), Batman and Robin, as Bruce Wayne and Dick Grayson, had begun to travel back—and occasionally forward—in time via the hypnotic powers (and sometimes the high-tech apparatus) of Professor Carter Nichols. Such stories were evidently popular, for they continued off and on for almost two decades, their last such journey transpiring in *World's Finest Comics* #138 (December 1963).

But in the Professor Nichols stories, Batman and Robin remained on

Earth. It was in *Batman* #59 (June–July 1950) that they journeyed not only into space, but into the future. "Batman In the Future!" by Finger, Kane, and Lew Schwartz had Batman and Robin accidentally sent into the future, rather than the past, by Professor Nichols (they wanted to travel to the past to " . . . stud[y] the Joker's ancestors . . . learn what hereditary influence affected him, and maybe reform him"). Finding themselves in the year 2050 they joined forces with the Joker's descendant, who was police chief of Gotham City, and foiled the schemes of space pirate Zarro using a space-ship redesigned into a "Bat-Ship," and a bat-signal projected from Earth onto the moon.

With the venue of science fiction and the subvenue of time travel firm-ly established—fantasy was seldom if ever seen anymore—numerous vari-ations began to be written on the same themes. These variations largely belonged to one of three categories, with some occasional overlapping:

1) Accidental time and/or space travel
2) Future or alien Batman imitators
3) Help-seekers from other times or places

For example, the events in "Batman In the Future!" transpired because Batman and Robin were accidentally sent into the future by Professor Nichols's mistake. The second and third categories are best epitomized by "The Lost Legion of Space!", by Finger, Sprang, and Charles Paris, in *Batman* #67 (October–November 1951). Batman appeared in only four panels of this story, which gave Robin center stage. The Boy Wonder, work-ing in the Batcave "while Batman is away" was startled by the appearance of " . . . a shimmering outline . . . which . . . materializes as a globe of gleam-ing steel!" This was a time machine piloted by Brane Taylor, who in the year 3051 had taken on the role of "Batman." "I studied micro-films of your and Batman's exploits stored in our museums, and I trained myself and my young nephew to duplicate them—thus another 'Batman and Robin' team was born—in the thirty-first century!" (Despite sharing the same name, it is clear that "Brane" from "The Year 3000!" and "Brane Taylor" are not the same character. If the similarity in names was even noticed by the editori-al staff, they probably assumed that in the intervening six years the reader-ship of *Batman* had turned over at least once, so no reader would notice.)

131

Learning that Brane Taylor's nephew had broken his leg while on a case, Robin took his place, also supplying most of the brainwork. The twentieth-century Batman appeared only at the end of the story, when Brane's identity as future Batman was about to be exposed.

Brane Taylor's actions as a Batman imitator pretty much set the standard for all others who would follow. He not only had a Robin, but a "Bat-belfry"—"because we of the future live so much in the sky"—which housed a Bat-Ship and a Trophy Room. In a few years Brane would return the favor Batman did him, coming to the present day to masquerade as the twentieth-century Batman when Bruce Wayne injured his arm, something that threatened to betray his secret identity to snoopy girl reporter Vicki Vale ("The Batman of Tomorrow!" in *Detective Comics* #216, February 1955, by Edmond Hamilton, Sprang, and Paris). Despite Brane's help, it fell to Bruce Wayne to preserve the secret of his and Dick Grayson's dual identities at the story's climax by his quick wits.

Possibly the most memorable of all the Batman science fiction imitators—who was also a help-seeker—was "Tlano, the scientist," the garishly dressed Batman of the far-flung planet Zur-En-Arrh (" . . . Located in a star system far from yours! I doubt if your astronomers know of our existence!"). "Through a powerful telescope, I've observed your every action!" explained Tlano. "It inspired me to play the same role here!" Though this story, "Batman—the Superman of Planet X!" by France Herron, Sprang, and Paris (*Batman* #113, February 1958), was set in the present day, it was one of the purest examples of Batman being set in a science fiction milieu. Batman, summoned to Tlano's planet to combat an army of alien invaders, found that on the planet Zur-En-Arrh he gained mighty superpowers: "Here on your planet, I become like my friend Superman, on Earth!" Batman explained, thus giving this story not only a Batman imitator, but making Batman a Superman imitator as well. Batman gave the invaders a run for their money, but it fell to Tlano, inspired by Batman's methodology, to figure out how to pierce the invaders' invisibility defense. When Batman was returned to Earth, he found he had been given as a souvenir Tlano's "Bat-Radia," a device that "issues electronic molecules that cause controlled disturbances in the atmosphere!" Tlano, like Brane Taylor, had a secret lair, an atomic-powered version of the Batmobile and a Batplane. Interestingly, his costume insignia was a bat on a yellow field, identical to the one that would be given to Batman in 1964 when editor Julius Schwartz (no relation) took over the Batman titles.

The methods by which Batman and Robin were sent—or taken—to other planets varied, lest the readers grow tired of the same formula. In "King Batman the First" (*Batman* #125, August 1959, by Finger, Sprang, and Sheldon Moldoff) a time-warp was utilized to provide transport, while in "The Winged Bat-People!" (*Batman* #116, June 1958, by Finger, Moldoff, and Paris) Batman and Robin, trying to penetrate the eye of a hurricane to obtain meteorological data, were caught up in the storm and were shifted to another dimension when the Batplane "passed the sonic barrier at a speed ten times greater than was ever thought possible." Fortunately, after defeating "bat-men" who could actually fly, Batman and Robin were able to ride the wave of an explosion back home.

In "The Captive Planet!" from *Detective Comics* #256 (June 1958, by Finger and Moldoff) Batman, Robin, and a group of Earthlings were kidnapped to the planet Torg, where they overthrew a dictator. The memorable aspect of this story came from the depth of the human interest: each of the other Earthlings taken to Torg had some unique aspect of their personalities that was serviced by the journey. Jim Rolfe, the big-game hunter, wished he could "get a shot" at a new species of animal. Harvey Baxter, a bored businessman, craved any kind of excitement in his life, and Pete Cole, "embittered ex-convict," wanted nothing more than revenge on the man who sent him to prison—Batman. There were others, all of whom found their lives changed for the better by their chance encounter not only with travel to another planet, but with Batman. (In the world of Batman, no one was ambivalent toward the Dark Knight; he was either admired or hated.) Character work of this detail hallmarked the story as the work of Batman co-creator Bill Finger.

"The Interplanetary Batman!" (*Batman* #128, December 1959, by Finger and Moldoff) belongs to none of the three categories. In it, Batman and Robin attempted to apprehend an alien criminal who had escaped to Earth, but were captured by alien lawmen who assumed the Duo to be the criminal's allies and took them to "an alien planet's moon prison," where they had to fashion an escape. Batman's resourcefulness in adapting to a strange world was showcased, as was the affection between him and Robin. When the alien criminal, Kraak, started to slap Robin around, Batman leaped to the lad's defense, despite a pronounced disadvantage in height. At story's end, the authorities proclaimed Batman "[n]ot only the greatest crime-fighter of your solar system, but also of ours," one of the rare science fiction Batman tales to overtly state the story's theme.

What ties this story to the others is more than just the science fiction milieu. In it, Batman was positioned as a nearly legendary figure, capable of inspiring men to higher aspirations, and in "Batman, Interplanetary Policeman!" and "Batman In the Future!" Batman's crime-fighting skills and quick, deductive mind were able to solve problems that the advanced technologies of the planet Mars and the far future could not.

Though these stories transported Batman to future times and to alien worlds, he was still depicted as a master strategist, a quick thinker, and the most formidable crime-fighter of any era, characteristics that are far more important to his character than setting.

Indeed, the reason the science fiction stories work so well, and result in such great reading (despite the potential ludicrousness of the settings), is that the unfamiliar, literally alien environs made it more necessary that the writers emphasize Batman and Robin's classic traits; this added emphasis resulted in some of the best character-oriented and character-driven stories of the time period.[1]

---

[1] Something similar, it could be said, was true visually—the unfamiliar settings required as compellingly realistic a treatment as possible. "The Year 3000!", "The Lost Legion of Space!", "The Batman of Tomorrow!", and "Batman—the Superman of Planet X!" were all penciled by Dick Sprang, one of the best of all the Batman artists. Though nothing Sprang drew ever looked like anything found in the real world—with the exception of machinery, which he excelled at drawing realistic depictions of, therefore adding credibility to his rendering of pseudoscientific devices—while reading his stories, his depiction of reality is totally convincing, which is the only real criterion of success for a cartoonist. Sprang's depictions of both modern-day Gotham City and alien science fiction cities were full of towering skyscrapers and vertiginous shots depicting fight scenes transpiring hundreds of feet above the ground. Even his modern-day cityscapes seem somewhat science fictional, which gave added credibility to his renditions of actual science fiction scenes. Every artist who drew Batman after creator Bob Kane was a better artist than Kane, but Sprang stands out even among the best.

Sprang's unique style also lent the illusion of realism to science fiction stories that contained no Batman imitators, such as "King Batman the First." Batman, Robin, and—unknown to them—a criminal they were hunting inadvertently wandered into a "time-warp" (though they did not seem to have actually traveled through time) and were transported to the planet Plaxius, where Batman temporarily became king after foiling the schemes of a would-be tyrant, Rakk. This story was also a variation on the usual formula in

Notably, a seemingly disproportionate number of science fiction stories appeared in *Detective Comics*, the magazine in which Batman premiered. It would seem more appropriate to place them in the *Batman* title, where a science fiction tale would be only one of three Batman stories in the issue; such a yarn, if deemed of inferior quality by a reader, wouldn't bring a whole issue down with it. But the Batman stories in *Detective Comics* were always longer than the individual stories in *Batman*, so perhaps the greater length was deemed necessary for plot exposition or, quite possibly, for character work to expand upon those vital aspects of Batman and Robin—the quick-wittedness, the camaraderie, the fearlessness—that editors may have felt needed emphasis when the characters were in such an alien environment.

Arguably the best of the Batman "alien" stories was something of a hoax—except in the impression it left in the minds of its readers—yet it is also perhaps one of the best examples of a science fiction setting providing the frame for a poignant character-revealing story. "Robin Dies at Dawn!" (*Batman* #156, June 1963, by Finger, Moldoff, and Paris) is considered a classic of its type, having been frequently reprinted, most recently in the 2005 collection, *Batman: The Greatest Stories Ever Told*.

Batman found himself alone on an alien planet, facing death until Robin charged in to save him. However, Robin died saving Batman, causing Batman

---

that Batman, Robin, and the criminal had no memory of the experience after being returned to Earth. The real impact of this story came in its final panels: when trying to figure out where the alien handcuffs that bound their prisoner came from, Batman said, "I'm afraid this trophy will be the one mystery we'll never solve." Though this could be taken as a denigration of Batman's detective abilities, it also serves to let the reader in on a secret even Batman doesn't know, making the reader, for a few seconds, Batman's equal.

It may have been that the other Batman artists cited in this essay were better at drawing the "real world" than Sprang, but that somehow worked against them when drawing aliens and alien planets. Perhaps Sheldon Moldoff, having been Bob Kane's official "ghost" for Batman throughout the 1950s and early 1960s, has drawn more pages of Batman art than any other artist. Certainly Moldoff's depiction of Gotham City and the numberless giant props used in the Batman stories are fondly remembered by many fans. But though his depictions of alien landscapes were generally good, his renditions of aliens never seemed quite credible. They were usually depicted as humanoid beings with exaggerated facial features, or bizarre physical attributes like scales, feathers, or beaks. The aliens of Lew Schwartz are not a great deal better, but are aided by the fact that his versions of Batman and Robin are more like Kane's than those of any other Batman artist. (In fact, as in "Batman In the Future!", Kane and Schwartz worked on several stories in tandem, with Kane drawing the Batman and Robin figures and Schwartz supplying everything else.)

to lose the will to live. The story pulled back, to find Batman the subject of a government experiment "that duplicates conditions an astronaut might undergo if he found himself alone on . . . a space flight!" But side effects of the experiment left Batman experiencing hallucinations that threatened to end his career until he was forced to go back into action to save Robin's life.

The science fiction elements existed only in Batman's mind, yet the scenes of Batman's hallucinations were vivid enough that the story is recalled as both a science fiction story and one of the best Batman stories of the 1960s—largely, one assumes, because of the script's emphasis on Batman's indomitable will and on the warm relationship between Batman and Robin.

Indeed, the better science fiction stories in the Batman canon are not only fondly remembered, but are among the best of the character's exploits. No matter where or when a Batman story is set, if Batman and Robin are true to their archetypes, it will be a story worthy of being added to the annals of the Dark Knight.

MIKE W. BARR has contributed to some of pop culture's most enduring series, including Sherlock Holmes, Ellery Queen, *Star Trek*, Star Wars, Doc Savage, the Shadow, and Batman. He's also created some, including the comic book series *Camelot 3000*, *Batman and the Outsiders*, *The Maze Agency*, and *Mantra*.

In 2003 he published the *Star Trek* novel *Gemini*, and is currently marketing two original fantasy novels. He has written numerous short stories; this fall his book on science fiction comic books of the Silver Age, *The Silver Age Sci-Fi Companion*, will be published by TwoMorrows.

He lives in a house with too many cats and not enough books.

Early in my tenure as the man in charge of DC's Batman line, I had to ask myself if I wanted to change the character's origin story, which might have been possible, since the company was in the process of reinventing a lot of its mythology. The answer, of course, was no. It wasn't broken and we weren't about to fix it. In fact, it may be the best origin story in comics. It's still being told today, with the general elements pretty much unchanged, but the way it's told, and the details, have been nipped and tucked to suit individual storytellers' purposes. Mary Borsellino will explain further.

GOTHAM'S FIRST FAMILY

Thomas and Martha Wayne

MARY BORSELLINO

Even if you know nothing else about the Batman tale, you probably know how it began: a wealthy family, walking home from an evening out, is mugged at gunpoint. The robbery goes bad, shots are fired, the mother and father die. Only their son is left behind—the young Bruce Wayne.

This is the prototypical myth of Batman, the origin story from which all others spring. The simplicity of it makes it primal, and allows it to be retold quickly and easily as often as required. With each of these retellings, new embellishments are suggested, and the myth evolves. Thomas and Martha Wayne, the ill-fated victims of street crime, have been written as kind philanthropists, blithe socialites, resigned martyrs, concerned parents, and heroes in their own right. They've died in the '20s, the '50s, the '70s, the '90s. Sometimes they haven't died at all.

By looking at some of the key stories about the parents of Bruce Wayne, written over a number of eras in the last century, we can see some of the ways in which Batman changes with his times—alter the origin story, and the hero born from it evolves as well.

The first version of the birth of Batman came six months after the character's comics debut. The mugging and murder of Thomas and Martha takes up only a few panels, but many of the elements seen in later versions were already present in their prototypical form. The Wayne family has been to a film and, on the walk home, is held up at gunpoint. The mugger wants Martha's pearl necklace. In the panic and confusion, Thomas is shot and killed. In this version of the story, Martha dies of shock rather than being shot. Bruce Wayne is left an orphan.

Rather than simply catalogue later iterations of the story chronologically, making note of the variations as they appear, let's break this scene down into its pieces, and examine how each of these fragments has been repeated and reworked as subsequent stories required it.

The Wayne family has been at the movies. Typically, this movie is *The Mark of Zorro*; whether it's the 1920 or 1940 version depends on the particular retelling. Bob Kane, creator of Batman, was hugely inspired by this movie in the creation of his own masked avenger. The Douglas Fairbanks version was particularly influential (another of the actor's films, *Robin Hood*, inspired Robin the Boy Wonder's name and tunic-style costume— Kane was a big fan of Fairbanks's work), and so to have the story of Bruce's transformation into Batman begin with a screening of *Zorro* is a nod to that inspiration—Batman literally emerges from Zorro.

Sometimes stories about Bruce's childhood before that night are told, and almost always these stories heavily foreshadow the birth and life of Batman. In Darwyn Cooke's graphic novel *Batman: Ego*, a young Bruce was given a Zorro toy for Christmas, which he treasured as a talisman against the dark. A similar backstory was offered in the Timm/Dini Batman cartoons of the 1990s, in which the young Bruce's hero was the Grey Ghost, a movie serial action star who incorporates elements of Zorro alongside those of other Batman forerunners such as the comic book detective Dick Tracy.

The Grey Ghost is voiced by actor Adam West, who introduced Batman to the medium of television in the 1966 series. The homage to earlier inspirations becomes layered and thick as Batman's story moves through the decades. Now it's not just antecedents such as Zorro who deserve acknowledgment; old Batman is the inspiration for the new Batman.

The motif of the mugger waiting outside the movie theater came full-circle in a series of comics set within the Timm/Dini animated version of

Gotham City: Bruce and his date, a young socialite named Veronica, took Veronica's son Justin to a Grey Ghost marathon at a downtown theater. On their way out, they were held up at gunpoint and mugged. Nobody was killed, but Veronica and Bruce's relationship was ruined when he ran off to "look for help." Batman caught the mugger and returned Veronica and Justin's stolen valuables to them. A few years and a few issues later, the reader finds out that Justin grew up inspired by a variety of heroes—Zorro, the Grey Ghost, and Batman—and that these role models taught him the bravery he needed to defeat the Scarecrow and thwart a bank robbery. The cycle goes on, with each new hero adding another layer to the list.

The reason it's worth looking at Justin's story as well as Bruce's is because the pair of them together demonstrates why the choice of film on the night of the muggings is important. This moment, just before the mugger steps from the shadows, is in a very real way the last second of Bruce's childhood. Once that gun goes off, he will have experienced adult grief and the uncertainty that comes with the loss of innocence and trust. The moment of violence forms him, and so we must look to earlier in his life to uncover what influences he had when he was still impressionable. The original Batman had one influence (Zorro), the 1990s Batman had two (Zorro and the Grey Ghost, an allegory for the earlier Batman), and the children of Gotham City have three (Zorro, the Grey Ghost, and Batman himself). The legend repeats—its power growing each time.

Sometimes the Waynes haven't been at the movies before the mugging. In the 2005 film *Batman Begins*, they have been at the opera. Their life is rarified, set apart from the ordinary experiences of the common people. The Bruce Wayne of *Batman Begins* is as much a fantasy figure for the audience as Batman is: his childhood, full of opera, mansions, maids, is not one that many viewers have had any kind of experience with.

By contrast, some versions of the Wayne family are designed specifically to be as normal and everyday as possible. In Jeph Loeb's Batman comics, Martha read bedtime stories—*Alice in Wonderland*—to her tiny son, and Thomas punished Bruce with grounding after Bruce snuck out to go exploring while visiting Metropolis.

One of the most divergent versions of the mugging scene took place in

John Byrne's *Superman & Batman: Generations 2* comic. In this story, Clark Kent's parents had access to "a chronoscope," a machine that showed them the future. Hoping to prevent Thomas and Martha's murder, the Kents told the Waynes about what was in store for them: the mugging, their deaths, and the eventual adult life of their son. The Waynes, however, went through with their night out at *Zorro* just as they had intended, knowing that their deaths were what created the hero Batman. "For the good of the city, darling. Perhaps the whole world," Thomas said, trying to comfort Martha as they set off to meet their doom.

This Thomas and Martha were not innocent victims of a random crime, but rather willing and knowing martyrs who had to die in order for Bruce to fulfill his heroic destiny as Batman.

In Greg Rucka's *Death and the Maidens* comic book miniseries, however, Martha's ghost appeared to Bruce and expressed her deep disapproval of his life as Batman. The core elements of Thomas and Martha Wayne are so bare—they can scarcely be called characters, serving solely as the catalysts for Bruce's transformation—that wholly contradictory thoughts and motivations can be built onto the same thin base by different writers.

Some stories have speculated on what Bruce Wayne and Gotham might have become if not for the death of the Waynes. Ed Brubaker's *Batman: Gotham Adventures* and Jeph Loeb's *Superman/Batman* both imagined worlds in which Bruce Wayne had grown up content but the world around him had crumbled—without Batman, Gotham had no hope, and any work that the surviving surgeon Thomas or the philanthropist Martha did was dwarfed in comparison to that never-was hero.

The 1981 story "To Kill a Legend," appearing in the five-hundredth issue of *Detective Comics*, treated the possibility of a living Wayne family somewhat differently. An adult Bruce and a teenaged Dick Grayson were offered the chance to travel to an alternate dimension, where time was twenty years behind and the Waynes were yet to make their fateful outing to the theater.

The young family that Batman and Robin found in this other world was far from the rose-tinted memory the Waynes are painted as in most stories. Little Bruce was a difficult child and Martha had to physically restrain the hot-tempered Thomas from hitting the boy. Dick had reservations about preventing the murder, worried—like the Thomas and Martha of *Generations*—that Bruce would never become anything useful without that terrible loss to overcome.

At the moment of disaster, as the mugger raised his gun, Batman stepped forward and prevented the tragedy. Rather than lapse into a spoiled playboy existence, however, the young Bruce Wayne was inspired by the sight of Batman to become a hero himself, much as the cartoon's Justin was by his and his mother's own rescue by Batman from mugging.

If it's possible to draw one single coherent message from all these different, and often conflicting, stories of the Wayne family's encounter with a mugger outside a movie theater, then the message is that it is not specifically the death of unlucky parents that creates a vigilante hero out of their surviving child, but rather that child's exposure to violent crime. If there's an existing hero around to save the family, then the child will be inspired by example, as seen in the cases of young Justin and the alternate-dimension Bruce Wayne. If there's no hero around, and things end badly, then it will be up to the children to create a savior out of themselves, and prevent others from losing family as they have.

Another element in the story of the Wayne family, introduced in the 1970s, is the character of Dr. Leslie Thompkins. Leslie is a colleague of Thomas's and, in some versions of the mugging story, she was the first person to arrive on the scene and comfort Bruce after the murders. She is a staunch pacifist and, along with Alfred, assumes guardianship of the young Bruce Wayne for the remainder of the boy's shattered childhood. She disapproves completely of Bruce being Batman, but will patch up anyone from Robin to Catwoman when they're in need of medical care. She is a dry, tough, no-bull character, the inner-city doctor with an under-funded clinic and no tolerance for nonsense. She fits into the world of Gotham City perfectly.

Leslie stands as a surrogate mother figure to Bruce, particularly because of the friendship she had with Thomas. When the editorial team at DC Comics decided that Batman needed to be cut free from any family connections, the decision was made to turn Leslie into a murderer as a way of removing her from the landscape of Batman's world. The teenager fulfilling the role of Robin at the time, a young single mother named Stephanie, was brought into Leslie's clinic with serious injuries.

Inexplicably, and against every other piece of motivation written for the character, Leslie didn't treat the wounds and instead let the girl die, in the hopes that losing Robin would finally put an end to Bruce's dangerous career as Batman. Leslie justified her decision by setting up a trust fund for Stephanie's orphaned daughter. Hearing this reasoning, Batman's mind flashed to the image of himself as a child, sitting forlornly beside the broken bodies of his parents in an alleyway, and he told Leslie that no amount of money could ever make up for losing a parent.

Here, then, we had Bruce facing conflicting loyalties for two stand-ins of his own lost mother. On one hand there is the fallen Stephanie, a victim of Gotham's criminal underworld, leaving behind a mourning child. But Stephanie's murderer, too, is an echo of Martha, which pits two strains of the legend at odds. Ultimately, Leslie was exiled to another country, ordered by Batman never to return. There's only room for one Martha in Gotham, and apparently that Martha needs to be a dead one.

Stephanie is not the only Robin whose story interacts with that of Thomas and Martha Wayne; rather, all four of the teenagers who have played the role of Batman's sidekick have had some direct connection to the pair. Dick Grayson, the first Robin, was taken in by Batman because he, too, was the single survivor of a criminal act that killed his parents. Jason Todd, the second Robin, met Batman on the anniversary of Batman's parents' deaths, when Batman returned to the alley where his parents died—Jason, a street kid, was living there. Tim Drake, the third Robin, comes from the same social strata as Bruce Wayne and began his career as Robin with both parents intact. Shortly thereafter, however, his mother was killed by a supervillain, leading Tim to wonder if this was the price required of all Gotham's heroes. The deaths of Thomas and Martha laid down the ground rules for the game, and echoes of them repeat in every new friend and ally Bruce encounters thereafter.

Although he's adopted three of his four Robins (all but Stephanie, who was a parent herself), Batman has never settled down to the family life that Martha is usually depicted as having wanted him to have. The seeds for this choice on Bruce's part, like so much else in the character, can be found in what little we know of his parents. In a number of stories, such as Cooke's *Ego* and Loeb's *The Long Halloween*, Thomas's work as a high-profile surgeon often intrudes on time and activities spent with his family. The young

Bruce is often resentful of, and hurt by, these demands that the outside world makes on his father's time, angry that this work Thomas does must come before the man's personal considerations.

In becoming Batman, Bruce has all but eradicated any chance he might have had for a personal life. All his romances are based either on lies, or on a shared world of the seedy underbelly of Gotham, neither of which make a good foundation for starting a family. Though Bruce has attempted to forge personal connections, these will always be a distant second to his calling. This is perhaps one explanation as to why Batman allows adolescents to fight alongside him as Robin—it permits these children entry into the part of their adopted father's life that is otherwise closed off, something Bruce was never able to have into his own father's life as a surgeon.

Throughout this exploration we have kept focus on the Wayne family, but the ways in which the myth of their mugger and murderer has changed with the times gives us equal insight into the shifting demands placed on this story.

As a general rule, the name of the mugger is Joe Chill. In some versions of the tale, Chill is hired by the mobster Lew Moxon to kill the Waynes, as a step in Moxon's quest to control all of Gotham's corporations and enterprises. Similarly, the 1989 Tim Burton film depicts the Waynes' killer as the hitman Jack Napier, a man who will later be doused in acid and become the Joker.

What these versions of the story do is remove the devastating randomness and meaninglessness from the deaths of Thomas and Martha Wayne. They allow the possibility that Batman will be able to take specific revenge against those who wronged his family, rather than the generalized quest for justice, the only possible response to an incomprehensible act of violence. If the murderer remains unknown, or is simply a thug looking to steal a strand of pearls, then the real villain of the piece becomes *Gotham*, the world that spawned this killer and which Batman will grow up to do nightly battle against.

The final issue of the comic *Batman Adventures* took place in a Gotham in which Joe Chill was nothing but a petty crook, one who had never recovered from the night his take went bad and two people died. He was slowly going insane, haunted by the twin specters of the famous socialite Bruce Wayne, whose very public life served as a constant reminder of that night for Chill, and the Batman, whom Chill had spent many a long year waiting for capture by for his crime. These two figures plagued every waking moment of Chill's life, until one night when he encountered Batman on a roof ledge.

Overcome to the point of madness by the meeting, Chill managed to push Batman's cowl off. There, staring back at him, was the face of his other personal phantom, Bruce Wayne. Convinced that he had gone insane and was hallucinating, Chill leapt to his death off the edge of the ledge. Bruce, bewildered, stared down at him, having no idea why the sight of his face had driven this man to kill himself. Batman had faced off against his parents' killer, but he would never know it. If there's one thing that really could destroy the Batman legend, it's closure.

The essentials of Batman's origin story are perhaps thought of as the bare ink lines of a sketch, which can be colored in a thousand ways by a thousand different storytellers: one night, a boy and his wealthy parents were mugged on their way home from the movies. Maybe the parents were kind, maybe they were harsh. Perhaps they could have all lived happily ever after, but maybe not. The mugger might have been a hired gun, or just a guy down on his luck in the big city. Maybe these specifics matter, but maybe not.

The parents were killed, the mugger fled into the night, and the boy was left alone. And what happened to that boy next, well, that's a story for another time.

MARY BORSELLINO lives in Australia and writes whatever and whenever she can. She's contributed to a number of essay collections about comic books, and founded the Web site Girl-Wonder.org in 2006. As much as she adores spending her days putting words together into thoughts, she also enjoys being distracted as frequently as possible, so please feel free to drop her a line at mizmary@gmail.com any time.

I wish that I'd had access to the following essay, or at least to Robin S. Rosenberg's research, back when I was Batman's boss, because occasionally I'd find myself debating whether or not our hero is bonkers. My answer was no, because what he does is volitional, albeit sometimes nutty, and in my private, never-to-be-written bio of Bruce Wayne, he hangs up the cape at around age forty and devotes himself and his resources to less flamboyant forms of altruism. Dr. Rosenberg's answer is more thorough, reasoned, and substantial—and much, much more interesting.

WHAT'S WRONG WITH BRUCE WAYNE?

ROBIN S. ROSENBERG

A family—mother, father, and their young son, Bruce—exit the side door of a theater and walk into a deserted alley.[1] A hoodlum with a gun demands the woman's necklace. The woman's husband tries to protect her, but the hoodlum shoots him, and then his wife,[2] instantly leaving their son an orphan. Bruce eyes the hoodlum, his parents' killer, and says, "They're dead! You killed them . . . you killed my mother and father . . ." and the narrator notes:

---

[1] There are minor differences among the versions of the story regarding how they all came to be leaving the theater. The family was watching either a theatrical production or a movie (in some versions, the movie was *Zorro*). In some versions, young Bruce is frightened by the performance and so the family leaves before its conclusion. In other versions, the family stays for the entire performance.

[2] There are also variations to this part of the story—in some versions, the woman has a weak heart and dies not from a gunshot but from heart failure after her husband is shot. In other versions, the killer is identified as Joe Chill, whereas in still other versions he is unidentified. Young Bruce was anywhere from six to eight years old, depending on the version.

> Something about young Bruce's eyes made the killer retreat . . .
> they were accusing eyes that memorized his every feature . . .
> eyes that would never forget. . . . The killer was never found, and
> soon after, a young lad made a grim promise. . . . (*Batman #47*)

At his parents' grave, the young man swears to "dedicate my life and inheritance to bringing your killer to justice . . . and to fighting all criminals!" From that tragic act were sown the seeds that would grow and produce the best-known superhero without superpowers: Batman.[3]

It's clear the enormous impact the murders had on Bruce Wayne—they cast a long shadow. He spent years acquiring the skills and knowledge that would enable him to avenge his parents' deaths and fight against injustice. The personal cost of his singular goal has similarly been massive: He has no personal life in the conventional sense, with the exception of his "Bat-family": Robin, Batwoman, Batgirl, and his butler-cum-superhero's executive assistant, Alfred. His crime-fighting endeavors *are* his personal life. Bruce Wayne—the billionaire playboy—is just a part that he plays. And let's face it, as Batman, he's a pretty weird guy. He's a loner. He broods and ruminates about how to get rid of Gotham City's criminal elements. He lives a dual existence—he's Batman and he's Bruce Wayne. What is most odd is that he's willing to spend his nights seeking out criminals and dangerous situations while walking and flying around in a custom-fitting black costume. Can this be normal? Let's take these "weird" characteristics one at a time.

IS BRUCE WAYNE MENTALLY ILL?

Wayne is a loner. He's antisocial, in the sense that he prefers to spend time alone. Many people are loners, but is being a loner a psychiatric disorder? The manual that contains the complete list of official psychiatric disorders is called the *Diagnostic and Statistical Manual* and is currently in its fourth edition, referred to as the DSM-IV. Although the DSM-IV includes a psychiatric disorder called *antisocial personality disorder*, this disorder involves a chronic disregard for the feelings and rights of oth-

---

[3] Captain American and Green Arrow, as well as the other crime-fighting members of the "Bat-family" (Robin, Batgirl, and Batwoman), to name a few, are also considered to be "superheroes" without superpowers.

ers, not a preference for avoiding the company of others. Wayne may disregard the rights and feelings of criminals, but he doesn't disregard the rights and feelings of noncriminals. Simply being a loner, then, is not a psychiatric disorder.

What about his brooding and ruminating? These mental activities are more common than you might think; most people think dark thoughts from time to time, and some people think such thoughts chronically. When persistent, brooding and ruminating can be indications of several psychiatric disorders, the most common is *depression*, marked by depressed mood or loss of interest or pleasure (American Psychiatric Association, 1994). Depressed people tend to ruminate about their own negative qualities or about their hopelessness that things will get better. Although Wayne isn't a joyful person, his mood isn't really depressed — he's just a serious person, even when acting the part of the carefree playboy. He doesn't appear to have the other symptoms of depression, such as loss of interest or pleasure in activities. His interest is always piqued by activities directed at crime-fighting. So a diagnosis of depression doesn't apply.

Some anxiety disorders also involve rumination, but in those cases, the ruminating takes the form of repetitive, preoccupying thoughts — such as a mental ritual like repeatedly counting to 100 — or unproductive and chronic worrying. In contrast, Wayne's ruminations are productive attempts at problem-solving. He cogitates or meditates on puzzles or problems related to crime in Gotham City, trying to fit together the pieces. So his brooding and ruminating aren't pathological, they just make him serious and thoughtful rather than lighthearted and impulsive.

Next: he lives a dual existence as Batman and Bruce Wayne. This characteristic is definitely high on the weirdness meter, but many people have dual lives, if less flamboyantly than Wayne. Individuals who are homosexuals or lesbians and are in the closet live a dual existence: one "self" is public and one "self" private, known only to a select few. Covert operatives and undercover police also live dual lives: they each have a cover identity and a "real" identity. On closer examination, then, having dual identities isn't, in fact, so strange.

Wayne's dual identities seem more extreme than those of other people, though. Could his identities be a manifestation of a psychiatric disorder? *Dissociative identity disorder* (formerly called multiple personality disorder) is the disorder that comes the closest to addressing dual identities; an individual with this disorder has multiple distinct *personalities* or *identities* that alternate controlling the person's behavior. Dissociative identity disorder doesn't really apply to Wayne for several reasons. First, although his millionaire playboy image is at complete odds with his Batman identity, the playboy image is simply that—an image. It's not a real identity; it's not how he sees himself. It's a "cover," much like a covert operative's cover—he can walk the walk and talk the talk, but it's an act. At a charity ball, Bruce can look and feel like a playboy, but he never believes himself actually to be one. Second, the Bruce Wayne and Batman personalities don't alternate control of behavior. His core personality (whatever name is most appropriate—Bruce Wayne or Batman) is always in control, sometimes acting as a playboy, sometimes acting as a frightening crime fighter. In short, Wayne doesn't have dissociative identity disorder. His two identities are well thought out, purposeful, and help him fight crime while deflecting any suspicion from his legal identity.

Finally, what about the fact that he seeks out danger and flies around in his costume? That's very high on a weirdness scale, and intuitively it seems that this can't possibly be normal behavior. The disorder that comes closest to explaining this aspect of Wayne's behavior is *posttraumatic stress disorder* (PTSD)—which involves anxiety and other symptoms that arise after experiencing a traumatic event. Let's walk through the diagnostic criteria for PTSD, and then decide.

PTSD: THE MOST LIKELY DIAGNOSIS

There are five basic criteria for the diagnosis of PTSD. In order to be diagnosed with the disorder, the individual—in this case, Bruce Wayne—must have symptoms that meet all five criteria.

Criterion #1: The person must have been exposed to a traumatic event.

In order to be diagnosed with PTSD, the person must have been exposed to a traumatic event at which:

1. The person saw, experienced, or otherwise encountered a situation that involved the threat of—or actual—serious injury or death to self or another person. *This was clearly true of young Bruce Wayne.*

2. The person then responded with horror, fear, or helplessness. *Bruce appeared to have all three responses.* The various comics that contain the origin story clearly show young Bruce's expressions of fear and helplessness. Immediately after his mother is shot, "The boy's eyes are wide with terror and shock as the horrible scene is spread before him" (*Batman* #1).

In fact, in inventing the character of Batman, his creators, Bob Kane and Bill Finger, reportedly declared that, "There's nothing more traumatic than having your parents murdered before your eyes" (Daniels 31).

Criterion #2: The traumatic situation is persistently re-experienced.

Memories, flashbacks, dreams, or nightmares are all ways that a traumatic situation can be re-experienced. For this criterion, however, these re-experiences must be persistent, distressing, and intrusive. Although Wayne—in various comics, films, or other incarnations—has had memories, dreams, nightmares, or flashbacks of his parents' deaths, these experiences aren't persistent, and the memories don't usually come to him unbidden; that is, they aren't intrusive, and he usually retrieves the memories in a normal way.

Criterion #3: The individual persistently avoids anything related to the trauma, and is generally numb.

This criterion has two difference facets: *avoidance* and *emotional numbing*. Symptoms of avoidance involve attempts to avoid stimuli, memories, or thoughts related to the traumatic event. This facet of the criterion definitely does not seem to apply to Wayne. In the 1989 Batman film, for instance, he visits the alley where the murder took place at least annually, and in none of the other versions of Batman does he generally shy away from many of the other trauma-related cues: dark streets, being at the wrong end of the barrel of a gun, encountering menacing people who intend to carry out nefarious deeds. He even goes out of his way to get himself into such situations.

The other facet of this general criterion is emotional numbness, which is indicated by:

- A sense of being detached from others;
- Not experiencing very strong positive feelings such as love or joy;
- A sense of shortened mortality, indicated by not expecting to live a long time or to have a family;
- Significantly less interest or participation in regular activities.

Wayne has significant and deep relationships with Dick Grayson and other young people who assume the role of Robin, Alfred Pennyworth, Superman, and Police Commissioner James Gordon (whom Wayne referred to as one of his "oldest friends" [Batman Special #1]). Moreover, there are women who have intrigued him, such as Selina Kyle, Kathy Kane, Talia Head, and Julie Madison.

You could argue that although Wayne has relationships, he's detached in all of them—even the closest ones, in which case the first symptom of emotional numbing could apply to him. And the second symptom of emotional numbing—a lack of strong positive feelings—could also seem to apply: it's rare to see Wayne with a full smile or genuine laugh, let alone a sense of joy or happiness.

It's not clear whether Wayne has a sense of shortened mortality, but he clearly wants to live as long as he can to fight against crime and injustice, so this symptom of emotional numbing doesn't seem to apply.

How about the last symptom of emotional numbing—less interest or participation in regular activities? This symptom is meant to indicate that the person has diminished interest in activities directly because of the traumatic event; that is, he or she has lost interest in things previously enjoyed. In dedicating his life to fighting crime, Wayne gave up the "normal" pursuits that he might have followed. So his single-minded devotion to crime-fighting comes at the cost of partaking in regular activities—an *indirect* result of the traumatic event. (In contrast, a *direct* result would be indicated by flashbacks or depression that interfered with a normal interest in activities.)

In sum, it seems that Wayne may have at least the first two symptoms of emotional numbing (detachment and muted positive emotions), but probably not the last two.

Criterion #4: Persistently increased arousal.

Increased arousal is indicated by *sleep problems, concentration problems, angry outbursts* and *increased irritability*, being *easily startled*, and being *hypervigilant for "danger."* In order to meet this general arousal criterion, the symptoms must not have been characteristic of the person before the trauma, but rather emerged after it.

Batman—a mere human—is considered a superhero because of his phenomenal physical and mental abilities. He is able to focus on the task at hand, use flawless logic and planning, and channel his emotions so that they help him to accomplish his goals. He doesn't panic, have outbursts, or appear to be irritable. Although prone to brooding, he is generally even-tempered. In fact, the only aspect of increased arousal that Wayne seems to have is a hypervigilance for danger. Like a police officer walking a beat, or a detective taking part in an undercover operation, Batman has his "antennae" up for possible danger, but hypervigilance is normal in that context. Batman is always on duty, and so it makes sense that he would be preternaturally attuned for possible threats. In addition, these threats aren't necessarily directed toward *him*, but toward other people.

Criterion #5: "Clinically Significant Distress or Impairment."

Once the person is found to have met all the above criteria for at least a month, he or she is still only diagnosed if the symptoms cause "clinically significant distress, or impairment in social, occupational, or other important areas of functioning" (American Psychiatric Association,

2000, 468). This is a part of the technical definition that can lead to varied opinions about whether Wayne suffers from PTSD. As a wealthy person without a 9–5 job that requires a moderately high level of functioning, he has a lot more flexibility than your average Joe. Given the fact that he is a billionaire whose time is his own, in what ways could it be said that his functioning is impaired?

His "work" life isn't impaired. He seems to carry out his duties with Wayne Enterprises and his charitable foundation, Wayne Foundation, effectively. Is he impaired because his life is narrowed by his devotion to fighting crime? What of heart surgeons or counterintelligence operatives who devote their lives (literally, in the case of the latter) to the same ultimate great cause—saving the lives of others? I don't think so.

Wayne's social life is no more impaired than that of many other extremely wealthy people, and if we compare him to other ridiculously rich people (think Paris Hilton), he looks downright stable. And he does succeed in having close friendships and intimate relationships with women—at least as intimate as is possible given the secret that he guards.

Wayne definitely suffered a traumatic event (Criterion #1), but does he have enough symptoms of PTSD to merit the diagnosis? The only symptoms he has are those related to emotional numbing (Criterion #3), and these may be a byproduct of the degree of emotional deadening necessary to dedicate his life to fighting crime as the Caped Crusader. His behavior and experiences don't meet enough of the criteria for him to be diagnosed with PTSD. So although Wayne is weird, he's not mentally ill.

RESILIENT MASTER WAYNE

Witnessing the murder of one's parents is clearly traumatic. So why doesn't Wayne have PTSD? Not everyone who has experienced a trauma goes on to develop PTSD; in fact, most traumatized people *don't* develop it (Breslau et al.; Shalev et al.). Most people emerge from a traumatic event without PTSD because the traumatic event they experienced was relatively discrete (versus chronic) and, in the relative scheme of things, wasn't severe; for instance, a natural disaster versus repeated rape (Bresau et al.; Dikel, Engdahl, and Eberly). People who don't develop PTSD after a trauma also likely possessed enough factors that protect against PTSD—factors that are associated with resiliency in the face of a trauma. One such factor is intelligence—that is, a high IQ—which provides people with more options for coping with the traumatic event (Brandes et al.). Wayne certainly has a high IQ.

Another factor relates to the way people cope after the trauma. Wayne coped the way many other trauma survivors do: by making meaning of the traumatic event. The risk of PTSD decreases if the traumatized person can understand the trauma in a larger framework about the meaning of life (Ai et al.; Frankl). Such meaning has three aspects (Park and Ai):

+ *Global beliefs*—beliefs related to justice, luck, and fairness (Park 2005; Reker and Wong). Before experiencing a significant trauma, most people believe that the world is a reasonably fair place and that they can control their lives; this belief may not persist after experiencing a traumatic event (Janoff-Bulman and Frantz);
+ *Global goals*—what people strive for: achievements, work, knowledge, or relationships (Emmons);
+ *Subjective feelings of meaning*—feeling that life has a purpose. This is often related to the individual's global goals (Emmons; Reker and Wong). Prior to experiencing a traumatic event, most people feel that they're achieving their global goals (Baumeister).

Traumatic events can call into question people's global beliefs, and cause them to question their global goals. The purpose of life goes up for grabs. To come to terms with trauma, then, people must make new meaning out of life. They must rethink their beliefs and question their goals. As their beliefs and goals come into new alignment, they often feel a new sense of purpose—the trauma has induced them to grow (Tedeschi and Calhoun; Updegraff and Marshall).

This growth process was true of Wayne. In dedicating his life to fighting crime, he gave his life new meaning: new beliefs (about justice and fairness), new goals (obtaining the skills needed to fight crime), and a new purpose (protecting innocent lives). And like many trauma survivors, Wayne's version of making meaning involves social activism, both through the efforts of his charitable organization (which seeks to prevent people from choosing a life of crime, and helps those who become its victims) *and* by putting his life on the line each night:

> I heard the cries of the dying . . . and the mourning . . . the victims of crime and injustice . . . I swore I'd do everything in my power to avenge those deaths . . . to protect innocent lives. (*Batman and the Outsiders #1*)

The manner in which Wayne has made meaning of his transformative traumatic experience lends itself to seriousness; lives are continually at stake. All the weird aspects of Wayne's life—being a loner, brooding, having dual identities, and seeking danger while dressed up in a costume—arise from his chosen path of social activism. Seen through the lens of meaning-making, Wayne's quirks of behavior lose their weirdness. They seem to be the consequence of an incredibly bright, talented, and altruistic young man's decision to give up the semblance of a normal life for a greater good.

The author wishes to thank Neil Kosslyn, Justin Kosslyn, and David Kosslyn for their incisive and helpful comments on an earlier version of this essay.

Robin S. Rosenberg is a clinical psychologist and co-author of *Psychology in Context* and *Fundamentals of Psychology* (introductory psychology textbooks) and *Abnormal Psychology: The Neuropsychosocial Approach* (abnormal psychology textbook). She has taught psychology courses at Lesley University and Harvard University and has a private practice in the Boston area. Her first foray into applying psychological theories and research to popular culture figures was for *The Psychology of Harry Potter*; she is the editor of the *Psychology of Superheroes* anthology. She can be found at drrobinrosenberg.com.

REFERENCES

Ai, Amy L., Toni Cascio, Linda K. Santangelo, and Teresa Evans-Campbell. "Hope, Meaning, and Growth Following the September 11, 2001, Terrorist Attacks." *Journal of Interpersonal Violence* 20.5 (2005): 523–548.

American Psychiatric Association. *Diagnostic and Statistical Manual of Mental Disorders*, Fourth Edition. Washington D.C.: American Psychiatric Press, 1994.

American Psychiatric Association. *Diagnostic and Statistical Manual of Mental Disorders*, Fourth Edition-Text Revision. Washington D.C.: American Psychiatric Press, 2000.

Baumeister, Roy F. *Meanings of Life.* New York: The Guilford Press, 1991.

Brandes, Dalia, Gershon Ben-Schachar, Assaf Gilboa, Omer Bonne, Sara Freedman, and Arieh Y. Shalev. "PTSD Symptoms and Cognitive Performance in Recent Trauma Survivors." *Psychiatry Research* 110.3 (2002): 231–238.

Breslau, Naomi, Ronald C. Kessler, Howard D. Chilcoat, Lonni R. Schultz, Glenn C. Davis, and Patricia Andreski. "Trauma and Posttraumatic Stress Disorder in the Community: The 1996 Detroit Area Survey of Trauma." *Archives of General Psychiatry* 55.7 (1998): 626–632.

Brewin, Chris R., B. Andrews, and J. D. Valentine. "Meta-Analysis of Risk Factors for Posttraumatic Stress Disorder in Trauma-Exposed Adults." *Journal of Consulting and Clinical Psychology* 68.5 (2000): 748–766.

Bryant-Davis, Thema. "Coping Strategies of African American Adult Survivors of Childhood Violence." *Professional Psychology: Research and Practice* 36.4 (2005): 409–414.

Cryder, Cheryl H., Ryan P. Kilmer, Richard G. Tedeschi, and Lawrence G. Calhoun. "An Exploratory Study of Posttraumatic Growth in Children Following a Natural Disaster." *American Journal of Orthopsychiatry* 76.1 (2006): 65–69.

Daniels, Les. *Batman: The Complete History.* San Francisco: Chronicle Books, 1999.

Dikel, Thomas N., Brian Engdahl, and Raina Eberly. "PTSD in Former Prisoners of War: Prewar, Wartime, and Postwar Factors." *Journal of Traumatic Stress* 18.1 (2005): 69–77.

Frankl, Viktor E. *The Will to Meaning: Foundations and Applications of Logotherapy.* New York: Meridian, 1969.

Gallers, Johanna, David W. Foy, Clyde P. Donahoe, and John Goldfarb. "Post-Traumatic Stress Disorder in Vietnam Combat Veterans: Effects of Traumatic

Violence Exposure with Military Adjustment." *Journal of Traumatic Stress* 1.2 (1988): 181–192.

Helgeson, Vicki S., Kerry A. Reynolds, and Patricia L. Tomich. "A Meta-Analytic Review of Benefit Finding and Growth." *Journal of Consulting and Clinical Psychology* 74.5 (2006): 797–816.

Janoff-Bulman, R. and C. M. Frantz. "The Impact of Trauma on Meaning: From Meaningless World to Meaningful Life." In *The Transformation of Meaning in Psychological Therapies: Integrating Theory and Practice*, edited by Mick Power and Chris R. Brewin. Sussex: Wiley & Sons, 1997.

King, Daniel W., Linda A. King, David W. Foy, Terence M. Keane, and John A. Fairbank. "Posttraumatic Stress Disorder in a National Sample of Female and Male Vietnam Veterans: Risk Factors, War-Zone Stressors, and Resilience-Recovery Variables." *Journal of Abnormal Psychology* 108.1 (1999): 164–170.

Linley, P. Alex and Stephen Joseph. "Positive Change Following Trauma and Adversity: A Review." *Journal of Traumatic Stress* 17.1 (2004): 11–21.

Park, Crystal L. "The Notion of Stress-Related Growth: Problems and Prospects." *Psychological Inquiry* 15 (2004): 69–76.

_____. "Religion as a Meaning-Making Framework in Coping with Life Stress." *Journal of Social Issues* 61.4 (2005): 707–729.

Park, Crystal L. and Amy L. Ai. "Meaning Making and Growth: New Directions for Research on Survivors of Trauma." *Journal of Loss & Trauma* 11.5 (2006): 389–407.

Park, Crystal L. and Susan Folkman. "Meaning in the Context of Stress and Coping." *Review of General Psychology* 1.2 (1997): 115–144.

Reker, G.T. and P. T. P. Wong. "Aging as an Individual Process: Toward a Theory of Personal Meaning." In *Emergent Theories of Aging*, edited by J. E. Birren and V. L. Bengston. New York: Springer, 1988. 214–246.

Shalev, Arieh Y., Tali Sahar, Sara Freedman, Tuvia Peri, Natali Glick, Dalia Brandes, Scott P. Orr, and Roger K. Pitman. "A Prospective Study of Heart Rate Response Following Trauma and the Subsequent Development of Posttraumatic Stress Disorder." *Archives of General Psychiatry* 55.6 (1998): 553–559.

Shaw, Annick, Stephen Joseph, and P. Alex Linley. "Religion, Spirituality, and Posttraumatic Growth: A Systematic Review." *Mental Health, Religion & Culture* 8.1 (2005): 1–11.

Tedeschi, Richard and Lawrence G. Calhoun. "Posttraumatic Growth: Conceptual Foundations and Empirical Evidence." *Psychological Inquiry* 15.1 (2004): 1–18.

Updegraff, John A. and Grant N. Marshall. "Predictors of Perceived Growth Following Direct Exposure to Community Violence." *Journal of Social and Clinical Psychology* 24.4 (2005): 538–560.

Batman movies have been around since 1943, just four years after Batman's debut in Detective Comics, *and they've varied hugely in quality, budget, approach, interpretation, box office success, and even genre—just because a guy wears a mask and cape doesn't necessarily mean we're watching him because we like to see movies where bad guys get caught. Film critic Daniel M. Kimmel here reflects on Batcinema and what its diversity might mean.*

THE BATMAN WE DESERVE

The Dark Knight on Film

DANIEL M. KIMMEL

There are not many film characters who constitute their own genre. When we talk of Tarzan movies or James Bond movies, we're talking about characters whose film careers span decades, and who have been tackled by a variety of filmmakers and actors. For the most part, a movie character is usually associated with a particular actor, so there is no Rocky without Sylvester Stallone and no Dirty Harry without Clint Eastwood.

Watching the eight live-action Batman films—ranging from 1943 to 2005, and Lewis Wilson to Christian Bale—becomes a journey through more than sixty years of American life. Some of the ways times have changed are obvious, as with a '40s dress code that has even the thugs in suits, ties, and hats; others are less so, as in the evolving depictions of the life of Batman's alter ego, Bruce Wayne. In exploring the movies, one thing becomes clear: each age gets the Batman it deserves.

The first two Batman films—*Batman* (1943) and *Batman and Robin* (1949)—were serials, a fact that reveals much about the era before a single frame is viewed. Although movie serials go back to the silent film era, by the 1940s they had been firmly established as kiddie fare. The fact that Batman was deemed fodder for the serials as opposed to a feature-length film shows that the character was dismissed by the studio executives and the adult world: Batman was not a legendary avenger like Zorro or the Scarlet Pimpernel, he was merely a comic book character. Like Superman, Flash Gordon, and Buck Rogers, the serials were deemed good enough. With the comic book series itself only four years old in 1943, the filmmakers—already constrained by the usual tight budgets of a serial—didn't bother to look too closely at the young Batman mythos. Instead, they present Batman and Robin as out to prevent a criminal ring headed by the Japanese Prince Daka from getting the radium they needed to complete a super-weapon. In chapter after chapter, Daka learns of some new source of radium only to be thwarted by "the Batman."

In 1940s America, white, male Americans were by definition the center of the universe, and anyone who was non-white, non-male, or non-American was inferior. It was wartime and movies demonized the enemy, especially when the enemy was Japanese. Some of this may be understandable because it was wartime, but when the action shifts to Daka's lair for the first time, it's hard not to gasp at the narration: "This was part of a foreign land, transplanted bodily to America and known as Little Tokyo. Since a wise government rounded up the shifty-eyed Japs it has become a virtual ghost street . . ." (*Batman* 1943). Over the course of the serial, Daka has to put up with being called a "Jap murderer" and a "Jap devil" before meeting his inevitable doom (*Batman* 1943).

Wartime propaganda aside, what may be most surprising is how dumbed down this Batman is. Heroes who had to keep their identities secret were not unusual; the Batman mythology was built on previous vigilante heroes who had civilian identities they kept separate from their masked roles. However, in the serials security is surprisingly lax. Robin repeatedly calls Batman "Bruce" after they escape danger ("Are you all right, Bruce?" [*Batman* 1943]), and they even change into their costumes in Bruce's car. Since Batman was merely a "comic book" hero for kids, the filmmakers were under no obligation to think through anything beyond the surface action. What was needed in 1943 was someone whom young viewers—particularly boys—could cheer on in fighting the "Japs." Even the choice of villain is revealing. Had Batman been fighting the Nazis, the filmmaker might have had to explain why our values were better than their values. Fighting "slant-eyed devils," however, required only a cartoon hero to fight a cartoon villain, the latter of which could be dismissed as alien. (After all, those Americans who might have identified with Daka—even if they remained loyal Americans—had been sent to detention camps.) Batman had been reduced to the barest minimum: a white, male vigilante protecting us from the 1940s version of the "Yellow Peril."

Six years later the war was over and the Batman comic book was well-established. The 1949 *Batman and Robin* borrows more heavily from the comic book, introducing the characters of Commissioner Gordon and photographer Vicki Vale. *Batman and Robin* also gives the Dynamic Duo a masked foe, the Wizard, who, even if he wasn't in the comics first, was easily recognizable as another megalomaniac with plans for Gotham.

Though the second serial is somewhat more sophisticated, the new serial's filmmakers agreed with their predecessors that, like Superman's, Batman's secret identity is merely a cover. This was an odd decision. In the case of Superman, he really is Kal-El, the survivor of Krypton who has superpowers on Earth. Clark Kent is simply a disguise he assumes so he can pass among Earth people. Bruce Wayne, on the other hand, is heir to the Wayne fortune and survivor of the tragic murder of his parents. Batman is the disguise he puts on for his crime-fighting chores. In the serials, though, Batman is the real person, the solid citizen who can be counted on to fight evil, support the establishment, and work with the authorities, while Bruce Wayne is a cowardly lay-about. It's one thing to use Bruce Wayne to throw people off track; it's quite another to make him so sniveling and unreliable that he becomes little more than a disguise that Batman adopts.

It is Batman, not Bruce Wayne, who stands for the values of 1940s white male prerogatives, and this becomes clearer in the 1949 film. In the first serial he protected us from the Yellow Peril. Now, besides fighting bad guys, he also makes sure that uppity women get put in their place. When photographer Vicki Vale grows suspicious of Bruce, even noting that Batman seems to get around in Bruce's car, Batman takes Vicki's own car keys to try and prevent her from following him. There's no romance here; Batman is what later generations would call a male chauvinist. In one scene he airily dismisses her, saying, "Don't worry about her. She's always taking pictures no one ever sees" (*Batman and Robin*). Bruce is more polite, but we're invited to regard him as a shallow wimp, merely Batman's mask. It's Batman we're cheering, and he lets us know that women need to be disciplined. This is the same year that Spencer Tracy and Katharine Hepburn would do *Adam's Rib*, and the battle of the sexes illustrated by Tracy and Hepburn's characters (the movie was years ahead of its time and still feels modern today) provides an interesting contrast. *Batman and Robin* offers a much more authentic view of contemporary attitudes.

Batman and Robin also shows us a world coming to grips with having entered into a technological age, where new and frightening powers are being unleashed. The Wizard has stolen a weapon allowing him to control all means of transportation in Gotham, and he communicates with his gang via two-way radio. He even manipulates the media: he controls a radio reporter who drives Batman and Commissioner Gordon mad with his ill-timed scoops. In contrast, the good guys are still playing catch-up. Tipped off to a criminal plot while outside Gotham, Batman and Robin hurry back to the city, with Batman instructing his partner, "Commissioner Gordon needs help. Watch for a phone" (*Batman and Robin*).

By the late 1940s America was what would soon be called a superpower, but we couldn't be sure that we had the upper hand. The Soviet Union had dropped what Winston Churchill dubbed "the Iron Curtain" across Eastern Europe, and their first successful atomic test took place in August of 1949. Although the serial began spinning out its chapters months before this, it reflects the unease that America was in a world it did not fully control. Batman's frantic search for a payphone reveals much about American anxieties at the time—the fear that we were being outthought and outmaneuvered by our enemies—providing a context for the rise of Senator Joseph McCarthy and his Red-baiting witch hunt the following year.

The launch of the *Batman* television series in January 1966 was a sensation. Obviously modeled on the old movie serials, each episode in its first season ran in two parts on consecutive nights, the first part always ending in a cliffhanger. Much of the mythology from the comics made it to the small screen: the eccentric villains, the Batmobile, the numerous gadgets and devices developed for fighting crime. What was new was the camp element, making it clear that Batman still wasn't being taken seriously. Now he was an earnest hero trapped in an ironic Roy Lichtenstein painting, complete with "Pow!" and "Biff!" captions during the fight scenes and appropriately arch dialogue. That first season, both episodes made the top ten in Nielsen ratings every week, and the series became a precursor to *The Love Boat* as a place for slumming actors and has-beens to pick up a paycheck, in this case, playing villains.

The 1966 *Batman* movie—originally conceived as a launch for the series but released the following summer when ABC ordered the show rushed into production—features a diabolical plot by four of the show's most popular villains: the Joker, the Penguin, the Riddler, and the Catwoman.[1]

The mid-1960s was a time when Hollywood was doing a lot of spoofing. *Get Smart* was sending up the spy genre on TV, while *Cat Ballou* (1965) lampooned the Western. This was exactly the wrong time to make the argument that Batman should be considered a dark vigilante, fighting crime in a way that society was unwilling or unable to handle. It wasn't an argument made in the comics, either. So Batman was treated even more like a cartoon character than he had been in the movie serials. The best-remembered moment in the movie is when Batman is trying to get rid of a bomb—it's the cartoon bowling ball with a sparkler fuse—and everywhere he turns he is stymied: by nuns, by a mother with a stroller, by young lovers, even by ducklings. "Some days you just can't get rid of a bomb," he complains, with viewers invited to see him as a clown (*Batman* 1966). He's a heroic clown to be sure, as compared to villainous clowns like the Joker and the Penguin, but a clown nonetheless.

Given the cartoonish nature of the movie, you might miss that it takes some of the issues of the Batman universe much more seriously. Here, Batman has been deputized by the police and thus operates under cover

---

[1] In the film Lee Meriwether played Catwoman instead of Julie Newmar, who had played Catwoman in the first season. Meriwether was cast because Newmar was already committed to making another film and wasn't available.

of law. For youngsters, this might have been reassuring: Batman was official now. For those who in a just a few years would be labeled part of the "counterculture," it indicated that our heroes had sold out and were simply posturing fools in costumes. Indeed, for those starting to grow cynical of a government that had gotten us into a war in Southeast Asia, it made perfect sense that this heroic buffoon was now firmly tied to the Establishment. Ironically, the 1966 *Batman* allowed Adam West to portray the best Bruce Wayne on film yet. He certainly looks the part, with his square-jawed good looks, and although Bruce is still a playboy he's also more of a philanthropist now. We're told he's a "do-gooder" and a "square citizen" (*Batman* 1966). West's wry performance made clear that he was in on the joke: Batman may be a clown, but Bruce Wayne is not. Almost by accident, the film shows Bruce Wayne as the real man and Batman as the disguise.

By making Batman such a ridiculous figure—in an era in which we would soon be questioning everything—the film suggests that Establishment values had all the depth of a comic book panel. While real life battles were raging over civil rights and Vietnam, Batman distracted us with a dream world, defending America against cartoon villains.

The four Batman films from 1989 to 1997 are a series despite the fact that three different actors played Batman and two different directors helmed the movies. While there was an obvious break between the first two and last two, from Hollywood's perspective this was a textbook franchise. The movies are what are known as "tentpoles," released at the start of the summer season in the hopes that they sustain the studio's (Warner Bros.) fortunes.

The first one did just that. In more than twenty years as a professional film critic, I can remember only one time where I was stopped going *into* an advance screening by a TV camera crew and asked for an opinion on the film not yet seen. That was for the 1989 *Batman*. The hype had been building for months, and audiences were primed to be blown away. Director Tim Burton did not disappoint. Although the casting of Michael Keaton as Batman was controversial among fans, he completely won them over with his earnest, deadly serious portrayal of the Dark Knight. He's less successful as Bruce, perhaps because we could see his face and it was hard to take the star of *Mr. Mom* (1983) and *Beetlejuice* (1988) in a serious role. As Batman, though, he is a creature of the night, striking fear into evildoers, and perhaps the only one who can stand up to Jack Nicholson's Joker.

The casting of a star of Nicholson's magnitude was a signal that this would be a very different *Batman*. Aided by production designer Anton Furst, Burton shows us a dark and evil Gotham City. This Batman is not a goofball, but a tightly controlled vigilante, doing what is necessary to fight crime. Burton had the clout to treat Batman seriously, and by 1989 the world of comic books had changed as well. Frank Miller had done *The Dark Knight Returns* in 1986, and fans—if not the general public— were primed for a Batman who felt real human emotions. No longer a clown or a character simply to thrill children, this Batman was a pained guardian, *driven* to fight crime. He donned the cape and cowl not mere- ly as a disguise, but because he *had* to. Such psychological motivations were no longer beyond the grasp of the comic book film's audience. Other genres, like Westerns and cop movies, had offered us revisionist heroes in the '60s and '70s. (Obvious examples appeared in Westerns like *The Wild Bunch* and *Little Big Man*, and cop movies like *The French Connection* and *Dirty Harry*.) Finally, the comic book film was ready to take the plunge. No longer kiddie fare, *Batman* was a movie squarely pitched to adults, who knew full well the ambiguities and compromises of real life and could handle a dark fantasy figure whose problems were merely shadowy versions of their own.

For Burton, the 1989 *Batman* was merely testing the waters. Would audiences accept a comic book hero—and villain—who acted from psy- chological motivations? Could they relate? They did. In the years after Watergate and Vietnam and, for that matter, the Iran hostage crisis, we no longer expected our leaders or our heroes to be perfect. It was enough if they could get the job done. As Bruce, Keaton is conflicted and vulnerable, finally revealing his secret identity to Vicki Vale, whom he also gets to take to bed, proving him a grown-up Batman indeed. Think you have troubles opening up to a lover? Look what *he* has to go through. Earlier Batmans were so tightly controlled they didn't even go to the bathroom; this one gets laid.

It wasn't until *Batman Returns* three years later that Burton and

Keaton felt fully comfortable delving into Batman's psyche. It's one thing to learn the Joker killed your parents and accept that you want revenge: it's another to find yourself attracted to someone with similar aims and motivations who's even less in control. The transformation of Catwoman into a fetishistic vinyl creation complete with whip shows us the continuum that Batman is on. Bruce saw his parents killed; Selina Kyle is killed by the evil industrialist Max Shreck, only to mysteriously come back to life as the Catwoman. Is she good or is she evil? Batman is drawn to her and even reveals his secret identity to her to try to shock her out of killing Shreck. He fails, but in the process it becomes clear that she's got her claws in Batman and won't let go.

By 1992, women had come a long way. Where Vicki Vale had to put up with Batman's putdowns in the 1949 *Batman and Robin*, *Batman Returns* is clearly a different world. Rescuing a woman being menaced by an assailant, Catwoman taunts the would-be rapist, "Be gentle. It's my first time." Later, battling Batman, she momentarily upsets him—and gains the upper hand—by playing to old stereotypes, "How could you? I'm a woman." She then uses Batman's courtliness against him, telling him, "Life's a bitch. And now so am I."

It's a brilliant, sexy performance by Michelle Pfeiffer, who may have haunted more twisted fantasies as a result than any actress since Diana Rigg in *The Avengers*. Whether she's licking herself because she "feels dirty" or assuring Bruce that normal guys have let her down—and then pouncing on him for a steamy kiss—she's a woman who will no longer allow herself to be victimized. That Batman accepts this says much about how times have changed. He's not threatened by Catwoman; he's turned on. A strong, fiercely independent woman is not a challenge to his masculinity, even if she's on the kinky side. It's not surprising to have such a film come out the same year that Bill Clinton was elected president. He would be impeached later for a fling with a White House aide and not only be acquitted, but retain the support of the country in the process. We hadn't quite turned into France, but we had become increasingly willing to forgive the sexual peccadilloes of our heroes—so long as they weren't hypocrites.

Clearly what was needed was a follow-up film focusing more on the Batman and Catwoman relationship—something hinted at in the

Batman Returns end when the bat-signal brings out the Catwoman, who has been presumed dead. Instead, Keaton hung up the cape and Burton turned over the director's chair to Joel Schumacher.

Though the Batman series continued, it would now reflect not the social or political *zeitgeist* of America, but instead how Hollywood had changed from the 1930s "Dream Factory," which turned out an unending stream of escapist fare, to the 1990s assembly line, manufacturing blockbusters to order. Schumacher is not a critic's favorite, in spite of such respectable films as *Lost Boys* (1987), *Falling Down* (1993), *Tigerland* (2000), and *Phone Booth* (2003), and he is certainly not a stylist like Burton. His two Batman films, *Batman Forever* (1995) and *Batman & Robin* (1997), demonstrate that he learned exactly the wrong things from the Burton movies. The later films are still dark, but where *Batman Returns* is practically a study in black and white, Schumacher made his films much more cartoonish.

Batman Forever gives us both Two-Face and the Riddler, as well as the addition of Robin. *Batman & Robin* keeps Robin, adds Batgirl, and offers up Mr. Freeze and Poison Ivy. Watching the two movies back to back makes it abundantly clear that they are virtually the same film; only the villains have changed. Robin's costume even gets the same fetishistic rubber/leather makeover as the Batman outfit (although it's interesting to note that when Batgirl arrives on the scene, her costume lacks the superfluous nipples that the Batman and Robin suits have).

What became clear with the Schumacher films is that the series couldn't hold on to Batman. After Keaton left, Val Kilmer and George Clooney each took the role for one film apiece, with Kilmer faring better, perhaps because he got to explore Bruce's dual personality with sympathetic psychiatrist Dr. Chase Meridian. The problem with the latter two films of the series is that they reflect the economic boom times of the '90s. They are all too aware that they are entries in a big studio franchise. When Two-Face invades E. Nigma's big party, Nigma—the Riddler's real identity—complains that Two-Face should have warned him so he could have pre-sold the movie rights. When, in *Batman & Robin*, the young crime fighter asks for his own car, there's this exchange:

ROBIN: I want a car. Chicks dig the car.
BATMAN: That's why Superman works alone.

It's like they can't make up their minds if they're in the *noir*ish world of the Burton movies or if they've slipped over into the wisecracking mode of an Arnold Schwarzenegger action film. The casting of Schwarzenegger as Mr. Freeze signaled which direction they were going; he made his entrance by declaring, "The Iceman Cometh."

The Batman of the Schumacher films is like the Johnny Depp of the *Pirates of the Caribbean* sequels: no one is interested in character and nuance any longer; now it's about feeding the public what they want. Trot out the wacky villains, do the action set pieces, and resolve everything so the next product can be put on the assembly line. There's a reason the momentum in Hollywood swung from the DC comic book heroes to those of Marvel (particularly X-Men and Spider-Man). The Schumacher Batman films told us more about '90s Hollywood and what it thought audiences wanted than it did about the audiences themselves.

What this quartet of Batman films are about, in the end, is the power of the box office. The first film was a blockbuster hit, taking in over $250 million in domestic receipts. *Batman Returns* proved a bit too weird for some, dropping to "only" around $160 million. To Warner Bros., it must have seemed that Schumacher got the series back on track when *Batman Forever* boosted the take to $180 million. Thus you can imagine their disappointment when *Batman & Robin*, which fully accepted the lessons of the third film, topped out at $107 million. On an estimated budget of $125 million, that made the film a certified flop, even if overseas box office and subsequent video and cable sales eventually balanced the books. It would be eight years before the Caped Crusader appeared again on screen—outside of animation—and it would be a reinvention that scraped away nearly everything that had come before.

Batman Begins (2005) is the best and most serious Batman put on film to date. Director Christopher Nolan seems to have asked himself, "What if this were real? How would it be done? Why would it be done this way?" The result is a movie that gives us credible explanations for every aspect of the Batman legend, from the armored suit, weapons, and

Batmobile, to where he got his fighting skills, why he wears a cape, and the source of his special bond with Alfred, Bruce's long-serving butler and the only one who knows that Bruce is Batman.

Indeed, by the end of the Burton/Schumacher quartet, the question was, who *didn't* know Batman's identity? He had revealed it to Vicki Vale, Selina Kyle, and Dr. Chase Meridian. The Riddler, Dick Grayson, and Barbara Wilson/Batgirl had figured it out for themselves. In *Batman Begins* his childhood friend Rachel guesses the truth, but it's not a big revelation scene. Instead it's a confirmation for both as to why a serious relationship between them has become impossible.

Nolan opens the film in a completely unexpected manner, showing Bruce Wayne as an inmate in a faraway prison. Slowly we get the story of how and why he is there, and how it leads him to the League of Shadows, where he receives his training from Henri Ducard. In answer to the Joker's famous query in the 1989 film, "Where does he get those wonderful toys?" we see him slowly acquire them from the basement of Wayne Enterprises, where military items that never went into mass production are his for the taking.

For a movie that dispenses with Robin, it makes some astute observations about male bonding. Just as a new generation of women accepted the changes wrought by "women's lib" but held "feminism" at arm's length, men of the '80s and '90s were trying to figure out if they were supposed to be sensitive or return to being macho, or come up with some new combination of both. The ideal man of the early twenty-first- century was now expected to be both macho *and* sensitive, which our hero turns out to be. Bruce is tortured by guilt over his parents' death—they left the opera and were gunned down after young Bruce freaked out seeing bats on stage—forcing him to work out his roles as both businessman/philanthropist Bruce Wayne and the dark crime fighter Batman. He has only two people to turn to, Alfred and Sgt. Jim Gordon. Alfred became Bruce's foster father, in practice if not in actuality, after he was orphaned. Their bond is expressed in typical male fashion, in the little jibes that make it clear that affection is being expressed by other means. When Alfred informs the newly returned Bruce that he has been declared dead, Bruce remarks that at least his property—which went to Alfred—has remained in good hands. Alfred drolly replies, "You can borrow the Rolls. Just bring it back with a full tank." Later,

Bruce is hosting a birthday party at Wayne Manor but has to run out as Batman just as the guests are arriving. Alfred wonders what he should do, and Bruce archly advises, "Tell them that joke you know."

Times had changed, and though the widespread cynicism toward the "wartime" leadership of President George W. Bush was not yet underway when the film was in production, or during its initial release, the movie certainly pointed the way. The system is corrupt in *Batman Begins's* Gotham, whether it's the military industrial complex (represented by the head of Wayne Enterprises), law enforcement (with Sgt. Gordon being the notable exception), the civil authorities (under the thumb of gangster Carmine Falcone), or even the educated elite (such as the duplicitous Dr. Crane). Where once we had faith that those in charge were trustworthy, allowing Batman to work closely with them and be considered a hero, now it was taken for granted that those with power could not be trusted, making it necessary for Batman to work outside the system. Outside the *film noir* genre, we wouldn't have hailed someone taking the law into his own hands during the complacent '50s under Dwight Eisenhower, or even in the idealistic early '60s under John F. Kennedy. However, in 2005, a Batman who made his own rules and saw those in charge as corrupt and venal required no explanation. It was the way American moviegoers were increasingly seeing the real world.

Batman's relationship with Gordon is significant, and will likely be developed in subsequent films. Gordon is the beat cop who comforted young Bruce after his parents were murdered. Later, Gordon is the rare honest cop on the force who defends Batman and whom Batman seeks out for assistance. Their big bonding moment occurs late in the film. Batman needs Gordon's assistance and asks him if he can "drive stick" before sending him off with the Batmobile, which we heard Gordon admire earlier. Married and a parent, Gordon is not interested in the car because it's a chick magnet. These are two men who are determined to fight the corrupt system and do what's right for Gotham, though they have chosen to do so in different ways. Batman recognizes Gordon as an honest cop and Gordon recognizes Batman as a vigilante who, nonetheless, feels constrained by the law. In a world of corruption, standing for the ideals the Establishment once espoused becomes an act of rebellion for them both.

When, at film's end, the newly promoted Lt. Gordon informs Batman of a mysterious new criminal who has left a Joker playing card behind at the scene, their friendship is cemented:

GORDON: I never said thank you.
BATMAN: And you'll never have to.

Modern men don't have to express emotions. They merely have to acknowledge them. Batman/Bruce Wayne's bonding—with Alfred, with Gordon—is all implied. If they are worthy of his trust, and they are, they don't need to say anything or ask anything. Their actions speak louder than any words.

Certain characters, because they are so endlessly adaptable, prove to be mirrors of their times. Character traits that mean one thing in one era mean something different in another. The Sherlock Holmes who asks Dr. Watson for "the needle" in the 1939 *Hound of the Baskervilles* is merely bored at having solved another mystery; the cocaine-abusing Holmes of *The Seven-Per-Cent Solution* (1976) is someone with a drug problem. The same is true for Batman. And what the eight Batman films demonstrate is a slow but certain journey from treating the character as a child's fantasy to accepting him as a fully adult character.

The Batman of the 1940s is an uncomplicated hero for children to cheer, just as those children's parents cheered President Roosevelt, a heroic wartime leader whose confinement to a wheelchair was largely kept from the public. The notion that someone could be a hero *and* have problems was left for more serious works.

Things changed with the Baby Boomers, a generation that famously refused to grow up—at least on their elders' terms. Where their parents learned to put "childish things" aside as they took on adult responsibility, the Boomers didn't want to make a choice. One could be responsible and yet still have fun with the things they enjoyed when they were younger. Comic book readers turned to "graphic novels," and filmmakers adapting Batman to the '80s and '90s assumed that adults who had grown up with the character would, in fact, be their audience.

These adults, both the ones making the films and the ones watching them, were ready to accept a complex, flawed Batman because the other once-simple heroes of their past had proven similarly complex. Sports stars use steroids. The rock star/actor/public figure who goes into rehab and emerges a changed person is part of our everyday culture. (Perhaps that explains why the public has lost faith in George W. Bush. He's trying to be a '50s politician who never has doubts and never asks questions in a twenty-first-century world where doubts and questions are all we have.)

It's interesting that, in the wake of the success of *Batman Begins*, two other movie icons were similarly reinvented in 2006: Superman in *Superman Returns* and James Bond in *Casino Royale*. In each case, but particularly with Batman and Bond, there was a conscious attempt to eliminate the camp and the cartoonish elements so that instead of focusing on the special effects, we focused on the character.

If each age truly gets the Batman it deserves, perhaps we're finally ready for a Batman struggling with the problems of what it means to be a man in the modern world, even if he has to wear a costume to do it.

DANIEL M. KIMMEL is a Boston-based film critic whose reviews appear in the *Worcester Telegram & Gazette*. He is the Boston correspondent for *Variety* and a past president of the Boston Society of Film Critics. He is an award-winning author of several books, including *The Fourth Network*, a history of FOX broadcasting, and *The Dream Team*, a history of DreamWorks. He is also a regular contributor to the *Internet Review of Science Fiction*.

Man and boy, I've been reading (and writing) about Batman for more than sixty years, yet in all that time I've never encountered a topic remotely like the one Alex Bledsoe addresses in the following essay. Take it away, Mr. B!

TO THE BATPOLE!

Alfred Explains the Facts of Life: Three Parodies

ALEX BLEDSOE

The influences that helped turn teenage millionaire Bruce Wayne into the vengeful, obsessed Batman have been endlessly analyzed, from the death of his parents to his discovery that bats are (gasp!) scary. But one small unemphasized incident might actually, as the Beatles would say, loom large in his legend. This haunted boy was "fathered" — in all but the biological sense — by a middle-aged English manservant, and at the onset of puberty this child of privilege would no doubt have turned to trusted Alfred Pennyworth for an explanation of the unexpected changes in his body, voice, and priorities.

For Bruce Wayne, "the Talk," as it is for any young person, must have been one of life's watershed events. It sends reverberations through our lives that Freud only glimpsed. But there is no single "Bruce Wayne," just as there is no one version of Batman. Bob Kane's creation has been modified, adapted, "reimagined," and tweaked by a succession of writers, artists, and filmmakers. So can the different popular incarnations of the Dark Knight, in all their shadowy variety, be traced back to this pivotal conversation?

What follows, though, are mere extrapolations. The actual conversations between Alfred and Bruce are the sole property of a mighty entity whose tendrils twine effortlessly around the necks of those who even dare breathe their name without permission. Just ask Dave Stevens.[1] What follows are parodies, humorous satirical imitations of serious writing. I swear.

A note: Just like the Caped Crusader, Alfred has gone through numerous incarnations, including a stint as a supervillain called "The Outsider." For the sake of clarity, we will deal with three popular, non-comic book interpretations: The *Batman* TV show, where he was played by Shakespearean actor Alan Napier; the Tim Burton films (*Batman* and *Batman Returns*) where Hammer Film Productions veteran Michael Gough took over the white gloves and tails; and Christopher Nolan's *Batman Begins*, which gave us a still-rugged Michael Caine as Wayne Manor's majordomo.

◆ ◆ ◆

In the *Batman* TV show (1966–1968) and its cinematic spin-off (*Batman: The Movie*, 1966), Alfred was the ever-proper, ever-helpful butler who, along with housekeeper Aunt Harriet, kept "Stately Wayne Manor" in tip-top shape. Privy to the secrets of Bruce Wayne (crime-fighting and otherwise, no doubt), he often stepped in to help, a domino mask hiding his identity. But at one time he must've dealt with something far less proper than battling the baddies bedeviling Bruce.

Imagine Bruce Wayne, in short pants and private school blazer, standing before Alfred in the mansion's library. This Wayne Manor is brightly lit, spotless, and filled with the works of art any respectable encyclopedia of the time would've called "great." It was created by set designers not concerned with psychological reality: Why, after all, would Bruce use a bust of Shakespeare to hide the red button? Surely, given his penchant for creatures of the night, Poe would've been a better choice. But thanks to the '60s insistence on educational basics like great literature, every schoolboy of the time knew Shakespeare on sight, and this bust told them that Bruce had also had to read *Julius Caesar* in junior high

---

[1] See "The Battle for the Rocketeer," page 12 in *The Comics Journal* #110 (Aug. 1986). Stevens ultimately won, but the cost for an independent artist to take on one of the majors (in this case Marvel) makes the victory probably Pyrrhic at best.

and wonder what the hell "ides" were.

Already a precocious (and chivalrous) lad, Bruce certainly would ensure that Aunt Harriet was either off to the market or with the other ladies getting her hair done. This is not a conversation for delicate female sensibilities.

"Alfred," he would say in his grim, vaguely breathless way, "there seems to be an untoward event happening that I can neither explain nor prevent."

"I see, Master Bruce," Alfred would no doubt respond, possibly fingering the furniture-polishing chamois cloth in his white-gloved hand. "And where is this event occurring?"

With hands clasped behind his back, Bruce might say, "In my trousers, Alfred."

"In your trousers, Master Bruce?"

"Yes, Alfred. It appears that a certain appendage has altered its appearance over an incredibly short period of time, although the appendage itself is no longer incredibly short."

Alfred would place his housekeeping items aside, and perhaps remove his glasses for a quick polish as he formulates his reply. He might even pour himself a discreet glass of port to help muster the resolve to address this issue, knowing that young Master Bruce has nowhere else to turn. At last he might say, "That does seem significant, Master Bruce."

"Can you explain this perplexing protuberance, Alfred?"

"Indeed, sir. It is the plain presence of proper puberty."

"Ah, yes, puberty. We studied this in science class. It means I have now experienced the first thrusts of manhood, does it not?"

"I believe so, Master Bruce. You should also have noticed an outgrowth of hair in new places, and I have detected a variation in your normal speaking tone."

"So all these examples are the expected exemplars of this extraordinary event?"

"Indeed, Master Bruce."

"Very well. I shall remove myself to my room to privately examine this perfidious protuberance more properly."

"I expect so, Master Bruce." Shortly, Alfred would no doubt see the unmistakable onomatopoeia hanging in the air outside Master Bruce's bedroom door, although perhaps *BAM!* and *OOF!* would be replaced by somewhat . . . squishier terms.

And so this version of Bruce Wayne would go on to don gray tights and a blue satin cowl with eyebrows drawn on it much in the style of an overplucked dowager's. He would also begin a long-term platonic relationship with a young man he insisted on calling "Dick" even though the boy's given name was certainly Richard, and who he encouraged to wear skin-tight green briefs in public.

Speaking of Robin, it seems unlikely that when the same problem arose (heh), Dick Grayson would approach cold, analytical Bruce Wayne. He, too, likely would seek out Alfred, although the conversation was probably much more energetic.

"Holy hardness, Alfred!" he might exclaim. "My Robin tights are tighter than ever!"

"I can see that, Master Dick."

"Holy sarcasm, is that a joke?"

A slight tremor, the very faintest of smiles, might be visible. "No, Master Dick, I assure you."

"Then stop *calling* me that! And tell me what to do about this! I can't go into Gotham City and fight villains looking like a sundial!"

"It is perfectly normal, Master Richard. All young men experience this."

"Even Bruce?"

"Indeed."

Robin's eyes might open wide. "Holy beefeater, Alfred, even *you*?"

"Well, I . . . ahem . . . it *has* been a very long time. My memory is a bit indistinct."

"*My* memory is as sharp as my tights! What do I do?"

"I believe, Master Richard, that short of self-control, there remains only one option. Thankfully we are not Catholic, although it is a temporary solution at best."

His eyes might open even wider. "Holy hand over fist! Is that the only cure?"

"Not so much a 'cure' as a 'treatment,' Master Richard. And for a young man of your tender age, most assuredly."

And so Robin, like Batman, would cultivate a fondness for satin and add his own quirks: disturbingly odd Peter Pan footwear and a tendency to smack his right fist into his left palm. Conventional wisdom assumes this was because he was spoiling for a fight with the bad guys, but perhaps it was really a way of strengthening his grip for something else entirely. And it does explain why two men whose lives often depended on their ability to hold tightly on to ropes and weapons might insist on those smooth silky gloves. . . .

◆ ◆ ◆

Michael Gough, in serving the needs of Michael Keaton in *Batman* (1989) and *Batman Returns* (1992) (we will completely ignore his stints with Val Kilmer and George Clooney under the aegis of Joel "Man-Goat" Schumacher[2]), gave us an Alfred whose main task seems to be compensating for his employer's frequent absentmindedness. In fact, he is so in tune with Bruce that he can anticipate even where his master might set down a champagne glass during a crowded party. This Bruce Wayne is so preoccupied with thoughts of his alter ego that when left entirely to his own devices, he simply sits around in the dark waiting to be summoned by the bat-signal. Only in costume does he become focused, certain, and relentless; in his civvies (or skivvies), his mind is always a million miles away.

It seems unlikely that this Bruce Wayne would consciously seek out Alfred at the onset of puberty. Instead, the loyal manservant might enter the main sitting room, where young master Bruce would be sprawled on the couch, legs askew, watching TV, and absently exploring his new priorities. After all, this Wayne Manor was a dark, grim edifice filled with shadows into which a vengeful young man would later vanish, only to emerge, Mr. Hyde–like, as a walking shadow himself. Why wouldn't the adolescent Bruce forget which room he was in, and presume privacy?

Suitably appalled, yet ever the loyal servant, Alfred would most certainly avert his eyes and say, "Master Bruce." Pause. "*Master . . . Bruce.*"

"Huh? Oh . . . hey, Alfred. What . . . uh. . . ." Young Bruce might be a bit surprised himself to be so flagrantly improper. "Hey, wow, where did that . . . wow."

---

[2] As so identified on page 225 of *Mike Nelson's Movie Megacheese*.

"Master Bruce, I believe it's time we had a talk."

"A talk. You mean about . . . oh! Yeah, I guess . . . sure." Bruce would sit up, hands clasped, elbows on his knees, ready to listen.

Another pause. "Your trousers, sir?"

"What? Oh. Sorry." Zipping sound.

Alfred would stand beside the couch, hands properly folded behind him. His eyes would focus on some point in the middle distance. "Wayne Manor is your home, sir. You may conduct yourself as you like. But I fear your penchant for distraction may one day do you a disservice."

"My . . . oh! Yes, you . . . yes. I see."

Alfred would choose his next words carefully. "Master Bruce, do you understand the concept of puberty?"

"Puberty, ah . . . yeah, I mean . . . in class we . . . so . . . sure."

Alfred would at last meet Bruce's gaze. "And do you realize you are experiencing it right now?"

Bruce might look down at his lap. "Huh. That explains it."

"Indeed. Do you wish to discuss it?"

"Talk about it? I don't . . . could . . . talk about it?"

"Yes. It can be a confusing time, and with your father gone, I thought you might need a sympathetic ear."

"An *ear*? Oh . . . you mean to listen with. Well, I guess . . . sure, if . . . sure."

A long pause might fill the room.

"You have to begin, Master Bruce," Alfred might point out.

"Oh! Okay, uhm . . . how long does it get? I mean *last*. How long does it last?"

"It is a permanent change, I'm afraid. Eventually you should be able to control it, but for awhile it may be quite a distraction." Pause. "Master Bruce?"

"What? Oh—distraction. Yeah."

"I'm certain we can find some medical texts to explain the exact biological mechanisms involved. It brings with it a set of responsibilities of which you should be aware."

"That might be good."

"And if you would like to discuss it further. . . ."

"No, that's all right, Alfred, I . . . thanks."

"At any time, sir."

This Bruce Wayne would compensate for his physical slightness by designing body armor and an array of gadgets that made him appear larger and more intimidating. Was this also a compensation for something else? Only Vicki Vale and Selina Kyle know for sure. . . .

◆ ◆ ◆

Christopher Nolan's *Batman Begins* (2005), unlike either the TV show or the Burton films, almost completely abandons stylization and places the Batman in as realistic a world as possible. This Wayne Manor is a home filled with sadness, but also love, memories, and a sense of purpose. The inner workings of Christian Bale's version of Bruce Wayne are not dark and mysterious, but methodical, well-reasoned, and clever. When he decides to dress as a bat, it makes perfect sense. This is a Batman we can all relate to, not the campy buffoon of Adam West or the brooding, shadowy loner of Michael Keaton.

Alfred is also substantially different. Both Alan Napier and Michael Gough portrayed the butler as an elderly, dignified man with the polish of a lifetime of service. Michael Caine, on the other hand, is a virile, active, and rough-edged manservant not above striking his own blows for justice. He also retains his native Cockney accent in the role, revealing the supposed lower-class roots of this most loyal of servants.

And as such, one can imagine him delivering a very different description of the facts of life to the spoiled, aimless Bruce Wayne. Alfred might pound on the bathroom door and say, "Aye, wot you doing in there, Master Bruce?"

In a cracked, embarrassed voice, Bruce might reply, "Nothing, Alfred, just. . . ."

"Hey, now, are you yanking on your Mars and Venus? Cor, lad, I'll be mopping up loads of Harry for a week. Get yer arse out here."

Bruce might emerge, fastening his jeans and nursing a serious blush. Alfred might put one meaty hand on the back of the boy's neck, grip it firmly, and say, "Master Bruce, you're coming of age. Soon you'll be wanting to have a bit of posh, and it's time you knew what goes where and when."

"Ah . . . Alfred, I swear, I was just brushing my teeth, and—"

177

"Your father, bless him, should be the one telling you this. But he left you to me, and it's me own fault for not speaking up sooner. Now pay attention." Deep breath. "When your three-card trick holds a standing election—"

"My what does *what*?"

An impatient sigh; these Yanks. "When you get an *ee-reck-shun*, it means you're wanting and ready to have sex with a girl. Do you still fancy Miss Dawes?"

Bruce might blush anew, start to protest, then nod sheepishly.

"All right, there you go. And who wouldn't at your age, she's got a lovely set of carpet and rugs and she's always thought you a right turtle."

"Rachel? She's just a friend, she's like my sister."

"But she's not, and I think you'll find it hard to think about her that way for awhile." He might chuckle at his own pun.

"Now, wait a minute, Alfred, I don't—"

"Master Bruce, please just shut your gob and listen. When a boy reaches your age, his body changes. You're now able to father children if you have sex with a girl."

"You mean I'm a man?"

Alfred might genuinely laugh. "Listen to you. *No*, you're not a man; you're a boy with a loaded gun who doesn't know how to aim or when to shoot. If you let that thing lead you around, it'll find its way into Miss Dawes's knickers, and then you and she could be in for some trouble.

"So, first: Don't do it. Second, if you're going to do it, wear a condom. Third, if you *do* do it and wear that johnny-bag, have the decency to call her the next day."

"I'm not going to try to . . . h-have sex with Rachel, Alfred."

"Well, why the bloody hell *not*?"

Bruce would stare, eyes wide, then realize Alfred was teasing him. Alfred would laugh, then pull Bruce from the chair and wrap a big arm around the boy's neck in a playful, affectionate headlock. "That's the way to be, Master Bruce," he might say. "That's sure the way to be."

This most natural, sensible, and "normal" version of Bruce Wayne would've heard a realistic description of what was happening to him given by a solidly loyal and caring Alfred. Unlike the other two Bruces, his decision to dress as a bat probably *can't* be traced at all to this moment, and his incarnation of the Caped Crusader bears few signs of any repressed or confused sexual issues. This Batman is a Dark *Knight*, kicking ass and taking names for justice, not Freud.

◆ ◆ ◆

So can a man who dresses up (in tights, rubber, or whatever) as a bat really be just like one of us? Probably not, in any real sense. But what makes the character so compelling is that his reason for doing so is something we can all, at the core, understand. Everyone has suffered an unfair loss; each of us has raged against the fates that took something or someone beloved from us. And certainly we've all had revenge fantasies. The nobler among us have probably considered how they'd fix the world so no one else would have to suffer as they did. But even they don't actually go out and *do* it.

Bruce Wayne does.

And we all have sexual histories that begin with self-discovery. Those histories inform our current selves in ways both subtle and (in every sense) gross. We all received the mixed signals of sexual information from the previous generation and tried to integrate it into our version of reality. We all felt the same terrors, the same thrills, and the same moments of sublime comprehension. Would Bruce Wayne, even with all his demons, really be any different?

Maybe that's why the new, reasonable Dark Knight of *Batman Begins* ultimately leaves me cold. While everything about the film is impeccable, from the solid script to the cast to the action, it finally gives us a Batman who is just a little *too* reasonable. Bruce Wayne's decision to dress as a bat and fight crime *does* make perfect sense in the film's context, but really, should it? Ever? Shouldn't it be an almost-unfathomable compulsion, just like that other compulsion we've been discussing?

In Burton's *Batman*, when Vicki Vale asks why he dresses as a bat, he replies, "They're great survivors," which is a total non-answer. And maybe that's the key: it's something that really can't be explained until you've experienced it yourself, much like our other topic. And if, like Vicki, you have to ask, then you've clearly never experienced it.

Selina Kyle, now, *she* gets it.

Next, we'll examine the meaning and symbolism of the Batcave. . . .
Just kidding.

ALEX BLEDSOE, author of *The Sword-Edged Blonde* (Night
Shade 2007), picked Batman as his favorite superhero around
age four, according to his mother. Except for those awful
Schumacher years, he's never regretted his choice.

REFERENCES

Nelson, Mike. *Mike Nelson's Movie Megacheese*. New York: HarperCollins,
2000.

In a reasoned fictional universe, Superman and Batman would not coexist, much less interact. They're different kinds of heroes, from different heroic traditions. But they do both coexist and interact, more because of historic accident than any other single reason. In his excellent essay, John C. Wright compares and contrasts them, tells us how and why they differ in everything from powers to sex appeal, and in the process defines their essences.

HEROES OF DARKNESS AND LIGHT

Or, Why My Girl Goes For Batman Over Superman

JOHN C. WRIGHT

1. DARK KNIGHTS AND WHITE KNIGHTS

My girl tells me that she would never date Superman.

She reads comics with a woman's eye, so perhaps she sees something I don't see, but she assures me that of the iconic superheroes of comic-bookdom, the one with the most animal magnetism, the one the ladies swoon over, is the Batman.

Why is it that Batman has the romantic allure of Zorro, whereas Superman has no more sex appeal than an Eagle Scout? On the other hand, if Batman has all the glamour, why is it that Superman has a steady girlfriend, and he does not?

The two heroes are as different as day and night. There is something in the souls of three generations of readers that reacts to these characters with a shock of delight and recognition: as if by instinct, we recognize that they are icons or archetypes, a modern pantheon of the demigods like those who fought before the walls of Troy.

Some dismiss cartoon characters as childish; and so they are, but not in the way that word is normally meant. Children, learning about a world as castaways might learn about an undiscovered mystical island, find out first about the most important things, the deep things from the roots of the world, the eternal things—it is for adults to concern ourselves with daily surface details. The noble self-sacrifice of heroes is one of the first things children read about when they read adventure tales. It is one of the basic truths of the world. When heroes act selfishly, or for personal gain, they lose what they cherish most: that is the message of every story about superheroics penned, ever since the day Achilles lost his temper.

This essay intends to explain the inexplicable, and say why glamour and mystery shroud the Batman, the most famous of the famous heroes of the night, and to contrast him against Superman, that most glorious of the brilliant heroes of the day. This essay will attempt to say in what part of the human psychology they find their roots.

The quickest shortcut to examining human psychology is to talk about romance, because it is the one issue that is touched by all others: find out what kind of girl a guy is attracted to, find out what kind of girl he attracts, and you find out all about him.

2. CRIMINALS ARE A COWARDLY AND SUPERSTITIOUS LOT

The Batman is all about fear.

Bats are one of those particular animals, like spiders, that give just about everybody the creeps. So why did Bill Finger and Bob Kane make a creepy creature like a bat into the mascot and icon of their pulp-style vigilante?

Well, one might as well ask why the Shadow wears black. The whole point of a vigilante is to terrify the terrible—to strike fear into the hearts of evildoers.

Human psychology has two basic reactions to images of darkness and horror: the first is to be horrified, as if we saw a monster; the second is to be curious what it would be like to horrify, as if we were the monster. For those of us who are not particular fans of stories told from the point of view of vampires, that curiosity can be made palatable if the horrific monster preys only on the guilty. Bats are creepy—but there are creeps in the world who deserve to be scared. For them, there is the Batman.

3. THE MAN IN BLACK

The idea is one with an ancient lineage. Before the Shadow was Zorro, and before them both was the Scarlet Pimpernel and even Spring-heel'd Jack (who, at least in the 1904 version by Alfred Burrage, was a nocturnal hero). As far back as Robin Hood, people have been telling tales and singing songs about dark avengers who step outside the law to right wrongs—remember that the gay and carefree Robin Hood was a highwayman, the very Prince of Thieves, and his Lincoln Green was originally meant as camouflage so he could blend into the green shadows of Sherwood Forest the same way Batman's black cape blends into the dark shadows of Gotham City. These men were good guys dressed in the uniform of bad guys—masks and hoods and black hats and black cloaks and so on.

The theme is one that gained popularity during the pulp era. The Shadow and Zorro inhabited cheap popular magazines in their heyday, and also appeared and appear in "Cliffhanger" serials, radio plays, comic books, paperbacks, and so on. Why the pulps? Because cheap popular entertainment is designed to entertain at the lowest common denominator. Pulps are childish in the same way comics are childish, by which I mean they have a simplicity and a mythic grandeur to them; they are about important things like justice and revenge and adventure that grown-up stories are too tired, too artistic, or too erudite to bother about.

4. DON'T THE IDLE RICH HAVE ANYTHING BETTER TO DO?

A common denominator of these nocturnal avengers is that they are rich boys. The Green Arrow, who is DC Comic's answer to Robin Hood, is Oliver Queen, millionaire; the Phantom, another non-superpowered crime-fighter with an eerie name and motif, in truth is the rich playboy Jimmy Wells; the Shadow is Lamont Cranston, millionaire playboy and world traveler (unless he is actually flying ace Kent Allard . . . only the

Shadow knows!); Zorro is Don Diego de la Vega, conceited dandy of the caballero class; the Scarlet Pimpernel is Sir Percy Blakeney, rich, empty-headed fop and titled aristocrat; Spring-heel'd Jack (in Burrage's 1904 version) is Bertram Wraydon, heir to 10,000 pounds a year; coming full circle, Robin Hood was the Baron of Loxley. All these are variations on one theme: What is it about the life of the idle rich that compels writers to cast them in penny dreadfuls and comic books playing the role of spooky masked avengers?

There are other parallels running between these masked avengers. Spring-heel'd Jack used his wealth to outfit his secret lair, where he donned an odd costume with mane and talons and special shoes outfitted to allow him the tremendous leaps that gave the character his name; Zorro had a secret silver mine, a cave where he kept the stall for his steed, Tornado; the Phantom had his secret lair in Skull Mountain; the Shadow had a mysterious sanctum somewhere in Manhattan, a chamber without lights, which is the closest one can get to a cave and keep it in the Big City.

Why a cave rather than, say, a headquarters on the eighty-sixth floor of the Empire State Building or, better yet, a Fortress of Solitude above the Arctic Circle, perhaps made entirely out of unearthly white crystal? That question answers itself: one can lurk in a cave, or brood in a cave; the cave is a natural habitat for dark monsters or dark men dressed as monsters. Remote super-fortresses and skyscrapers equipped with scientific wonders are reserved for a different type of hero altogether.

One reason why the recurring Dark Avenger is always one of the idle rich is for the convenience of the author, who need never explain where he gets all those wonderful toys with which he fights crime. Do you know how much a 1955 Lincoln Futura costs, once it is outfitted with an atomic motor, particle-beam weapons, armor, battering ram, mobile crime lab, and six varieties of Bat-shark-repellent?[1]

Another reason is the author's sense of ironic contrast: No one is more worthless to society than a rich fop spending his father's hard-earned wealth, whereas no one is more needed by society than a champion of the poor and an avenger of the oppressed. No one is more unlikely to

[1] Editor's Note: To find out, see Darren Hudson Hick's essay, "The Cost of Being Batman," in this book.

possess the steel-eyed cunning, the iron discipline, the brazen nerve, the sheer brass, and the undefeatable mastery of his weapon, whether it be a Toledo steel rapier, a .45 automatic, or a bat-shaped boomerang.

Another reason is the character's own sense of ironic contrast. He is the last person Sergeant Gonzales, Shiwan Khan, or Two-Face will ever suspect of being his nemesis.

The sheer absurdity of the conceit is part of its appeal. An ex-marine taking up the arms he is skilled with to join the police force and go fight crime is heroic, but not dramatic; a lazy playboy driving himself to be as tough as a marine, to dress up as a giant bat to go fight crime, is both heroic and dramatic. Comics and pulps are not about the likely things that happen every day. Newspapers are about that. Comics and pulps are about the things so unlikely that they make a great story: things that happen once in a lifetime, or once in human history, or things that never could happen, but we wish they would.

5. SO YOU'RE IN LOVE WITH ADAM WEST? . . .

The Batman stands out from his fellow dark knights due to the severity of the personal tragedy that marred his life: Zorro did not as a child have his parents murdered before his eyes.

Girls take note: A guy with no emotional scars has nothing in his life that needs fixing. Such guys it might be wiser to marry, but not so much fun to fall in love with. Let's face it, guys: women tend to look at potential mates as fixer-uppers.

One problem that plagues any attempt to talk about a character as old as Batman, who has been under the direction of so many artists and reinterpreted in so many media comics, serials, radio plays, television, movies, even video games (is there anything he hasn't been in?) is that there is no canonical version of the character.

There ought to be two different words for the word "character." One word should refer to someone like Hamlet, who stars in one sequence of events, under the pen of one Shakespeare, in one play, and that is that. Such a character cannot be studied separate from the one play in which he appears, and there is only one artist who created him.

Another word entirely should refer to characters who exist, and are meant to exist, in eternal and episodic form. There is no one definitive version of the Shadow—can he cloud men's minds or does he merely use a black cape and stage magician's sleight of hand to disappear? The radio play said one thing, and the pulp magazines said another. These eternal champions have one adventure after another, never age and never die, or at least not for long. They cannot marry or change costumes for that long, unless the audience is willing to accept the change; otherwise it is only a matter of time before the next artist, or the next movie version, goes back to the better known original roots of the myth.

6. ONE CHARACTER IN MANY HANDS

But no matter the state of the English language, the Batman is such a character. If you think of Adam West, or George Clooney, you have a very different mental picture from the Dark Knight of Tim Burton. Some variations were camped up and played for laughs; others were grimmed down and played for darker emotions. But no matter the variation, certain themes and motifs remain ever-present.

Even in the campy television version, criminals were a cowardly and superstitious lot, frightened of the Batman; he was still the world's greatest detective, even though his deductions were goofy leaps of logic aided by a goofy-looking version of the Batcomputer; he still was unbeatable in fisticuffs, even if the sound effects were written on the screen for comic exaggeration; he was still the most dangerous man on the planet, even though he was played by a slightly hammy actor.

But, to be honest, no girl is really going to flip over the campy version of Batman; he is not meant to be taken seriously. Part of the humor of having the jaw-droppingly gorgeous Julie Newmar, her perfectly formed, statuesque five-foot-eleven squeezed into a skintight black catsuit, making eyes at Batman, was that Batman was played utterly straight-laced and square, unable to react to any of the glamour Amazon's alluring advances with other than strict Victorian courtesy. It was played for laughs, but even so, the television show still portrayed Batman as strong and intelligent and ergo attractive to women (more than one supervillainess or gun moll or lovely Russian reporter from the *Moscow Bugle* cooed over this strength). It was merely funny that he was.

7. BATMAN'S BROWNSHIRTS

It should be noted that the opposite extreme, Frank Miller's militaristic take on the caped crusader in *Batman: The Dark Knight Returns*, is equally unappealing to the fair sex. The glamour and drama of a dark avenger of the night drop away when he becomes a bloodthirsty vigilante, not merely stepping outside the law to right a wrong but rejecting the law altogether. Miller's Batman is a personification of anger, a living embodiment of the idea that society is corrupt, policemen and politicians are too small and too inept to deal with the chaos of a broken world, and only a strong man on a white horse (Frank Miller actually puts the dark knight on a white horse in one scene), only, I say, the strong leader chosen by destiny—can trample the laws and constitution that have failed the people and lead the world to a glorious destiny . . . once the subhuman rabble have had their backs broken in a bare-knuckle brawl.

While I acknowledge Mr. Miller's genius as a storyteller, I would have preferred he not depict a character beloved of generations as some sort of cross between Mussolini and a cage match wrestler.

As if the parallels were not sufficiently clear, at one point Batman actually rounded up street thugs, the Mutant gang, and turned them into Brownshirts, the none-too-subtly named Sons of Batman (S.O.B.s get it?). He then used them to restore order during the hyper-inflation caused by the incompetence of the Weimar government . . . oh, excuse me, I mean the social chaos that followed a nuclear detonation blotting out the sun, of course, and the incompetence of the American government.[2]

If I am in a mood for anger and gore I can read about Miller's version of Batman with some pleasure, but he seems to me no more related to the real Batman than Alan Moore and Dave Gibbons' Rorschach from *The Watchman* was like Steve Ditko's the Question. Ditko's character was

---

[2] Yes, I am not kidding, the U.S. government is the villain in Mr. Miller's little morality play, the one that sent Superman to take down Batman because Batman's success had become an embarrassment to the administration. And we all know Supes is a mindless thug obeying his corporate Masters, because anyone wrapped in the flag or salutes it must be evil, right, Frank?

an intelligent but pitiless Ayn Randian; Moore and Gibbons dismissed Randianism as lunacy and portrayed Rorschach as a lunatic. A brutal, sick, twisted version of the character might be interesting for a four-issue mini-series, in the same way a "what if" story where Superman was raised by Communists and used his power to crush truth, justice, and the American Way rather than support it might be interesting. But Miller broke up the friendship between Superman and Batman because the limitations in Mr. Miller's personal philosophy could not allow him to take such a friendship seriously. To Miller, Batman is a symbol of the brutality he worships and fantasizes about, the chaos of the night creatures; Superman is a symbol of law and order incompatible with the night-beast. Law and order, here, is depicted as selling out to the military-industrial complex. And so Miller broke up the oldest and best friendship between the World's Finest heroes, something for which Mr. Miller should never be forgiven. Batman defeated Superman, faked his own death, and then led a private army into caves beyond the Batcave in order to continue his fight—this time not against criminals, but against everything Superman stands for.

Miller's bloodstained version of the character has no more sex appeal than Adam West's campy Victorian version, but for the opposite reason. The television Batman is too perfect to want or need a woman to improve him; the Miller version is too broken. The point of the character, or of any dark avenger of the night, is to scare the villains with villainy greater than theirs while protecting the innocent—to wear the monster's mask but have the heart of a hero beneath. The point is not to be a monster. The comedy version of this character is not scary; the heartless version is too scary.

But let us not stray too far from the main point: In the spectrum from campiness to brutality, the essential character of the Batman remains, even if one artist or another exaggerates a particular characteristic of the character for comic or tragic effect. He is supposed to be the most dangerous man on the planet, the smartest and toughest.

8. HEROES OF THE DAYLIGHT

The opposite, or the complement, to DC's flagship character Batman is, of course, the superhero who invented the superhero genre: Superman.

In the way that Batman is all about fear, Superman is not at all about fear. He is about chivalry. To be blunt, he is all about the strength of character it takes to stomach humility.

The idea of a superman, the next step in human evolution who would be to us as we were to apes, is one that has fascinated the imagination ever since Darwin. Any author who addresses this concept betrays his thoughts on what gives mankind its evolutionary advantage. H. G. Wells portrayed his invading Martians as creatures composed entirely of brain, cool and ruthless, rational and dispassionate—for, to him, dispassionate reasoning was the essence of man. Nietzsche, who first coined the term "superman," identified the next step in evolution with ruthless pagan heroics—a strong-willed beast able to shrug aside the fetters of common morality and notions of decency, and to do whatever his roaring heart desired, while lesser men fawned and cowered and were amazed. Both these men portrayed a repellent ideal of superhumanity: intellect unchecked by pity, might unchecked by scruples.

Jerry Siegel and Joe Shuster, two Jewish immigrants of humble origins and big dreams, boys who penned a comic book for kids, understood the concept better than these high-minded European philosophers and literati. For them, the Superman is a hero who helps others, taking no reward and asking none. Even the reward of public recognition is denied him—Clark Kent gets no parades. For these two comic book writers, the next step in evolution meant a figure with greater moral stature than human, not less.

Now, a character who is invulnerable, invincible, and perfect does not allow much scope for tension and drama. When your character is undefeated in battle, the battlefield is not where his drama lies: Lancelot's drama is in his love life, in how his loyalty to his friend and king is at odds with his painful, hopeless, dangerous, dishonorable love for his queen. Achilles cannot be hurt; we are not on the edge of our seat, fearing his downfall, when he fights Hector, but we are fascinated when Priam comes in secret to beg the body from the proud hero's blood-stained, invincible hands.

Siegel and Shuster made a character even more puissant than Achilles or Lancelot, but they added a twist that neither the king of Phthia nor the aristocratic queen's champion would recognize. (But which the mighty Thor or Arjuna, the hero of the Hindu poem Mahabharata, might; Thor and Arjuna spend at least part of their lives in humble disguise.) The whole point of Superman is that he is not really Superman; he is Clark Kent. He is not really the last son of Krypton, a planet that brought forth a race of highly advanced superbeings; he truly is the son of a Kansas farmer and an All-American boy.

9. ALL-AMERICAN BOY

Superman has never, in any incarnation, acted mysterious or alien. He has never acted like a man from another planet. He has never looked, either with pity or condescension, on human beings as an inferior species. That is because, in his heart, he is Clark Kent, humble farm-boy.

One of the more interesting interpretations I have heard recently of the psychology of Superman came, oddly enough, from the bloody samurai movie *Kill Bill: Vol. 2*. Bill, the villain of the piece, says Kal-El dresses like Clark because that's what the Last Son of Krypton thinks human beings are really like: weak, ineffectual, mild-mannered goofs in glasses. The interpretation is interesting, but dead wrong, and the movie was honest enough to put this interpretation in the mouth of a remorseless killer. If that were the true interpretation of the character, there would be no character—that is, no dramatic tension, no paradox between his super-identity and civilian-identity. Superman would be merely mocking us, the under-men, by pretending to be us. He would be like Tarzan wearing an ape suit in order to get along with the lower order of life who raised him, or Mowgli wrapped in a wolf-pelt, pretending not to know how to use fire; the superhuman with contempt in his heart for the subhuman is a character of no drama and no interest, except, perhaps, as villains, in, say, the *War of the Worlds*.

Kal-El at heart is and must be Clark Kent first, and Superman only in emergencies, in order for the character to be true to the American Way he represents.

10. JUST A WORKING STIFF FROM SMALLVILLE

Americans, as a nation, have never been comfortable with the role of the nobility—we are the only superpower in history that has turned its back on Empire. No matter how little we interfere with other nations (or rescue them, take your pick), even a little, for many among us, is too much. We are a Clark Kent nation at heart: we don't mind turning into Superman when "This Is a Job for Superman," but we want to put on the glasses, battered hat, and the red tie as soon as possible, and go back to our daily jobs. That was certainly the sentiment during and after World War II, when Superman first became popular.

As an idealized version of the All-American, one thing Clark Kent cannot be is an aristocrat. He is not rich; he is not famous. He is a mild-mannered newspaperman who cannot get a date. He lets himself, when he is Clark, get shoved aside. Men cut in on him when he is dancing. He waits in the traffic jams on the way to work just like every other working slob.

One of the most worshipful and puissant knights of the Round Table, the invincible Sir Beaumains, is here disguised as a kitchen drudge, and still must woo and win the fair but proud Elaine, who looks down on his low station with disdain. Clark is the champion playing the court fool. The whole point of Lois Lane, the thing that gives her character her particular dramatic twist, is that she is a high-class lady. She is a Big City gal, a prize-winning reporter, sharp-witted and good-looking. She is everything the bumpkin from Hicksville looks up to and cannot approach.

11. EVOLUTION AND ETERNAL RETURN

There is the answer, by the way, why Superman has a steady girlfriend.

Comic book characters undergo changes and revisions as they pass from author to author and medium to medium.

Some things are added and stay as part of the myth: Superman's famous line about "This is a job for . . ." (drop voice an octave) " . . . Superman!" was added as an audible cue in the radio play to tell listeners he was now in his cape and tights. Superman could not fly in the comics until the Max Fleischer cartoons; before, he jumped over an eighth of a mile and leaped tall buildings, but jumping looked silly in the moving pictures.

Other things, like being killed or turning into a being of blue electricity, don't last. By and large, readers like the old ideas best; when Supergirl is an artificial life form merged at death with a girl and an angel of fire, created by Lex Luthor in a pocket universe that, uh . . . then she travels back in time to become her own mother, so that . . . never mind. Next time she's revived, Supergirl is Superman's cousin again. Some changes don't stick.

Lois Lane, on the other hand, no matter what the reboot or the change of medium, is always going to be Superman's girlfriend. His character has no innate drama without her; Superman would be just one more teen power fantasy, were he not in love with the one girl he cannot have, who only loves his secret hero identity. The two-sided love triangle was so successful in Superman that nearly every other superhero book copied it: Hal Jordan loves Carol Ferris who loves Green Lantern; Diana Prince loves Steve Trevor who loves Wonder Woman; and so on and so forth.

Superman is all about chivalry: if he ever chases another woman, if he looks at another woman, it breaks the archetype. He is a hero of the daylight, pure and chaste and good as a knight of old. He cannot play the playboy or ladies' man for the same reason he cannot be wealthy and famous in his secret identity—the contrast with his hero identity, and thus the drama, is lost.

There was a short-lived Saturday morning cartoon called *Super President*; the concept was (you guessed it) after managing the affairs of state in war and peace, vetoing bills, and acting as commander-in-chief, President James Norcross, equipped with powers born in a cosmic storm, would don his cowl and cape and fly off through a secret exit buried under the White House to fight space monsters, evil scientists, and mutants. Never heard of him? Not surprising. When your "Clark Kent" has the arsenal of the Free World at his fingertips, it is really pointless to rocket out in your Omnicar to engage in fisticuffs with the mad genius known as Witch Doctor.

Super President lacked the basic chemistry of that super, mild-mannered little man. Because we have all, at one time or another, been the mild-mannered nobody and we have all sometimes wondered what it would be like to pull the shirt of our conventional appearance aside and reveal the brawny chest and blazing insignia of a champion. For the chemistry to work its magic, Superman has to be secretly what we secretly wish we were, and openly the same as we are openly, just one more shy jerk in glasses mooning after Lois, the most popular girl around. The drama is that Superman could very easily win any girl on the planet, most likely, but he has to remain totally devoted to the one he cannot have, as pure as a White Knight of old.

12. HEROES OF THE NIGHT

Batman is not a White Knight but a Dark one.

He is as dangerous as a panther at night, and as silent. This stealth is unnatural, spooky. In every comic book and animated cartoon put out recently, Bats has the eerie ability to slip out of sight even while people are talking to him. The normal mortal pauses to light a cigarette or look at his watch or something and Batman is gone, making no more noise than a ghost. If Bruce Wayne did not actually learn the power Lamont Cranston has to Cloud Men's Minds when he was away studying in Tibet, he might as well have.

Like the Shadow, Batman is stealthy and creepy; like Zorro, he is cunning like a fox. Like Sir Percy Blakeney, he plays the fop.

Batman playing the playboy is different from Superman playing the fool, but the need for contrast is the same. Why?

The Dark Knight has to be dangerous—the kind of man who might, just might, throw a crook off a rooftop. The Batman's mission in life is to dress in the uniform of a villain, black cape and all, to show the villains what it feels like to be on the receiving end of villainy. Superman is all about mercy. Batman is all about justice—and it is a grim, dark justice, too, or else the drama is lost.

One aspect of justice that makes it dramatic is its implacability: No one escapes it. No one deceives it. The Batman can track you in the dark because he has a Bat-tracer on your car. Do you think you can get away? The Shadow *Knows*. Even the Pimpernel is damned and elusive. The vigilante who might be anywhere might as well be an angel of vengeance who is everywhere.

13. THE CODE AND THE CIPHER

Here we see the full contrast. Superman is merciful because, since he is as strong as a god, it would be so tempting and so easy for him not to be merciful.

Clark Kent has to look weaker than he really is, or else there is no superhuman humility. Without humility, there is no drama. Like most virtues, humility is what makes life dramatic, for the drama is whether a man can be strong enough to be weak. He is his own foe, and so the forces are evenly opposed. The stakes are the highest—his soul hangs in the balance. On the other hand, vices are boring, and pride is the most boring of all. Anyone who has ever listened to a braggart can tell you how unexciting a prospect it is.

The drama for all the Dark Knights, not just Batman but any character of that archetype, is the temptation all policemen, jurors, and judges face in real life: it is the temptation to be unjust in the name of justice. The temptation to go too far, to say the ends justify the means.

The reason why a portrayal of Batman merely as a brutal vigilante—no matter how well told—is treason against the character is precisely because this essential element of the drama of virtue drops out. Justice is a difficult balancing act in the soul, and therefore dramatic, the only real drama in life; brutality is easy, therefore boring.

The Dark Knight turns pride on its head. It is the arrogance of the criminals that will prove their downfall. No one suspects the worthless millionaire playboy.

Be strong and be meek! So says the code of the White Knight.

Be dangerous and look weak and worthless, so that your foe will underestimate you and be destroyed. So says the stealthy strategy of the Dark Knight.

14. THE ANIMAL MAGNETISM OF THE BAT

Having said all this, the reason for the sexual appeal of the untamed beast of Bruce Wayne over the White Knight of Clark Kent should be plain to see.

By the very nature of what it means to be a dark vigilante, all such Zorro-types are rebels who play by their own rules. They are "bad boys" who dress like villains even to the black hat and black cape. Hence, they have the romance of a villain without actually being a villain. And women find villains alluring—look at how many pirates and bold highwaymen appear on the front cover of lurid paperback romances. Women sigh over the "bad boy" even if they end up marrying the good boy.

Batman's civilian identity cannot be a mild-mannered normal working-man for the same reason Superman cannot be Super President. Drama requires a sharp contrast: the dark avenger needs must appear in the eyes of the world as a lazy, self-indulgent playboy in order for the contrast with his inner steel to be clear.

In order to maintain this contrast, in order to play the fop while being the deadliest blade in Spain (or the deadliest batarang in Gotham), the dark avenger must be a man of absolutely stern conviction, utterly devoted to his cause.

Devoted? Or driven? For Robin Hood, the injustice of the usurping King John drove him to his career of vengeance; for Zorro, it was the injustice meted out to the peons; for Batman, it was the death of his parents.

To be truly dark, the dark avenger has to be tormented by inner demons. He is a man of unparalleled passion and conviction, his true nature repressed, hidden beneath an icy cold exterior. He is like some sleeping volcano seen in the distance, crowned with snow and seemingly calm, but beneath, an inferno. Batman is the Rhett Butler of the comic book world.

If that does not explain the appeal to women of the Batman, dear reader, all I can say is that you maybe read too many comic books, and not enough lurid romance novels.

JOHN C. WRIGHT is a retired attorney, newspaperman, and newspaper editor. The spectacular unsuccess of these ventures drove him into science fiction writing. He presently works as a writer in Virginia, where he lives in fairytale-like happiness with his wife, the authoress L. Jagi Lamplighter, and their three children: Orville, Wilbur, and Just Wright.

His works include *The Golden Age* (2002), *Last Guardian of Everness* (2004), and Nebula Award finalist *Orphans of Chaos*. His authorized sequel to A. E. van Vogt's *World of Null-A* is called *Null-A Continuum*. His short fiction has appeared in anthologies and magazines, including *Year's Best SF 3* (David

Hartwell, Ed.), *Year's Best Science Fiction* (Gardner Dozois, Ed.), *Year's Best Short Novels* (Johnathan Strahan, Ed.), *The Night Lands* (Andy W. Robertson, Ed.), *Absolute Magnitude*, and *Asimov's Science Fiction*.

So there I am, reading Kristine Kathryn Rusch's contribution to this book, having a reservation here and there but agreeing with most of what Ms. Rusch wrote, and enjoying it, when I come to this one sentence and have one of those focusing moments: She's absolutely right! And then: Why didn't I think of that? You'll probably recognize the sentence when you get to it and, depending on your politics, be either celebratory or aghast.

BATMAN IN THE REAL WORLD

KRISTINE KATHRYN RUSCH

irst, a disclaimer: I like Batman. He is my favorite superhero. He's not true blue and loyal like Superman, but then he's not in love with the dumbest reporter on the planet, either. He's also not a young kid given incredible powers (by a radioactive spider, no less) who learns to properly use those powers while whining about it.

Batman doesn't whine. He never whined—not when his parents were murdered in front of him, not when he realized he was the only one who could save Gotham City from itself, not when he had to sacrifice love and a personal life to do his real job.

Unlike Superman, Batman never professes to be doing what he does for truth, justice, and the American Way. I'm not sure Batman believes in any of those things—except his truth and his justice.

And, oddly enough, that makes him the most American of all the superheroes. And the most terrifying.

Yeah, yeah, I know. When Superman is influenced by red (or is it black?) Kryptonite, he gets really mean. We learn what a Kryptonian villain could be like. But meanness is not part of Superman's core personality, so we understand that eventually he will return to his very good self.

When Spider-Man becomes Venom, we realize that we're better off when Peter Parker whines. Venom forgets about the great responsibility that comes with great power. He simply uses that power the way all supervillains do—for evil.

Batman already straddles the line between good and evil. He uses the darkness in service of the light. That's why Frank Miller's *The Dark Knight Returns* did so well in the mid-1980s, because Miller went back to Batman's roots. Miller found Batman's essential nature.

And at his core, Batman is—like most iconic American heroes—a mean, violent son of a bitch.

HEROISM, AMERICAN STYLE

Let's talk a little bit about the ideal American. Let's look at the traits (good and bad) that our collective past has given us.

Trait #1: Americans Rebel Against Authority

It's bred into our bones. From the Boston Tea Party to the Declaration of Independence to the Revolutionary War, Americans have fought against the established order from the moment we identified ourselves as Not-British.

Trait #2: Americans Have Our Own Way of Doing Things

Also bone-deep. A different way to state this is that once we've overthrown the establishment, we take charge. The Founding Fathers led the country that they created. They wrote a great document delineating rules for governance (so that the country wouldn't fall back on its evil Old World roots)— and then they proceeded to change, break, ignore, and refine those rules just because they could.

Trait #3: The American Way of Doing Things Is Often Violent

Our nation was born in war. We slaughtered our way across this continent, conquering natives as we went. We created frontier justice—which was essentially the rule of the strongest.

We cling to our guns, not because we're all homicidal maniacs but because we know in our cowboy roots that those guns might come in handy some day. To defend our home. To defend our land. To get rid of the bad guys, whoever they might be.

Trait #4: Americans Believe in the Power of the Individual

It's built into our Bill of Rights, which protects individual rights, sometimes at the detriment of the state. No other nation protects its individual citizens as much as we do. Individuals moved West, sometimes establishing homes on a barren prairie with no one else around. Individuals established towns and counties and states.

Individuals created this great nation and, by gum, we're going to make sure we can continue on our individual ways—or America just wouldn't be America anymore.

Trait #5: Americans Believe We Are Always Right

We know we were right to break away from the Old World. We claimed the moral high ground then, and we've never let go of it. The Old World is tired; we're still a young, strong, and vibrant nation. The Old World happened; we were created. Our creation, by men of intellect and men of strength (sorry, ladies, historians don't give us a lot of credit in the nation's founding), makes us unique. And better than everyone else.

We learn that in school. And because we're surrounded by oceans on two sides and a permeable border with a country that has modeled itself more on us than its mother country (sorry, Canada) and a country that can't seem to govern itself effectively (you know who you are, Mexico), we rarely have citizens of other nations pouring across our borders to contradict us. We're right. We know it because no one argues with us.

And really, who can?

Traits the Other

There are tons of minor and major corollaries that I could list for pages and pages. For example, Americans don't trust inherited wealth (too Old

World) but love the self-made man (very New World); Americans are inventive (from Benjamin Franklin to Thomas Edison, from Henry Ford to Bill Gates, American inventors have changed the world in ways that no other inventors have); Americans have a can-do attitude, which probably comes from all our natural wealth (which we stole and slaughtered for, but we don't discuss that).

In short, America's national character is self-righteous, violent, and powerful. On the surface, we seem to be frivolous and fun-loving (we invented the movies and video games and baseball), but only if everyone else stays out of our face.

When someone pushes us, we get mean.

And behind that meanness is an incredible national darkness—a tolerance for all sorts of nastiness so long as the ultimate goal is noble.

Or maybe, so long as we believe the ultimate goal is noble.

STREET JUSTICE

What does this history lesson have to do with Batman?

Everything.

Superman might stand for truth, justice, and the American Way, but he's an alien—an illegal one at that. Superman works hard at maintaining all the best traits of Americans—a can-do attitude, the kindness we all believe ourselves capable of, a deep loyalty. But he's not us and he never has been.

Batman is.

Batman is a self-made man. No radioactive spider gave him superpowers. He's not a mutant, nor is he an alien conveniently dropped into a Kansas field.

He chose to become Batman.

This is an important—and American—distinction.

Bruce Wayne started as a victim—a child who witnessed his parents' murders. He becomes a powerful crime fighter, both feared and trusted by those he helps.

Bruce Wayne built his alter ego from nothing—less than nothing, despite his inherited wealth. He lacked the very thing that Clark Kent got by landing in Kansas—a loving, supportive family.

From that frightened, grieving child, Bruce Wayne pulled the most formidable of emotions.

A desire for vengeance.

Retribution.

Revenge.

Batman is not about serving the greater good. Truthfully, he doesn't care that great power brings great responsibility. Bruce Wayne understands responsibility. He nods at it. But he swore vengeance as a child, and a creature of vengeance is what he has become.

Bruce Wayne could have used that incredible brain of his to improve his investments. He could have put all his money into various trusts—trusts that would help the homeless, try to eradicate poverty, educate underprivileged children.

Instead, he only put some of his money there. Wayne, despite his playboy image, is Gotham City's most important philanthropist—and, we're led to believe, its most generous.

Yet he spends about 3.5 million dollars every year on his Batman alter ego, at least according to a *Forbes* article published just before *Batman Begins* premiered (Forbes.com).[1] Three and a half million dollars that could heal the sick or improve lighting in Gotham City. (Street lights alone would probably eradicate half the petty thefts in that dark place.)

But Bruce Wayne is not, as those lovely commentators on *FOX News* would say, a namby-pamby liberal who believes that social programs will change the truly evil among us. He believes that some criminals are just bad. Some are evil. And some are truly monstrous.

Social programs won't change the evil or the truly monstrous. Social programs will only stop the average criminal. Give that average criminal good health care, enough to eat, a good education, maybe someone to love him, and he'll grow up to be a model citizen.

But the Penguins, the Two-Faces, the Jokers of the world, they'll never be reformed by a full belly and a comfortable place to sleep. They'll want more—and someone will have to stop them from taking it.

Someone good, like Batman.

---

[1] Online at www.legionsofgotham.org/FeatureHISTORYbeingbatman.html. Editor's Note: You can also see an alternate accounting of how much it would cost to be Batman in Darren Hudson Hick's essay, "The Cost of Being Batman," in this volume.

In this, Bruce Wayne is quintessentially American. We give more money to impoverished nations than any other nation in the world. Yet we're quick to judge a less advantaged nation "evil" and, at least in recent years, even quicker to take military action against it.

Or, let's take this out of the international arena and into the national. These days, no one advocates a strictly social solution to the nation's ills like some politicians (and sociologists) did in the 1960s. Now even namby-pamby liberals won't propose providing our poorest citizens' basic needs without also recognizing the need to beef up police presence and to have enough jails.

Americans still believe that people should be held responsible for their actions and that no one should get a free pass just because of extreme poverty or a terrible upbringing. We do what we can to alleviate both, but we also expect people to pull themselves up by their bootstraps (what an American expression) and conquer the challenges of their youth.

After all, we can all cite examples of someone who grew up poor and has become a scion of society, or someone who was horribly abused and has gone on to become a great humanitarian.

So Batman's roots make him a traditional American. But does he have the traits listed above, the ones historically tied to Americans?

1. Batman Rebels Against Authority

He believes that the government of Gotham City has broken down. Indeed, in the early Batman comics, Gotham City has no real government. It's a chaotic, lawless place where the people who try to maintain the rules are a laughingstock or worse, as corrupt as the people who break them.[2]

Because the government has broken down, Batman has no use for its services. He doesn't call the police when something goes wrong. He

---

[2] This, by the way, is a very accurate 1930s view of the world. Batman made his first appearance in *Detective Comics* #27 in May 1939. The Depression still raged. People had lived with hopelessness for a very long time. Most city governments were ineffectual if not corrupt. Who wouldn't look for a hero to solve these problems? But the hero would have to be equal to the darkness.

solves it himself.

And that is pure rebellion—dissing authority and doing something that authority disapproves of.

2. Batman Does Things His Way

After he grew up, Bruce Wayne saw a problem in Gotham City. Crime was just as bad as it had been when he was a child. And what did he do?

Better to ask what he didn't do. He didn't run for election—which he could easily have done with all his millions. He didn't join the police academy or the FBI. He didn't go into law enforcement.

He became something other. That something other was also quintessentially American—and I'll get to it in a moment.

For now, let's continue down our checklist.

3. Batman's Way of Doing Things Is Often Violent

Well, duh.

4. Batman Believes in the Power of the Individual

Another "well, duh."

5. Batman Believes He's Right

Because he almost always is. And that's the fiction part, which we will get to shortly.

All these elements combine to create a superhero who is different from the other superheroes (at least in the Golden Age pantheon).

Because of his lack of extraordinary powers, Batman isn't really a "super" hero. He is something else.

Something as American as apple pie.

Batman is a vigilante.

VIGILANTES, SUPERHEROES, AND THE AMERICAN WAY OF JUSTICE

The word "*vigilante*" is Spanish, and it means watchful.[3] When used to describe a man or a woman, it means watchman or guard.[4] My handy-dandy *Encarta World English Dictionary*, thoughtfully provided by my software company, describes "vigilante" as used in English thusly: "Someone who punishes lawbreakers personally and illegally rather than relying on legal authorities."

This definition implies but doesn't expressly state an important part of being a vigilante: vigilantes punish lawbreakers using whatever means necessary.

And that's where it gets ugly.

Vigilantes or vigilante groups in American history run the gamut from bounty hunters to the Ku Klux Klan. The word itself, in its English usage, comes from the American South. In the 1830s, "vigilance committees" formed to silence (read: arrest or kill) blacks and abolitionists. The people who composed those committees were referred to as *vigilantes* (Barnhart and Metcalf 157).

Vigilantes aren't by definition criminals. In fact, criminologists have had a hard time figuring out exactly what vigilantes are. One of the first real attempts to define vigilantism came in 1975, and the conclusion sounds quite familiar to the loyal Batman reader: Vigilantism represented "'morally sanctimonious' behavior aimed at rectifying or remedying a 'structural flaw' in society," usually in a place where the law was ineffectual or completely unenforced (Brown).

The difference between acting like a vigilante and acting in self-defense is that acting like a vigilante is premeditated. If Bruce Wayne had somehow taken the gun from that robber who murdered his parents and shot the man, Wayne would have been acting in self-defense. Instead, a few nights later, Wayne made a vow—"I swear by the spirits of my parents to avenge their deaths by spending the rest of my life warring on all criminals" (quoted in Jones 154).

---

[3] El esta vigilante. "He is watchful." Or in English, "He is vigilant."

[4] El es un vigilante. "He is a guard."

And one more thing about vigilantes, at least according to those criminologists (who are just starting to figure out that they'd better study this phenomenon)—vigilantes do not care about the law. They care about justice—as they *define* justice.

Which is where the entire idea breaks down.

You see, what places Batman in the same category as the Grand Wizard of the Ku Klux Klan is that personal definition of justice—and the fact that the justice must be meted out quickly. There are no courts, no real investigation, and no room for error.

The person being punished is wrong, at least in the eyes of the vigilante. And if the vigilante is wrong, well then, the person he punished has already suffered.

Fortunately, Batman is always right.

BATMAN FOR PRESIDENT

By now, some of you are thinking, "What the heck is with this woman? I thought she said she liked Batman."

And I do. He is my favorite superhero, which is why I had the disclaimer up front.

But in the real world, Batman and his ilk are often not just on the wrong side of the law, but on the wrong side of justice—and, equally bad, the wrong side of history.

If you go to Google's Advance Search and type in "Batman," "vigilante," and "George W. Bush," you will get several hundred hits. And that's no accident.

President George Walker Bush is the closest thing we've had to Batman in a long time.

Think about it. Bush comes from money. He was, once upon a time, a millionaire playboy. He had to redefine himself in the face of his own past. He rebels against authority. He has no respect for the law—often taking it into his own hands to the chagrin (and now anger) of Congress, the Supreme Court, and a vast majority of the American people.[5]

---

[5] The polls issued the week I write this give Bush a 32 percent approval rating. Which by my math makes his disapproval rating somewhere around 70 percent.

Writers—from the odd blogger to reporters, from the magazine *The Progressive* to Reason Online—have taken this analogy farther. They point out that Bush, in his response to 9/11, repeated the essential flaw in the Batman origin story.

That flaw is this: When Bruce Wayne's parents are murdered, he doesn't seek revenge on his parents' killer. He seeks revenge on all criminals for all time.

After 9/11, Bush didn't go after the terrorists that attacked the World Trade Center. Instead he went after all terrorists, and plans to continue until they're gone.[6]

I could go on. The bloggers and the writers and the comic geeks do.[7] But that's somewhat beside the point.

Because Bush, as the world acknowledges, is practicing cowboy diplomacy. He's acting in a quintessentially American fashion—one anyone who consumes American media understands.

He's mining our stories to conduct his foreign policy and his presidency. I think he truly believes he's right in everything that he does.

And early on, Americans supported him in this behavior.

We believe in the lone wolf. We believe in the man who, for moral reasons, reacts in a solitary and often violent manner.

We believe in him—if he's always right.

And therein lies the rub.

Batman is a fictional character. He's on the side of good.

"We should remember that this is a comic book," writes Kristian Williams in a very political review of Frank Miller's *The Dark Knight Strikes Again*. "Superhero stories, however politicized, are still superhero stories. In them, unusually gifted and virtuous people (superheroes) fly around in ridiculous outfits saving the world from unusually gifted and vicious people (supervillains)" (Williams 39).

The problem comes when we start believing our own press. When we—as Americans—believe that we are always on the side of good and

---

[6] He has said repeatedly that the war on terror might not ever end.

[7] For example, see Thom Hartmann's "A Fistful of Kryptonite Against SuperGeorge . . ." at www.commondreams.org, or Ziauddin Sadar's "Holy Terror! Batman versus Bin Laden!" at www.newstatesman.com, or Pab Sungenis's "The Politics of Superheroes" at www.democraticunderground.com. Or just put "Batman," "vigilante," and "George W. Bush" into Google yourself. You'll be stunned. I was.

other people (who some of our politicians now call "the bad guys") are on the side of evil.

In the real world, such things aren't that simple.

If they were, George W. Bush wouldn't be president. He'd be living in a gothic mansion in one of our nation's largest cities. He'd have an older manservant who keeps him on the straight and narrow. He'd have a secret bunker in the basement. He'd have one of the coolest cars on the face of the Earth. . . .

Wait.

Scratch that. Some in the left-wing blogosphere could and do argue that Bush isn't president (by popular vote anyway), that he does live in a mansion in one of the nation's largest cities, a mansion with a secret bunker in the basement, and has access to some of the coolest cars on Earth. We're only stretching the analogy when we call Dick Cheney a manservant. . . .

And when we assume that Bush—or any other American—is always right.

Batman is the stuff of fiction.

And maybe that's why I like him when it should be pretty obvious to you, dear reader, that I don't like George W. Bush.

Batman is understandable. He comes from a dark place. He lives to avenge his past. He has created his superhero self from nothing. In other words, he was an ordinary boy until he turned himself into an extraordinary man.

And yes, I have to admit, I like the fact that he's always right. In the end (unless we're dealing with some of the nihilistic and dystopian comics), he always stops the worst criminals. He saves the world, just by being himself.

It's fantasy.

It's a fantasy I like.

Except when it creeps into the real world.

KRISTINE KATHRYN RUSCH is a bestselling author who has won everything from the Hugo Award to the World Fantasy Award. Many years ago, she wrote stories for several Batman anthologies. Her latest book is *The Recovery Man* from Roc books.

REFERENCES

Barnhart, David K. and Allan Metcalf. *America in So Many Words: Words That Have Shaped America*. Boston: Houghton Mifflin, 1999.

Brown, Richard Maxwell. *Strain of Violence: Historical Studies of American Violence and Vigilantism*. New York: Oxford University Press, 1975.

Forbes.com. "Being Batman." Forbes.com Magazine. <http://www.forbes.com/digitalentertainment/2005/06/20/batman-movies-superheroes-cx_de_0620batman.html>

Jones, Gerard. *Men of Tomorrow: Geeks, Gangsters, and the Birth of the Comic Book*. New York: Basic Books, 2004.

Williams, Kristian. "BATMAN versus THE MAN." *The Progressive* 67.3 (2003): 38–39.

Batman's childhood caregiver, Leslie Thompkins, was introduced not only to fill in a gap in Bruce Wayne's biography, but also to give the mythos a voice that denied the value of violence. By Leslie's standards, every time Batman slugs someone he's failed. And a psychotherapist might argue that Bruce's failure to let go of his childhood trauma constitutes an ongoing failure. So, from certain angles, the Caped Crusader's life has not been the unalloyed triumph many people think. David Seidman gives further examples in the following essay.

BATMAN, THE FAILURE

DAVID SEIDMAN

On March 30, 1981, John W. Hinckley shot President Ronald Reagan and his press secretary, James Brady. Brady and his wife, Sarah, took their pain, sorrow, and rage, and channeled them into a crusade against gun violence. Their lobbying succeeded: on November 30, 1993, President Bill Clinton signed the Brady Handgun Violence Prevention Act, a law requiring a five-day waiting period and background check on all handgun purchases. The Bradys continue to run the Brady Center to Prevent Gun Violence, which fights for gun control.

On July 27, about four months after the Brady shooting, someone kidnapped six-year-old Adam Walsh from a Florida department store. Sixteen days later, local authorities identified a small corpse as Adam. The boy's parents, John and Revé, took their pain, sorrow, and rage, and channeled them into a crusade against child abuse and other crimes. They founded the National Center for Missing and Exploited Children (NCMEC); John's television show, *America's Most Wanted*, has uncovered hundreds of criminals; and John led the charge for the Adam Walsh Child Protection and Safety Act to track and apprehend sex offenders, which President George W. Bush signed into law in 2006.

About fifteen to twenty years ago, depending on how you calculate it, a mugger killed the parents of young Bruce Wayne. Bruce took his pain, sorrow, and rage, and channeled them into a crusade against crime. Blessed with a brilliant brain, enormous wealth, and other resources, he put on a gray unitard and leaped off window ledges to punch muggers in the face.

If Bruce sounds a little silly next to the Walshes and Bradys—well, he is. It's not exactly a fair comparison, of course. The Bradys and Walshes were adults when they suffered their tragedies, and Bruce was only a child. More importantly, the Bradys and Walshes are real people, and Bruce is a fantasy hero. He exists to create thrills, not legislation.

Still, Batman isn't utterly a creature of myth and fable. His writers have worked like demons to make their star believable. They've probed Batman's personality as intimately as Georgia O'Keefe explored lilies. They've filled Gotham City with landmarks lifted from real-world New York. They've detailed the Batmobile's technical specifications, crafted fights (both physical and emotional) full of genuine pain, and developed a man and a world that have grabbed readers for generations. They've made Batman so convincing that it's simply right and respectful to treat him as if he were real and see how his world matches up to reality.

As it happens, Bruce isn't entirely different from real counterparts such as the Walshes and Bradys. He has his own version of the Brady Center and the NCMEC: the Wayne Foundation, which funnels his money into preventing crime and helping its victims. He's even had chances to change laws and government policies. In *Detective Comics* #179, he was mayor of Gotham City for a while. In *The Brave and the Bold* #85, he temporarily became a senator.

But he got out of those positions as soon as he could because they interfered with his crime-fighting, which is like the head of the United Way quitting his job because it interferes with his charitable work. And while Bruce funds the Wayne Foundation, he doesn't seem to put much time, attention, or passion into it. He'd rather be out on the streets as Batman, hitting people.

Unfortunately, all that hitting hasn't done much good. After all, Gotham City isn't getting safer. If anything, its criminals have grown more numerous and more vicious.

To be sure, Batman works hard at his holy war. But he works just as hard to hobble his own efforts.

Take the Batman costume. But first, think about other people who regularly put themselves in danger: infantry soldiers, riot cops, warplane pilots, mountain climbers, skydivers, and NASCAR drivers. Do they wear tights?

Heck, no! Leotards are great for ballerinas, but they're not very protective. I'll grant that Batman could devise tights a lot tougher than any Danskins. But he hasn't done it; his stories have shown gunfire, acids, and knives shred his suit.

Most people who put themselves in danger protect their heads with specially made helmets. Batman's cowl covers his head as thoroughly as any helmet, but it fits so snugly that it can't include the thick layers of protection that other headgear uses. As Batman observed in *The Dark Knight Returns*, "[I] can't armor my head." At the same time, the cowl covers his ears—not the smartest choice for someone who has to listen for ambushes.

The cowl's mask is even sillier. If you had to watch for sudden attacks from any and all directions, would you restrict your vision to two little eye holes? In *The Killing Joke*, the Joker even stuck his fingers through the holes and pulled the mask down. How he managed to do that without gashing out Batman's eyes is a mystery. In any event, the action blinded Batman long enough for the Joker to brain him with a two-by-four.

Flowing seamlessly from the cowl is the cape. Capes are dramatic, mysterious, impressive, and ridiculous. Why does Batman give his opponents something to grasp and pull—especially something connected to his neck? Even worse, it stretches out behind him where his eyes can't see and his arms can't reach. And have you ever tried to run in one of those things? Aerodynamic drag will pull you backward and slow you down. A decent gust of wind will yank the cape and push you off balance. And heaven forbid you have to pull off a quick pivot or about-face to reach out and hit somebody; the cape will get in your way and bind your arms.

Despite its oddities, Batman's not about to give up his costume. After all, it hides his identity as Bruce Wayne.

Except when it doesn't. Any number of people have uncovered Bruce's secret. The authoritative Batman volume of Michael Fleischer's *Encyclopedia of Comic Book Heroes* lists dozens of people who have discovered Bruce's identity, and the book covers only the period from 1939 to 1965.

The tradition has continued since. Some people have found the secret by research and deduction, including the villains Ra's al Ghul in *Batman* #232 and Hugo Strange in *Detective Comics* #471. Even a kid could do it; Tim Drake, the current Robin, doped it out at age nine, according to *Batman* #441. Others have done it by spending time with Bruce, like his bodyguard Sasha Bordeaux in *Detective Comics* #756. Still others found out because they knew whom to talk to. *Batman* #619, for instance, explained that Bruce's friend Tommy Elliott got it from the Riddler.

Finally, plenty of people simply stumble across Bruce's secrets. Blame Wayne Manor; the place practically invites people to find a hidden passageway to the Batcave. Alfred Pennyworth, Batman's butler—originally something of a buffoon—found the cave by sheer chance during *Batman* #16. The same thing happened to Jason Todd, a kid with no special deductive skills, in *Detective Comics* #526. (Jason would build up his brain after Batman took him in and made him the second Robin, but that transition came later.)

Wayne Manor is, in fact, a pretty loopy place for an urban adventurer. How Bruce can see Commissioner Gordon's bat-signal from there is hard to fathom, since the house sits in the suburbs more than a dozen miles outside the city limits. (Batman left the cave for an urban skyscraper in *Batman* #217, but he gradually came back.) Unless the Batmobile can fly, there's no way that Batman can reach a crime scene before Gordon's forensic team and the local *FOX News* affiliate probe every inch.

The Batmobile's a problem in itself. Imagine trying to push that giant brute through thickets of shoppers hunting for parking spaces, taxicabs trolling for nightclubbers, and squads of red-jacketed valets heading for parking lots. It doesn't even use a siren or flashing lights like any self-respecting police car.

Batman recognized the problem himself in *Detective Comics* #233. He was driving the Batmobile toward a robbery in progress when a new heroine, the Batwoman, whipped past him on a motorcycle and detoured off-road to beat him to the criminals. She shouted that her vehicle "can go where your Batmobile can't!" and Batman admitted, "That Bat-Cycle does give her a chance to short-cut." Although Batman has occasionally used motorcycles himself, he usually sticks with the bulky Batmobile.

Batwoman didn't stick around long, but other allies have. And in this area as well, Batman's judgment proves flaky. As his closest aides, he takes on Robin and Alfred: a small boy and an old man. Are they the best troops for someone going all-out to win a war?

Robin in particular is a weird choice. In 2005, comics journalist Matt Brady reported a talk by Bat writer Frank Miller and artist Jim Lee at the Wizard World Chicago comics convention. "Lee and Miller were both asked if they were bothered by the aspect of Robin as an underage kid in a brightly colored costume getting shot at, and Miller asked, 'Oh, you mean Robin, the Boy Target?'"

The boy doesn't even have decent clothes. His costume has left his legs, face, and arms largely bare—pretty sad protection for someone who leaps toward brick buildings, crashes through windowpanes, and gets dangled over bubbling vats of acid. Thank God Batman has wised up and changed the boy's outfit to something more sensible and protective.

The poor kid. So bright and eager and quick, but when he's piped up with the solution to a mystery, Batman has usually said, in effect, "Nice try, but wrong." And that was only the mildest of Robin's humiliations. In *The Dark Knight Returns*, Batman recalled that the villain Two-Face called him "Robin, the boy hostage." The Joker even murdered the Jason Todd incarnation.

Other allies don't get much better treatment. Alfred, for instance, seems to tend all the immense Wayne Manor and vast Batcave by himself, while his peers in the butler game probably supervise entire staffs of cooks, chambermaids, chauffeurs, maintenance workers, flunkies, and gofers.

Commissioner Gordon, who has eternally aided and protected Batman, gets no great consideration, either. Batman has often vanished while Gordon talked to him, let imposters play Batman without telling him, and left town during crises without so much as a phone call. A remarkable sequence from *Batman: Legends of the Dark Knight* #125 finally ignited a long-simmering confrontation between the two.

BATMAN: You're my partner.
GORDON: Don't blow smoke at me.
BATMAN: It's true—
GORDON: It's what you'd like to think—that doesn't make it true. Partners are equals, Batman! When have you ever treated me like your equal? Partners, for example, tell you their plans! They keep you informed! And they sure as hell don't walk out on you in the middle of a sentence!

(To his credit, Batman tried to make good, even offering to let Gordon in on his secret identity.)

But if Batman has treated Gordon roughly, that's nothing compared to the people who could help him the most: his fellow costumed heroes. Superman, for example, has sometimes been Batman's most trusted friend, but in recent years the man with the cowl has often sneered contempt at the Kryptonian's schoolboy ethics and Boy Scout methods.

Batman has given other superheroes even less respect. Back in the 1960s and '70s, when he was on friendly terms with his comrades in the Justice League, they would have happily offered him weapons and powers that would supersize his ability to fight crime, but he apparently wasn't interested. In 1983's *Batman and the Outsiders* #1, Batman angrily quit the League when its members refused to help him rescue the kidnapped Lucius Fox, Bruce Wayne's CEO. (The Leaguers declined the job because rescuing Fox would have meant breaking international law, but Batman didn't care much about that.) Since the late 1980s, he's treated various teammates like scatterbrained children who don't understand the seriousness of the struggle against evil. In the first decade of the 2000s, he took to spying on his colleagues and cataloguing their weaknesses. When his data networks fell into evil hands and later became evil themselves (it's a long story), death and disaster followed.

Though Batman has been hard on his allies, he's sometimes been remarkably flexible with his enemies. For one thing, he hands them to the police even though experience shows that gullible officials or legal technicalities will put them back on the streets sooner or later.

Sometimes, he goes even further. He's occasionally let the thieving Catwoman simply go free, starting in *Batman* #1. After blocking Robin from catching her, Batman smiled and mused, "Lovely girl! What eyes!"

Even murderous monsters have gotten his mercy, like Two-Face from *Batman Annual* #13. In that story, Batman broke Two-Face out of jail, took him to an island far from any American authority, and let him loose. (It was all in a good cause, but still. . . .) Possibly the most infamous case came from *The Killing Joke*, where Batman offered to help the Joker regain his sanity and ended up laughing with him as if they were old pals—only hours after the Joker had shot and crippled Batgirl, and tried to drive Gordon insane.

Batman may even inspire his enemies. Stories set during his early years, like *Batman: The Long Halloween* and *Batman: Prey*, have pointed out that his flamboyant persona may excite and stimulate dangerous nuts such as the Joker. In *The Dark Knight Returns*, a touchstone of modern Bat-myth, the aging Batman's return to action after years of retirement revived the long-passive Joker into waves of mass murder.

The most explicit description of Batman's power to stimulate criminals has come from Henri Ducard, an assassin and gun-runner who trained Bruce Wayne. (He's also another of the people who have figured out that Bruce is Batman.) In *Detective Comics* #600, Ducard soliloquized:

> He functions as a lightning rod for a certain breed of psychotic. They specialize in absurdly grandiose schemes, and whatever the ostensible rationale—greed, revenge, the seizure of power—their true agenda is always to cast Batman in the role of Nemesis. Hence the puns, the riddles, the flagrant clues they scatter in their collective wake—daring their foe to penetrate the obvious.

Ducard went on to a bigger point. "True evil seldom announces itself so loudly. The dangerous ones set their subversive goals, and achieve them, bit by bit . . . invisibly, inevitably." He added, "While Batman busies himself with petty thieves and gaudy madmen, an abyss of rot yawns ever wider at his feet. He's a Band-Aid on a cancer patient."

Bruce himself recognized the problem in *Batman* #217. He pledged to wipe out "[a] new breed of rat—[who] uses the modern weapons of 'phony respectability'—'big-business fronts'—'legal cover-ups'—and hides in the fortress towers of Gotham's metropolis!" And then he ignored his own words and tracked down a second-rate thug who shot a doctor.

Bruce probably couldn't stop himself. Writers throughout his history have traced the maze of his psychology, starting with his parents' murder. Fleischer's *Encyclopedia*, for instance, provides a Freudian explanation:

> In the unconscious mind of the young Bruce Wayne, he was unworthy of his parents' love, and so they deserted him. . . . [Bruce's] anger at his parents for having deserted him, and at himself for having been unworthy of their lasting love, finds socially acceptable expression in Batman's hatred for the underworld and in his lifelong crusade against criminals. Seen in this light, the life of socially sanctioned violence in which Batman has embroiled himself is not a freely chosen occupation at all, but rather the acting out of an unconscious, violent compulsion, for Batman's war against the underworld is in reality a war against his parents. And, in the sense that the inner compulsion to wage this war has deprived Batman of his own freedom, in particular the joys of ordinary life that he claims to envy, it is also a war against himself.

It makes sense that Bruce would push himself to become everything that the once-helpless little boy wanted to be or wanted his parents to be: a fearless avenger who could stop any criminal.

But it also makes sense that he'd punish himself for failing to save his parents. No wonder he's put himself through painful training and suffered any number of wounds. No wonder he's taken on a war that he's doomed to lose. (No one can wipe out crime as long as human beings are greedy and violent—that is, as long as they're human.) And no wonder he fights his war in ways that can't work very well.

Back here in the real world, the concept of a man of immense ability and equally immense flaws is nothing new. Ask Richard Nixon, one of the shrewdest politicians in American history, why he let a third-rate burglary bring him down. Ask Bill Clinton, who promoted his wife as his partner when he ran for president, why he risked his marriage and his career over a bit of hide-the-cigar. Ask corporate chieftain Ken Lay or televangelist Jimmy Swaggart why they let their tawdrier urges topple them from heights of wealth, fame, and power. Ask Bruce Wayne why he'll never win his war on crime.

Bruce will keep fighting—not just because DC Comics wants to keep pumping out issues of *Batman* and *Detective Comics*, but also because of something more fundamental in his personality. It's something that makes Batman appealing to generations of readers and audiences. It's something that sets him apart from other superheroes. It's something that he holds in common with Clinton and Nixon and Lay and Swaggart and you and me:

He is only human. Like us, Batman has flaws and blind spots and uncontrollable needs. He can't win his war on crime, just as we can't win our own battles to avoid death or live without worries or attract and hold the admiration of everyone around us.

But he never gives up. He struggles and suffers but keeps on going. And so do we.

Yes, Batman's a failure. But aren't we all?

DAVID SEIDMAN has been a comic book writer, a publicist for the comics publishers NBM Publishing and Claypool Comics, senior editor of Disney Comics, a teacher of comics writing at UCLA, and an author of storybooks and other fiction starring superheroes such as Spider-Man and the Fantastic Four. As a journalist, he's written about comics for publications ranging from the *Los Angeles Times* to the trade journal *Comics and Games Retailer*. In addition, he's authored more than thirty books on subjects as diverse as Christmas lights, longevity medicine, teenage life in Iran, relocating to Los Angeles, and the F/A-18 warplane.

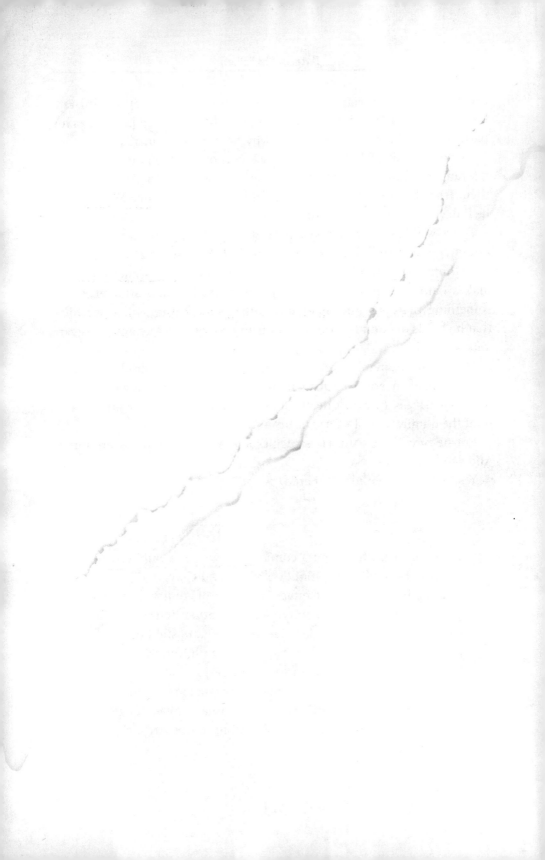

ACKNOWLEDGMENTS

The publisher thanks Robert Greenberger, the author of *The Essential Batman Encyclopedia* (coming June 2008), for his assistance with the manuscript.